To all my teachers.

Bradford Fitch   Jack Holt, Editor

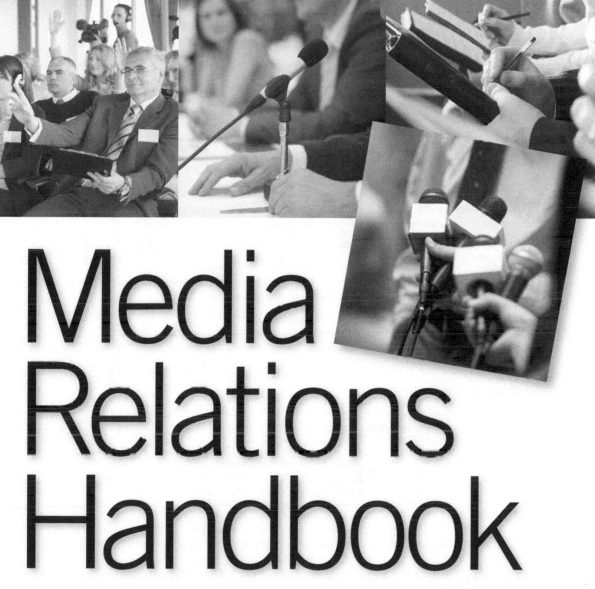

Media Relations Handbook

for Government, Associations, Nonprofits, and Elected Officials

Second Edition

TheCapitol.Net

For more than 30 years, TheCapitol.Net and its predecessor, Congressional Quarterly Executive Conferences, have been training professionals from government, military, business, and NGOs on the dynamics and operations of the legislative and executive branches of the U.S. government and how to work with them.

Our training and publications include congressional operations, legislative and budget process, communication and advocacy, media and public relations, testifying before Congress, research skills, legislative drafting, critical thinking and writing, and more.

Our publications and courses, written and taught by current Washington insiders who are all independent subject matter experts, show how Washington works.™ Our products and services can be found on our web site at *<www.TheCapitol.Net>*.

TheCapitol.Net is a non-partisan firm.

Additional copies of the *Media Relations Handbook for Government, Associations, Nonprofits, and Elected Officials* can be ordered directly from the publisher. Secure online ordering is available on the web site, *<www.TCNMRH.com>*.

The Training Edition of *Media Relations Handbook for for Government, Associations, Nonprofits, and Elected Officials* is used as course materials in several of the media training programs offered by TheCapitol.Net. See our web site for more information, *<www.WorkWithTheMedia.com>*.

Citation Form—URLs

We use a standard style for all web addresses, also known as Uniform Resource Locators (URLs). URLs appear in text next to the first mention of the resource being described, and are surrounded with open and close angle brackets.

Web addresses that have the standard web addressing form at the beginning of the URL of "http://www." we show only the initial "www." For example, the URL "http://www.domainname.com" will appear in text and tables as "*<www.domainname.com>*".

For URLs that begin with anything other than "www.," such as "http://thomas.loc.gov", the URL will appear in text and tables as "*<http://thomas.loc.gov>*". For example, the URL "http://www3.domain.gov" will appear in text and tables as "*<http://www3.domain.gov>*".

Design and production by Zaccarine Design, Inc., Chicago, IL, *zacdesign@mac.com*.
Ebook conversion by Paula Reichwald *<igossi.com>*.
Index by Enid Zafren *<IndexingPartners.com>*.

ISBN:
Softcover: 978-1-58733-167-1
Hardbound: 978-1-58733-171-8

Ebook ISBN:
Amazon Kindle: 978-1-58733-253-1
B&N nook: 978-1-58733-254-8
Google Editions: 978-1-58733-262-3

Editor's Note

Communication vs. Communications

Human communication is a constant, continuous, and dynamic phenomenon. You cannot not-communicate nor can you un-communicate. For an individual entity, there is only ONE communication. Not multiple, not varieties, only one. That one communication is the culmination of all that has been communicated by the entity until the "now" in time. You cannot go back and un-communicate something. You can only begin from the "now" to create the intended outcome. That outcome is always a negotiation with the receiver/audience/community to cultivate an agreed understanding.

For a communication professional, understanding this fact is essential. No matter where you work, someone has been communicating something before you began. You cannot un-communicate it. You cannot create a new beginning; but you can begin now to create a new outcome.

Communication Professional Careers

There are many facets to the communication professional's career environment. Here is a primer on some of the different career positions.

Press Secretary: works for an individual in a public office to help manage that individual's public profile. Duties typically include:
- Primary advisor for public affairs policy
- Speechwriter
- Editorial writer
- Spokesperson
- Media representative
- Public affairs staff supervisor

Public Affairs Officer (PAO): works in the public sector for a government agency to help manage the agency's public profile. Duties typically include:
- Primary advisor to leadership on public affairs operations
- Primary point of contact for news media
- Media representative for the agency
- Agency journalist
- Spokesperson
- Public Affairs Event/Media Planner
- Public Affairs staff supervisor

Public Information Officer (PIO): works in the public sector for a government (usually state and local) agency to help manage the agency's public information activities. This position is sometimes a secondary duty for a professional from another field within the organization to assist the leadership with public information activities in the event of an emergency or crisis. In some agencies the duties typically include the same duties as the public affairs officer but with activities scaled back:

- Emergency/Crisis communication principal
- Spokesperson on-scene
- Media representative
- News release writing

Public Relations professional: works in the private sector for a company, industry, or nonprofit organization. Duties typically include:

- Primary advisor to leadership for developing public relationships
- Primary point of contact for news media
- Organization spokesperson
- Organization journalist
- Media representative
- Press/news release writing
- Public events planner/supervisor

This is by no means an exclusive list. Communication professionals may find themselves in any, sometimes all, of these roles at any point during their careers. As you see, many of these roles are common among each type of career position. So what is the difference? Focus.

The Press Secretary focuses on the reputation of the individual for whom he works. The Public Affairs Officer focuses on the public understanding of what the agency is doing and how tax dollars are being spent. The Public Information Officer usually focuses on specific events or types of events to ensure that the public stays informed as a public safety measure. The Public Relations professional focuses on the organization's reputation and relationship with the public as typically reflected in the bottom line of the financial statements.

Difference between the Internet and the World Wide Web

It is helpful to understand the difference between the Internet and the "world wide web." The Internet is the core structure on which the web is built. The web is an application that runs on the Internet. To get to the web you must first be connected to the Internet. Not everything that runs on the Internet is available on the web, but everything on the web is available on the Internet. A bit of history may help here. The Internet was first established in the late 1960s between a computer at UCLA and another at SRI International. More connections were added over time; in 1982 the Internetworking Protocol Suite (TCP/IP) was standardized and commercial Internet service providers began to emerge in the late 1980s. In the early 1990s Tim Berners-Lee used the inter-linking of hypertext documents to create the World Wide Web (www, web). So, while the Internet is the backbone, it is the web that powers our online communication.

The Media Environment

What would you consider to be the first, high-speed Internet? This question usually conjures up a variety of responses. I submit to you the first, high-speed Internet was hard-surface Roman roads. This technology, built by the govern-ment for a military purpose, and laid out in public, changed the way Roman citizens lived their lives. No longer relegated to subsistence farming, the roads gave rise to farmers trading in agricultural goods. It opened new industry, changed commerce, and empowered the individual citizens with the ability to diversify their holdings, increase their wealth, and build their own personal economies of scale. This new technology gave rise to other new technologies that also increased the speed and reach of communication at the level of the individual. Cultural change happens at the speed and reach of individual com-munication.

We are in a time of great change. Today's Internet has given rise to the web, which has given rise to the social web, commonly known as Web 2.0. The social web is giving rise to the "semantic web," becoming known as Web 3.0. What next? The "sentient web"? Know one really knows.

What we do know is that this new media has changed people's behavior. It allows us to do things we could not do before. We can broadcast ourselves on YouTube, find long-lost friends and relatives on Facebook, post about our daily life, thoughts, and concerns on Twitter, Blogger, WordPress, Tumblr, and any number of online platforms. We can find jobs and become thought lead-ers on LinkedIn. We can do all these things without leaving our living room. These interconnected online technologies have increased the speed and reach of communication at the level of the individual, creating cultural change.

With this in mind we present this Second Edition of *Media Relations Handbook*. While some examples may seem dated, the examples are still valid. Research continues into the changes wrought by the Internet and public expectations that are experiencing mercurial change. As best practices are now being developed, it is our hope that we are able to give you guidance and ideas that will spark your innovation and that we may find you setting the examples to be published in the Third Edition.

Jack Holt

Acknowledgments

While this text aims to collect the accumulated wisdom of hundreds of public relations professionals, there were a few friends and colleagues who provided invaluable guidance, reviewed drafts, answered countless questions, and gave the author both support and friendship during the writing process. I am grateful to these people, who understand and appreciate the communication profession as a crucial part of the democratic process: Jim Berard, Paul Bock, David Carle, Mike Casey, Deb DeYoung, Kathy Goldschmidt, Ed Henry, Marci Hilt, Dennis Johnson, Jim Kennedy, Kathy McShea, Mike McCurry, Margo Mikkelson, Congressman Tom Sawyer, Kristy Schantz, James Vaughn, and Pat Wood. My wife, Susanne Fitch, has been a sounding board, editor, and advisor through the first and second editions. And, this book would have been considerably weaker if it were not for the enormous and important contributions of fellow public relations professional Beth Gaston, who also is a contributing author to Chapter Eleven, Communication in a Federal Agency.

Aiding me in researching, updating, and editing the second edition was Zach Goldberg, a veteran of the congressional, association, and agency media relations worlds. Zach's discipline and research skills were invaluable to the finished product (and it helped that we both share a kind of snarky humor).

Finally, I owe my highest praise and gratitude to my editor and publisher, Chug Roberts of TheCapitol.Net. For years I've read authors praising editors in the front of books—thinking it merely a polite necessity. I now know different. This book would not have been written without Chug's initiative, encouragement, guidance, and support.

Bradford Fitch

About the Author

Bradford Fitch is president and CEO of the Congressional Management Foundation. He has spent twenty-five years in Washington as a journalist, congressional aide, consultant, college instructor, Internet entrepreneur, and writer/researcher.

Fitch began his career as a radio and television reporter in the 1980s. He began working on Capitol Hill in 1988, where he served for thirteen years. He worked in the House and Senate for four members of Congress, serving as press secretary, legislative director, and chief of staff.

He left the Hill in 2001 to work for the Congressional Management Foundation (CMF), a nonprofit, nonpartisan organization that advises congressional offices on how to improve operations and enhance the relationship between citizens and Congress. As deputy director of CMF, he served as a management consultant for members of Congress, offering confidential guidance, conducting staff training programs, and writing publications on enhancing the performance of individual congressional offices and the institution. He left CMF in 2006 to form a new company, Knowlegis, in affiliation with Capitol Advantage. Knowlegis is now a part of CQ-Roll Call, where Fitch served as a vice president until 2010, when he returned to CMF.

Fitch is the author of *Citizen's Handbook to Influencing Elected Officials* (TheCapitol.Net, 2010); *Pocket Guide to Advocacy on Capitol Hill* (TheCapitol. Net, 2010); "Best Practices in Online Advocacy for Associations, Nonprofits, and Corporations," a chapter in *Routledge Handbook of Political Management* (Routledge, 2008); and articles on communication and advocacy. He also served as editor of *Setting Course: A Congressional Management Guide* for the 108th Congress and 109th Congress editions. He taught journalism and public communications at American University in Washington, DC, for thirteen years, where he served an adjunct associate professor of Communications. He received his B.A. in Political Science from The Johns Hopkins University and his M.A. in Journalism and Public Affairs from American University.

About the Editor

Charles J. "Jack" Holt, APR. Jack Holt is a recognized leader in successfully formulating, implementing, and managing communication programs for very large organizations, including both the Department of Defense and other U.S. federal government agencies. He created, developed, and produced the DoD Bloggers Roundtable and DoDLive web communication concept, co-authored the OSD policy memorandum DTM 09-026 for the Responsible and Effective Use of Internet-based Capabilities, and is co-founder of the DoD All Services Social Media Council.

Jack has more than twenty years of communication policy development and application experience, teaches at the graduate level, consults, and collaborates on how to effectively use the new and emerging media in meeting business needs, including improving customer relationships, implementing change management, and developing innovative organizational environments. He also has more than twenty years of direct experience as a leader, coach, teacher, and mentor in policy analysis and development, communication, and business strategy development, organizational design, knowledge management, and workforce training and development.

Jack has his own communication consulting firm, is the director for Policy Analysis for Blue Ridge Information Systems, adjunct lecturer at Georgetown University, and a member of the faculty for TheCapitol.Net. He also teaches at the NATO School and has taught sessions on Communication, Journalism, and New Media strategies and tactics at the Defense Information School and the Naval Postgraduate School. He is a member of the PRSA Counselors Academy, The PRSA Counselors to Higher Education Committee, and served as the 2009 Chair for the PRSA National Capital Chapter Public Affairs and Government Committee.

Summary Table of Contents

Back of the Book

Table of Contents

Chapter Three:
Developing a Message and Communication Plan

Chapter Four:
Interacting with Reporters

Chapter Five:
Overview of the Media:
Print, Radio, TV, and the Internet

Chapter Six:
Online Communication

Chapter Seven:
Dealing with the Principal

Chapter Eight:
Interview Preparation

Chapter Nine:
Internal Issues: Experts, Policy, Numbers, Leaks, Lawyers, and Language

Chapter Ten:
How to Interact with Congressional Campaign Operations

Chapter Eleven:
Communication in a Federal Agency

Chapter Twelve:
Crisis Communication in Public Affairs

Chapter Thirteen:
Honest Spin: The Ethics of Public Relations

Back of the Book

Introduction

America was founded by a public relations campaign. Certainly General George Washington's army played an important role as well in freeing the colonies from British tyranny. But it was Thomas Paine's pen, through his pamphlet *Common Sense*, which motivated thousands of colonists to join the rebel army to fight for the cause of liberty against their British cousins.

It's strange to think that public relations existed two hundred years ago, yet *Common Sense* was the first mass-media campaign on American soil. In a nation of three million, more than 500,000 copies of the forty-page pamphlet were printed. That would be the modern-day equivalent of about half of all voters watching the same thirty-minute documentary calling on them to overthrow their government—and most of them supporting the idea.

From cave drawings to the printing press to the Internet, leaders and their acolytes throughout human history have combined persuasive ideas and available technology to communicate those ideas to those they wish to influence. In a democratic context, the process takes on larger meaning, as the goals of the persuader are often intended to better the human condition, right a social wrong, or protect an unsuspecting public from some menace.

We think of *public relations* as a craft invented in the twentieth century by people like Edward Bernays, sometimes called the "Father of Public Relations." The writings and tactics of this first great thinker and practitioner in the industry redefined both government and corporate communication in America. Bernays (who was also the nephew of Sigmund Freud) defined the topography of our profession through his concept of "engineering consent," and the fundamental tools of press releases and photo opportunities that he perfected are still staples today.

Yet whether we use pen, pamphlet and horseback, or web site and satellite to carry the message, the basic principles remain the same. The great journalist Walter Lippmann said the question his communication profession faced was "what to say and how to say it." Communicators using public relations face the same question, but must add a twist: "to what end?" In public affairs, our objective must have some purpose, because the results of our work can have significant consequences. Through the communication of certain facts and how they are presented, people will vote for a candidate, contribute to a nonprofit, join an organization, or take up arms against their government.

This book is for those who are seeking the most effective means to communicate on behalf of a government agency, a national association or nonprofit, or an elected official. It will help you channel your hot passion with the cool guidance that has been gleaned through others' experience.

The author professes no unique insight into media relations in public affairs. Rather, this book is an amalgamation of the collective wisdom of hundreds of public relations professionals in the worlds of government and politics. It is an overview of the ideas that have become the accepted rules of communication in Washington, presented in one volume.

Soon before his death in 1995 at the age of 102, Edward Bernays was asked for his definition of a "public relations person." He scoffed at the notion that anyone who could write something down in a press release and hawk it to a newspaper could qualify for what he considered a meaningful calling. "A public relations person . . . is an applied social scientist who advises a client or employer on the social attitudes and actions to take to win the support of the publics upon whom his or her or its viability depends." (Stuart Ewen, *PR! A Social History of Spin* (New York: Basic Books, 1996).)

In the world of public affairs, the "viability" of the cause often has greater meaning to us and to others than those causes in related public relations fields. We are not selling soap—we're selling ideas to improve the world. We promote a member of Congress who wants to cut taxes; a nonprofit executive who wants to stop a timber company from clearing a thousand-year-old forest; an association executive trying to build a coalition to lobby against federal regulations; or a federal agency trying to convince an industry that those same regulations might save lives and property.

The public relations profession in Washington is often derided as populated by nefarious characters, willing to say anything to promote their agenda. Like most caricatures of Washington politics, this is exaggerated and largely inaccurate. We may not be the direct descendants of Thomas Paine, but our lineage is closely connected. We mostly advance our employer's objectives because we *believe* in their causes; we share their faith that our goals are just and their achievement will make things better . . . if only a little bit. We like the idea that we can make a difference.

To do that, you have to know how. This book is a tool in that undertaking.

Media Relations Handbook

for Agencies, Associations, Nonprofits and Congress

Chapter One: First Steps

> *"Public sentiment is everything. With public sentiment nothing can fail; without it nothing can succeed. He who molds public sentiment goes deeper than he who enacts statutes or decisions possible or impossible to execute."*
>
> Abraham Lincoln

First Steps

§ 1.1 Introduction

On my first day as a press secretary, I walked into the office filled with enthusiasm, the intention to do the right thing, and a small amount of knowledge about the public relations profession. To me, the decision to work for a member of Congress was an easy progression. I was interested in government, I had a background in journalism with solid writing skills, and it seemed like a natural transition to translate these abilities into another form of communication work.

The office was a typical congressional environment in 1988. I had a desk, phone, computer, and maybe eight square feet of office real estate I could call my own. All my teenage and adult life I had watched and studied government. And five years as an intermittent radio and television reporter, a political science degree from a university, and two whole years in Washington made me feel that I was prepared for the job of press secretary.

As a new public relations professional, I did not fully understand the impact press secretaries could have on the content of the news. This is not to diminish the dominant role of the news media in communicating information to the public. Network television, major daily papers, web sites, blogs, and a host of other avenues are the primary filters for information the public receives. However, public relations agents for corporate, political, and governmental figures also play a significant role in the positioning and content of much of the news the American public hears about its government.

The communication professionals who serve in government, a nonprofit organization, or any group that operates in the world of public affairs have the rare position of supporting a mission, a cause or individual, and advocating those ideas using their communication skills. Public relations specialists are a crucial link in the chain of communication between leaders and citizens, and our ability to translate those high ideals into language and images that impact people and cultivate understanding often makes the difference between the success and failure of those ideals.

§1.2 Matching Convictions with a Job

Trying to match up your personal beliefs to a cause or individual is usually the first major hurdle in any public relations career. As they enter the profession, most communication professionals dream of fighting the great fight for a cause or person they believe in, with all the best resources, and all the best people. The real world is a little more complicated, and public relations people often find themselves with either a shortage of resources or nobility in their cause. Nonetheless, it's best to find some healthy balance where you are given the tools to grow professionally, do an effective job for the organization or individual you represent, and feel that your work has some meaning.

There is a vast array of people and organizations that are in desperate need of good communication work, so there's likely to be something that you can connect with. Working in politics is one way to feel meaningful in a public relations job, but not the only way. Some of the happiest public relations professionals I know are doing sports information and entertainment press work. The important point is that you share some common beliefs with those whom you represent.

As a general rule, not just applicable to public relations professionals, you want to find a functional office—one that has good internal communication among staff and is solidly managed. It's often hard to get a clear picture of the internal politics of any organization until you're fully accepted as a member of the team. Still, there are warning signs to watch out for. If you get a really bad vibe from the supervisor you interviewed with, you should probably go with your gut and pass on the position.

Most important, communication specialists succeed most often when they are working with leaders who understand the importance of communication. Some public figures are obsessed with the media. They love the camera, will never turn down interviews, and berate the press secretary if the headline is below the fold instead of above it. Others really don't care about the press and consider it an afterthought, not central to their mission. It's hard to say which one is more difficult, but I would rather try to slow down a moving train than get it going from a dead stop. Leaders who are shy of the media, or who just don't understand the impact, are not good candidates for sophisticated communication work. Employers don't all have to be perfect spokesmen, but they do have to think that it is important to communicate professionally and effectively.

Finally, when you attach yourself to an individual or organization, you're attaching your reputation as well. If the individual or organization succeeds, you succeed. If scandal or failure should envelop your employer, you will be painted with the same brush, at least temporarily. Finding yourself spokesperson for a corrupt or scandal-ridden politician doesn't necessarily have to destroy your career. Mike McCurry worked for a U.S. senator who resigned over a bribery scandal and a president who was impeached. Yet, McCurry's reputation as one of the best public relations practitioners ever remains intact. As you consider whom you will advocate for, the principal's character is probably one of the most important qualities to consider.

§1.3 Getting to Know the Principal

In many public affairs-related operations, there often is one person who will be the leader, and therefore the chief spokesperson for the organization. They may be called member of Congress, president of the association, executive director of the agency, Undersecretary of Something Important, Grand Poobah of the Ascension of Moose Antlers, or some other title that makes them worthy of quoting in the news media. This means that much of the communication that you're responsible for creating will have to flow through one person: the principal. The communication that you create is the voice of the organization through the principal.

It's important that you get to know your boss on many levels. You must develop a trust between one another, so that your principal has confidence in your ability to deliver the message, and you have confidence that your hard work to create the message will be advanced by a solid leader. You must identify the strengths and weaknesses of the principal, assessing which forums and public relations vehicles work best, and develop a strategy for improving her skills. And, you must appreciate that you're dealing with a human being, whose emotions will occasionally interfere with sound judgment when dealing with the media. Nothing creates more joy or despair among principals and organizations than media stories. Public relations professionals must be prepared to handle these roller coasters of emotions, recognizing the real problems and smoothing over the false ones. For more detail, see Chapter Seven, Dealing with the Principal.

(Federal agency public relations professionals may not have one, key principal, but many representatives who can speak to the media. This structure and the challenges associated with it are addressed in Chapter Eleven, Communication in a Federal Agency.)

§1.4 Assessing Your Strategic Position and Historical Record

Early on in their tenure, new press secretaries should assess how the organization, candidate, or public official is positioned in the media's and target audience's opinion. In other words, before you determine where you're going, you must first figure out where you are. For a candidate, this historical baggage is usually a resume, public statements, and a host of other details that make up her life. For some individuals and groups this history would fit in a single file; for others it could take up a library.

Regardless of the available material for review, new public relations professionals should do all that they can to learn about their new boss and organization. The best source is your predecessor. A candid conversation, best done outside the office environment, is probably the quickest path to clarifying the challenge ahead. Your predecessor can outline your new boss' strengths and weaknesses, tell you which reporters are smart and which ones are dangerous, and outline the basic terrain of the internal office politics. Hopefully, this conversation will not result in a later "what did I get myself into" conversation with yourself, but instead will be a helpful benchmark.

There is another selfish reason to get to know your predecessor: his work is one of the standards that you'll be judged by. Whether fair or not, all public relations professionals are measured, in part, by the person whose shoes they fill. While it may sound strange, it is often best to follow in the footsteps of someone with extremely small feet. You sometimes can look incredibly intelligent by doing the simplest things right if your predecessor screwed them up. On the other hand, following a professional has its advantages as well: good relations with the media; a seasoned team of colleagues who appreciate the importance of public relations; and an up-to-date press list.

New press secretaries also must become thoroughly knowledgeable about a principal's or organization's record. The easiest and most thorough way is by reading all past newspaper articles. If the history is too extensive, perhaps a new colleague could give you the key highlights of recent events for you to peruse. Also, review any major television stories or recorded events on video. Watching candidate debates is one of the quickest ways to get an assessment of a member of Congress in one of the most challenging communication settings ever created.

Try to watch any relevant video that is available on the Internet. You-Tube, Google, and Google News in particular, are great tools to learn more about your principal. There are a number of sites that track mentions on blogs (such as *<Technorati.com>*). You should also visit social media sites. This is especially important if the principal has had unfettered access to Twitter or an office Facebook page. Those off-the-cuff comments are excellent ways to assess your new boss' personality and see if there are any hidden land mines you might need to defuse.

Another one of the clearest ways to get a quick view of the terrain is through internal polling. How to integrate polling into the message of the organization is discussed more fully in Chapter Three, Developing a Message and Communication Plan. In assessing your position, polling is also valuable to a new press secretary for an entirely selfish reason: it is one of the few quantifiable measurements of our craft. Since public relations is an art, and not a science, results can often be subjective. With a poll, you have a statistical assessment of how your campaign or message or product has done with the public. For a congressional office, the poll is the ongoing report card for communication operations (outside of elections). For nonprofits, polling can help clarify public opinion on primary issues, suggest strategy and language that resonates with audiences, and is invaluable in creating a communication plan. For associations and agencies, it can help define a strategic course about the interests and desires of target audiences.

Finally, your own principal's or organization's web site is also a valuable resource, particularly to identify what interests your audience. Using web analytic programs, you can determine what people are interested in. Is there high traffic for the newsroom page? The issues section? The "contact" page? By assessing your web site traffic, you can determine what is most interesting to visitors.

§1.5 Learning the Office Strategic Goals

As part of the development of a communication plan, new press secretaries need to know what the office is working on and where it wants to go. Well-run offices and organizations usually have gone through some kind of strategic planning process. The results may include a mission statement, statement of purpose, or some other fundamental declaration of the office goals. It's important to get a quick understanding of how important strategic goals are to the office and how they are integrated into the day-to-day operations. Some strategic plans do not have "buy-in" from the entire staff, and are promptly ignored by management and employees as soon as the ink is dry on the paper. These plans still may be valuable to public relations professionals—if only to understand the once-stated goals of the leader, even if they are not matched with the work of the office.

Whether the office has clear goals or not, you must have them. For the purposes of your initial assessment of your new environment, you'll need to keep in mind the need to narrow your mission to two or three goals or messages. In reviewing the office or strategic goals you inherit, think about how best to translate the goals into communication themes. What communication vehicles are best to project the message? What was tried by your predecessor? Which goals are most attractive to reporters? Are there spin-off mini-objectives tied to broader goals that can be encouraged and developed?

As you work with the office goals, keep in mind that communication professionals have a responsibility to point out opportunities and even to suggest strategic initiatives. This may cause internal political problems because policy experts usually hate it when "flacks" muck about in their well-tilled policy gardens. Nothing more riles an over-educated, masters-degree toting, bespectacled policy wonk during a strategy meeting than some brash spin doctor chiming in, "Maybe we could do it another way that could get us more press." But, in spite of the hateful stares and lost lunch invitations, that's part of your job. Press secretaries are responsible for translating policy into message, and that sometimes means we must tinker with the policy product to make it salable to the media and public.

§1.6 Assessing the Issue Terrain

As public relations professionals come to learn about their new job, usually a clear set of target issues will become apparent: the member of Congress will have committee assignments that revolve around agriculture and foreign policy; the nonprofit organization is responsible for advocating pay equity for women; the federal agency has a mission and policy initiatives to achieve.

As spokesperson, communication specialists are expected to have a fair amount of knowledge about their boss' and organization's area of expertise. This can be extremely awkward for new spokesmen, since they usually don't have a lot of experience in specialty areas. As you become an expert on your new boss' or your organization's history and goals, you must also become an expert on the issue terrain, the stage on which you'll perform. The crash course in your new office's mission could include lots of articles, seminal writings, and other research that everyone in your new world has known about for years.

One simple analysis for examining your environment is to break issues and groups into categories: threats and opportunities. The opportunities analysis is the fun one, and you can usually get help from colleagues in the office to aid with this research. Organizations usually try to build their goals around environmental opportunities. A big push for worker safety legislation makes the time ripe for a key amendment your organization has been seeking for years. A major tax bill is seen as likely to pass, requiring your staff to engage in a coordinated legislative and communication effort. Public affairs opportunities are the gold that policy and press wonks mine for, and the digging is the stuff that makes governmental and non-government organizations hum.

The less enjoyable analysis is a review of potential threats in the environment. One employer I worked with offered this blanket assessment: "Threats? There are no threats." While this rosy assessment did much to buoy spirits in the office on a regular basis, it did little to prepare staff for potential problems. Communication threats often come in the form of political opponents, organizations that oppose your mission, or even reporters bent on drumming up news. The blogger with few facts and a nasty disposition also could be a problem in the making. By anticipating potential threats and preparing for them, your organization and boss will be in a much better position to handle adverse events. We will address crises in much greater detail in Chapter Twelve, Crisis Communication in Public Affairs.

Your environment is also filled with like-minded people and organizations. Get to know your friends and allies. Washington is filled with vast, interlocking networks of entities that have overlapping goals and interests. Good communication professionals—especially those with limited resources—learn how to hook up with those allies and use their strengths. Especially for public relations professionals new to a position, finding an experienced communication ally in another organization or office can be like a unexpected gift.

§1.7 Conducting a Resource Assessment

Every press office usually can also count among its assets a variety of administrative and technical tools in its communication cupboard. Even before joining an organization, prospective employees should inquire what resources they will have in order to accomplish their job.

The most fundamental asset to a communications specialist in charge of an operation is a budget. Many organizations will have thought this through and will provide reasonable funds to accomplish communication goals. These include: money to hire staff, existing contracts for specialty work (such as video news releases), and funding for contingencies and emergencies that tend to crop up in public relations. Unfortunately, others who have not mapped out a central role for communication in their operation may only have ad hoc arrangements for funding communication initiatives. They'll hire one or two people for their "press shop" and expect them to get the word out with a phone, email, fax machine, and web site. "When you want to put out a newsletter, just show me a draft, and we'll see if we can afford it." Or, "Why do we need a web site designer? Billy knows computers, he just got out of college." It's best to negotiate a budget before you accept a position. It's a lot tougher to ask for things after you're tethered to a steady paycheck.

If you're not in a position to demand a budget as part of your hiring agreement, at least raise issues related to resources in the interview process. Pitch prospective employers on the need to invest in their communication operations. You probably won't get everything you want, but you'll be putting your new boss on notice that you're aggressive in your advocacy of your part of the mission, and most good employers will appreciate that kind of enthusiasm.

Even if you're not working on the Starship Enterprise of PR shops, you're probably going to have one or two toys to play with. Take an inventory of what's in the file cabinets, storerooms, and computers used in the communication process. Broadcast-quality digital recorders and microphones, digital cameras, pocket recorders (audio, photo, and video), and database software—all these are the basic tools of modern public relations. Keep track of the age of the equipment, as the march of technology is quickening its pace—yesterday's neat gadget will become tomorrow's relic in no time.

As a communication professional in the twenty-first century, your primary tools are your computer when you're in the office and your smartphone, laptop, or tablet when you're outside the office.

These are the "machine tools" in your factory that manufacture all of your products, and they are your link to the rest of the world. Given rapid technological advancements, it is often difficult to stay current with the latest technical marvel in the communication world. While you do not have to be a computer geek able to write code, basic technical knowledge is essential for public relations professionals. You should know what you can do with your computer, and be comfortable with the current email, word processing, database management, and web site updating programs. Avoid the desire to try out every technical innovation. It's more important for communication professionals to be functional than current. At the same time, don't let valuable technology developments pass you by.

It's also a good idea to be on good terms with the computer expert in your office, as you will likely need her help in a variety of ways: coordinating databases, building mass mailings, updating the web site, etc. With the assistance of someone who understands the office computer system and knows how to make it sing, you can geometrically increase your reach.

As you become familiar with your word processing, spreadsheet, database management, and email programs, make sure you are able to seamlessly integrate these tools. A good press database should have the flexibility to manipulate the data and be merged with your email program. Categories should be created for type of media, geographic region, issue interest, or any other logical issue that could separate reporters. Ideally, the database should merge well with your email and word processing programs. Some organizations maintain association member or constituent databases that are set up to manage correspondence and contacts—and it's possible to adapt these for communication professionals' needs. However, most communication professionals are more comfortable maintaining their own press databases because of the flexibility they require, and the ability to conduct media outreach—mass or targeted—using the database. A list of items to include in a media database is provided in § 1.10.

As your office's communication professional, you are likely responsible for maintaining the web site and keeping it up-to-date. Even if you have a staff member or systems administrator who is tasked with updating the web site, you should be familiar with the web site management program. Web sites and electronic communication are addressed in Chapter Six, Online Communication. For the purposes of your asset inventory, you should know how to post

§1.8 Asset Inventory

- Desktop computer
- Laptop computer or pad
- Smartphone
- Printer
- Fax machine
- Television
- DVR
- DVD
- Word processing program
- Database program
- Email program
- Presentation software (PowerPoint, Keynote, FlipShare, etc.)
- Web site editing program
- Media directory (online or offline)
- Digital audio recorder
- Digital video recorder
- Digital camera
- Easel

press releases, update the issue pages, provide new information about constituent services, etc.

You also may have the responsibility of creating and sending the organization's e-newsletter. If so, learn the software that manages the content, how to create "stories," and include links and photos. Many of these programs are intuitive, but that has a downside: it makes it easy to hit "send." Make sure you learn how to save content and delay sending so others can check your work.

The reality of your job is that it doesn't end when you leave the office. At any given hour on any day (weekends and holidays included), you may be required to respond to a reporter's inquiry, draft and distribute a press statement, or update the web site. That's where your smartphone, laptop, or tablet comes in. These tools allow you to do your job essentially anywhere in the world. You may need to work with your systems administrator to sync your smartphone with the tools at your office (such as your media lists), but there is no reason you need to come in the office to send a press release on a Sunday.

Your office also may have access to research tools, such as Lexis-Nexis, Factiva, WESTLAW, CQ.com, or Bloomberg Government. As a communication professional, you have to be one of the best general researchers in your office. You must know how to use the research services available, how best to use common search engines, and how to quickly download and transmit the data to colleagues. You also may determine that these services aren't worth the cost. The House of Representatives canceled its Factiva contract in 2011 because House offices were using Google News searches instead of Factiva.

Fortunate communication operations also will have use of television facilities. They could consist of a contractual relationship with a company that produces video news releases (VNRs), or be full studios at your disposal, such as in the U.S. House, the Senate, and some federal agencies. If television production is part of the communication strategy of the office, methods and practices will exist for using this asset. For new public relations professionals, working as a "television producer" can be one of the most rewarding aspects of the job. Identify the television assets the organization works with and consider how they may be expanded to enhance the organization's goals. For more on this topic, see § 2.21, Video News Release (VNR).

§1.9 List Building

For most communication professionals, their most tangible asset is their press list. The White House press secretary probably isn't fretting over whether his list of the local Iowa weekly editors is updated, but someone in the

§1.10 Sample Database Checklist

Databases should be designed to capture all relevant information for a news organization. Ideally, they should be laid out using software that allows the user to:
- Have data easily input by individuals not versed in computer software (such as interns);
- Merge with other office software to build letters, fax cover sheets, or customized emails;
- Create flexible forms so that fields can be added to the database when appropriate; and
- Possess clear search and list-building capabilities.

All Media
- Organization
- Phone Number (main)
- Fax Number (main)
- Address
- Subject Area (for news organizations that specialize in certain issues)
- Geographic Region (if appropriate)
- Media Type (daily newspaper, television station, etc.)
- Primary Contact
- Phone Number (direct)
- Fax Number (direct)
- Email Address
- Deadlines
- Notes/Special Instructions
- Preferred Delivery Method of Releases (email, fax, postal mail)

Talk Shows Only
- Host(s)
- Show Time(s)
- Booker(s)
- Format

Television Stations Only
- News Director
- Executive Producer
- Assignment Editor
- Newscast Producers (Create fields for each producer of a particular newscast, such as "5 PM Producer, 6 PM Producer.")
- Newscast Times
- Newscast Lineup Meeting Times (when news staff make choices for story lineups in upcoming newscasts)
- Reporters (Include specialties or beats, if appropriate.)
- Special Programs (Include information on public affairs programs the station may produce; you may wish to create a separate record for this program.)
- General Manager

Print/Wire Services Only
- Publication Frequency (daily, weekly, monthly)
- Time/Date of Publication
- Editor
- City Desk Editor
- Other Editors (Create fields for each editor of a particular section of the publication.)
- Other Reporters

Radio Stations Only
- News Director
- Newscast Times
- Special Programs (Include information on public affairs programs the station may produce; you may wish to create a separate record for this program.)
- Program Director
- General Manager

New Media Only
- Editor
- Blogger(s)
- Frequency of blog posts
- Type of post (opinion/reporting)
- Political leaning (if appropriate)
- Accept guest posts?
- Social media accounts

§1.11 Media Directories and Software

- BurrellesLuce
  <www.burrellesluce.com>
- Gebbie Press
  <www.gebbieinc.com>
- The News Media Yellow Book
  <www.leadershipdirectories.com>
- Hudson's Washington News
  Media Contacts Directory
  <www.greyhouse.com/hudsons.htm>
- Vocus <www.vocus.com>
- Cision <http://us.cision.com>

White House probably is. The press list is the pure definition of your target audience. It should be up-to-date, complete, comprehensive, and in an electronic format that can be used to create letters, send out emails and faxes, and rapidly make phone calls. As the new press secretary, you inherit the list of your predecessor, making you completely vulnerable to the professionalism, or lack thereof, of the immediate past occupant of your chair.

You must first determine what is in your computer and in the files. Does the press list encompass the full universe of media that you wish to target? Are all the specialty reporters who might have occasional interest in your issues included? Are news organizations, reporters, and bloggers coded, based on a logical breakdown of issues and interests? Are all the characteristics of the news organizations accurately recorded? (editors' names, deadline times, circulation, satellite feed preferences. See § 1.10, Sample Database Checklist, for a detailed list of all possible characteristics.) While your predecessor's press list may be in rough shape, it's still better than starting from scratch.

After you've assessed what you have, start looking for more information. Press lists can always benefit from an infusion of new data. There are probably other individuals or groups that are collecting the same press lists and might be willing to share data. For example, House and Senate offices from the same state all have overlapping territory. If you work for a Republican congressman in a state with two Republican senators, your Senate press secretary colleagues might lend you their portion of the state press list that covers your congressional district. Similar nonprofit organizations would probably benefit from sharing reporters' names and interests; or, federal agencies or departments may have overlapping missions. However you acquire it, make sure your press list is as up-to-date as possible.

For public relations professionals new to their posts, the tasks of updating a press list and making the rounds of introductions to key news media can be combined. If you can't beg, borrow, or steal your way to a shiny new list, you'll have to go through the labor-intensive process of calling each organization on your list to determine if it's current. As you review your list, make sure you have all relevant numbers of each news organization. Most important, make sure you have direct dial numbers and email addresses for television assignment desks, radio station news departments, and newspaper news editors (sometimes called the "city desk"). For reporters who cover you on a weekly basis, try to get cell and home phone numbers and email addresses. They'll likely want to exchange for yours, so be ready to give up some evenings for reporters' phone calls.

As you review your data, it's important to ensure that the software format that contains the data is compatible with the regular communication tasks you'll perform. Technology used to maintain press data and distribute press materials has evolved in the Internet Age, but it's up to you to determine the most effective and user-friendly method (sometimes those two concepts don't align). Some offices rely on an email program like Microsoft Outlook to keep media contacts and to create press lists, such as one for TV news assignment editors or Washington-based reporters for local newspapers. Others prefer to keep a press list on a spreadsheet and use mail merging to disseminate information. Another option is to use the same online program used to distribute the email newsletter. Rarely, but occasionally, offices use faxes to distribute materials. You should ask media outlets how they prefer to get information.

You should use the format that allows you to regularly carry out communication tasks, including keeping an up-to-date list and sending out press releases on short notice. You don't have to be a "tech expert," but you must know your way around your system and be able to perform basic functions. If your current technology doesn't afford you these basic functions, you may need to have the list converted to another format. To do this, it's best to have your systems administrator or computer vendor help. Databases and spreadsheets are generally malleable and can be converted in a variety of ways. It usually means that you or your assistant will have some clean-up and you will have to eyeball each record. But that's another way of getting to know your media outlets.

§1.12 Getting to Know Your Reporters

Next to your new boss, the most important people in your life are the reporters who cover your office. These are the keepers of your reputation, and building a good relationship with them will be one of the key criteria you'll be judged by. As you start a new job, the list of key reporters will become self-evident. For a congressional office in Washington, there are usually a handful of reporters who cover the state delegation, though fewer of these reporters remain in Washington each year—as newspapers downsize, Washington bureaus are often among the first to be cut. For agencies, there are reporters for major papers or wire services who cover a beat that encompasses the agency mission. The list will probably be in descending order, based on newspaper circulation, television ratings, or blogger's importance—and that's an appropriate way to get to know your new friends. Every press office either mentally or in a written plan prioritizes the reporters who cover them. This doesn't mean you have to play favorites all the time; but it does mean that you understand who has the greatest reach and who has the greatest impact on your target audiences.

Getting to know the reporters who cover you is a little like learning about the new teacher you have for a tough course. You want to check them out surreptitiously, try to get on their good side without doing much work, but you're always kind of wondering when they're going to slam you with a pop quiz. The friendlier and more comfortable you are with your reporters, the better job you can do for your boss.

One way to get to know reporters is to do a "media tour" by setting up appointments and visiting them on their turf. Since a press secretary's primary link to the media is through reporters, this is a rare opportunity for you to get to know the editors and news directors who pull their strings. It may also be your only chance to meet face-to-face with the radio voices who will regularly call you at 6:00 a.m. for a sound bite. Visiting news organizations is a great way to demonstrate that you appreciate and respect the work that reporters do. If you're a former reporter, you can establish a rapport as common practitioners of a trade. It's important that you convey your credibility in these meetings and try to build both a professional and personal connection.

§1.13 Internal Politics

Early in your tenure as a new communication professional, the internal politics of your organization will become visible. Whether you're a press assistant in a nonprofit association with a hundred people, a press secretary in a congressional office with fifteen, a federal agency department with a half-dozen staff, or a two-person public relations firm, internal politics exist in any organized association of humans. People with apparently equal titles will appear to have different status with the boss, some policy people may have sign-off authority on communication matters, or the executive assistant will review every document that flows in and out of the office. However the power flows, it's a good idea to get a handle on it as soon as possible.

Internal political games can be some of the most self-defeating and depressing aspects of a career in public affairs. People who gravitate to the work are often very intelligent, highly motivated, and have a strong sense of public service. This can often translate into people enthusiastically expressing their beliefs and sticking by them. We'll address how to handle some of the more common internal office issues related to communication in Chapter Nine, Internal Issues: Experts, Policy, Numbers, Leaks, Lawyers, and Language. In your first week, size up the situation and don't make a bad impression. Sophisticated personnel interaction should wait until you get settled in.

Any review of internal political issues should include a check on outside groups or individuals who carry weight on communication issues. Nonprofit organizations have boards of directors, members of Congress have political consultants, and federal agencies have lawyers, *lots* of lawyers. You'll want to identify early on those who feel they have a piece of the communication operation and set up a procedure for working with them. As you do, consider two questions: 1) who *should* have input, and 2) who *thinks* they should have input. How you manage the answers to those questions probably will have a significant impact on your interpersonal relationships in the operation.

§1.14 Creating a Communication Plan

Often, one of the most important early tasks for new communication professionals is the development of a communication plan. We will address this task in much greater detail in Chapter Three, Developing a Message and Communication Plan. Nonetheless, it's important to recognize that much of your initial research, reviews, and interviews with staff will lead to the development of this important written product. Without a plan, your proactive press work will be rudderless. Sometimes you will enter a press shop that has a communication plan, and your primary responsibility is to help implement it. Many times, if you are the senior (or only) press liaison, you'll be expected to chart the message course and will have to draft a plan.

When drafting a communication plan, first consider the message you want to convey, the strategic goals of the principal or organization, the history of communication on the issue, and the tools you have to communicate with. You may have communication goals tied to a timeline—either a legislative calendar, election campaign, or other major series of events.

Communication plans cannot be created in a vacuum. Staff who are genuinely terrified of dealing with the media will suddenly want to get very involved in crafting the particulars of a communication plan. Recognize who the players are when considering the internal politics, and think about who needs to review the plan in order to make it a reality.

§1.15 Finding Teachers and Allies

Someone once said that wisdom begins with the statement, "I don't know." Even the most seasoned professional starting her fifth senior communication position needs help, especially at first. If you work in a public relations firm, large federal agency, or trade association, friends in the profession can often be found in the cubicle next to yours. However, many public relations professionals are islands in a sea of policy wonks.

You'll need to find someone to bounce ideas off, learn from, even just gripe about the challenges you face. Your logical allies will likely work regularly with your office. Congressional delegations, common policy coalitions, other similar agencies, all have communication professionals who will want to help you succeed. Building personal relationships, professional ties, and networking are all necessary for a successful career.

When I was a new press secretary, I was intimidated by the breadth of my responsibility. It seemed awesome, the potential for good or mischief, huge successes or humiliating failures, all at the end of the phone or the computer keyboard. With luck, you'll find yourself in an office that also employs a person who has more communication experience than you.

I was fortunate in my first job working for freshman Congressman Tom McMillen of Maryland. His administrative assistant was Jerry Grant. Jerry was one of these political operatives out of central casting. His resume was filled with work for presidential candidate Senator "Scoop" Jackson in 1976, administrative assistant to Senator Jim Sasser of Tennessee, and he attended every Democratic political convention from Kennedy to Clinton. He had been lured back into politics from semi-retirement by a brash young candidate. McMillen, a former NBA player, University of Maryland graduate, and Rhodes Scholar, was beginning his political career, and won a House seat in 1986 with Jerry's help.

Jerry Grant split his day between the Capitol Hill office and making the rounds in suburban Maryland, handling district political and congressional business. His usual attire consisted of casual shirts and docksiders, with a good cigar nearby. Jerry's brutal and often wonderfully profane honesty about political communication was the real-world hardball course I needed. Jerry knew all the messy communication problems a young press secretary could get into, and he helped me avoid most of them. When I wanted to fire back at an editor who (I thought) had unfairly criticized the congressman in an editorial, Jerry gave me my first political rule: "Never get in a pissing contest with someone who buys ink by the barrel." His humor and wisdom guided me through many crises. He wasn't always right, but having someone to talk things through with is invaluable in any communication situation.

Jerry Grant developed bone cancer some years ago and passed away after a five-year struggle with the disease. I attended the funeral in Annapolis. The political pros from four decades were in the pews—congressmen, senators, governors, sitting and retired. Seems like I wasn't the only one Jerry taught political communication to.

§1.99 Chapter Summary

- Find an organization or boss who shares your values. You'll be a much stronger advocate for the mission if you believe in it. (§ 1.2)
- Research the organization's strategic position, historical record, and key issues. Use your predecessor as a resource. (§ 1.4)
- Learn the principal's or organization's strategic mission. Are they following a written strategic plan, or some unwritten yet well-known goals? (§ 1.5)
- Assess the internal and external environment from a communicator's perspective. Identify strengths and weaknesses of the principal and staff; scan for potential opportunities and threats. (§ 1.6)
- Conduct a resource assessment. List the hardware and software you have to work with. (§ 1.7)
- Review the press list, update and build on it. It is the most important asset to a public relations professional. (§ 1.9)
- Make an effort to get to know the reporters who regularly cover your organization. If possible, visit them in their offices. (§ 1.12)
- Try to get a handle on the internal politics of the organization. Who is involved in communication strategy? Are there outside advisors who need to be consulted? (§ 1.13)
- Consider how you'll form a communication plan. Identify broad themes as you conduct other reviews of your external and internal environments. (§ 1.14)
- Find teachers and allies. Everyone needs someone to talk to and bounce ideas off. (§ 1.15)

Chapter Two:
Tools of the Craft

Tools of the Craft

§2.1 Introduction

Communication is the act of conveying a message from one person to another. In public relations, that message is conveyed through a variety of vehicles that make up the public relations practitioner's tools. The White House press secretary has many staff, television studios, vast computer assets, web site managers, and a host of other resources. The communication assistant for a small nonprofit organization may only have a phone, computer, fax, and his charm to convince a reporter to write a story for *The New York Times*. The vehicles for conveying the message vary from organization to organization, but there are some basic tools that are common to most public relations shops.

Like any craftsman, becoming skilled at using the tools of the craft makes you a more valuable worker. In public relations, there are certain skills that everyone must master, such as writing a press release. Others, such as designing a web site, lend themselves to specialty experts. This chapter will give an overview of the essential tools of public relations and how to use them.

§2.2 The First Tool: The Written Word

At the core of all communication vehicles is a written product. Whether it's a ten-page speech delivered with hundreds of reporters frantically scribbling notes, a set of talking points for a television interview, or a press advisory that will be read by two or three weekly newspaper editors, something written is usually the starting point. Every new college graduate hears stories from business leaders about how they can't find enough people who write well— and there's certainly some truth to that complaint. That makes it all the more important for a public relations practitioner's writing to be clear, crisp, and

§2.3 How to Test Your Document's Readability

A readability test of your writing is available in the Microsoft Word software. The Flesch Reading Ease test was developed in the 1940s by Dr. Rudolph Flesch to test the readability of writing. It uses a formula based on factors such as length of sentences and complexity of words in order to determine the amount of mental work a reader would have to do. A score of 60 or 70 is considered "plain English"; a score of 20 to 30 is more difficult to read. Microsoft Word allows you to run this test on any document. In Word 2003, under the "Tools" menu, select "Options," then select the "Spelling and Grammar" tab. At the bottom of the screen, check the box for "Show readability statistics." In Word 2007, click the Microsoft Office button, select "Word Options," select "Proofing," and check the box next to "Show readability statistics." The next document you run spell check on will produce a score on the Flesch scale.

flawless, especially for those new to the business.

Most organizations will follow some stylebook, such as the *Associated Press Stylebook*. This is the most common one, but agencies also use the *United States Government Printing Office Style Manual*. Soon after getting the job, make sure you have two of them—one for the office and one for home.

Writing is not something you learn once and carry with you throughout life. The best public relations writers work at their craft, constantly edit their work, ask colleagues for input, and carefully examine each sentence as if it were a work of art. Anything leaving the office, such as a press release or a blog post, also needs to be error-free. The need for perfection is not just a by-product of the obsessive-compulsive personalities that tend to flock to public relations work. Each written product goes onto the public record, for all to see, absorb, and usually criticize. Barely a week goes by in Washington when *The Washington Post* or *Roll Call* doesn't fillet some flack or staffer who wrote a dumb memo, misspelled an important person's name in a letter, or had a typo in a press release. Worse yet, it's likely if you make this kind of mistake, it will be your boss or organization with egg on its face, compounding your error.

Finally, with the Internet, any written mistake committed by an individual in public affairs can be discovered and saved by the media with ease. In an age of overflowing information distribution, attention to good—if not perfect—writing and detail is essential.

§2.4 Press Release

The fundamental tool in public relations is the press release. The primary goal of the press release is to convince reporters to do a story. However, the press release has morphed into a communication tool that is read by more than just mainstream media. Bloggers, policy experts, even the public rely on press releases for the basic—and often definitive—information on public policy. For this reason communication professionals must consider all potential readers of this fundamental communication tool.

The first audience, reporters, is the most common one. Reporters need to review information quickly. A press release should tell a reporter in one or two sentences whether the story is worth pursuing. Therefore, the wording of the headline and lead are paramount. Like newspaper headline writing, it's often a good idea to wait to write the headline until the release is done, much like putting a bow on a wrapped gift. You will want to come up with good phrases and eye-catching buzzwords in the release-writing process that you can emphasize in the headline. The press release headline is similar to a newspaper headline, only it can be a little longer—up to ten words. You also have the flexibility to write a sub-headline, either emphasizing the main thrust of the release, or elaborating on a different central point. The headline is a tease, designed to get reporters to read the release and convince them to write a story.

The lead of the release is similar to a newspaper lead, and most releases should use a summary lead, condensing the most important information. Good press release leads are usually one or two sentences long and no more than three to four lines in length. The lead summarizes the overall thrust of the story and should be rigorously edited, as it is the second most important part of the release. Weak leads that don't catch the reporter's attention are a disservice to your principal and organization; slave over them, as they are the keys to good coverage.

What comes next in a release depends on the story and the public relations goals. Generally, press releases work on the same principle as newspaper stories—using the inverted pyramid as a guide. The most important information goes first, with everything flowing underneath in a descending order of importance. With elected officials, or agencies and organizations with high-profile leaders, it's probably best to include a quote in the second paragraph. The quote should not convey fact, but opinion or emotion. This is the part of the release that communicates feeling. The goal is to give the quote some zest or attractiveness that will make a reporter say, "This guy would be a good interview."

§2.5 Email Press Releases

The advent of email has changed many aspects of a press release. Most reporters would rather get information via email than in paper form. Some basic format information remains the same, but, like all electronic communication, email differs from the printed word. Here are some tips on writing email press releases.

- **Avoid attachments at all costs.** Unless a reporter is expecting an attachment of a release, or requested it, all releases should be in the body of the email text message. Some firewalls at large organizations will automatically block emails with attachments for fear of viruses.

- **The subject line of the email replaces the headline as the most important line of the release.** You've got five words to sell the story.

- **Include URL links to more information.** This is the greatest advantage of an email release. You can link the reader to additional information on your subject.

- **Keep the basic format of the release, with contact information up top, a headline, body of the release, and so on.** Reporters are still accustomed to the "old" format and expect it.

- **Keep media-targeted releases short—less than 500 words, or about four to six paragraphs.** If you've got more to say, include URL links to the additional information. Releases targeted to expert audiences and the public can be one to two pages long.

- **Do not include any text formatting, such as bold, underline, or even tabs.** Many email programs eliminate them. The only formatting flexibility you have is to use all capital letters. Use dashes (—) or stars (*) in place of bullets.

- **Test out the release by sending it to yourself.** Email formats vary, and usually require a shortening of the length of lines to about seventy characters. Send it to your own account and to your personal accounts on Yahoo and Hotmail to see how it will look.

- **When sending to more than one reporter, always include all the addresses as "blind cc's."** Reporters don't like having their email addresses broadcast around the world.

- **Try to send the release at the reporter's least busy time.** For most news organizations, this is between 10:00 a.m. and noon.

There is more on electronic-based communication in Chapter Six, Online Communication.

§2.6 Sample Press Release

 **NEWS RELEASE**

U.S. Small Business Administration

PRESS OFFICE

1 | **Release Date:** July 28, 2003 | **Contact:** Roger Hopkins, 202-205-6567 | **2**
Release Number: 03-52 | **Internet Address:** http://www.sba.gov/opc |

Regulatory Agencies Earn Improving Grades from SBA **3**

4 **5** WASHINGTON, D.C. – Federal regulatory agencies are doing better at creating and maintaining a small-business friendly attitude toward the nation's small businesses, according to the fiscal 2002 annual report to Congress from the U.S. Small Business Administration's National Ombudsman.

More than 30 agencies and their divisions received ratings from National Ombudsman Michael Barrera on their resolution of complaints about excessive enforcement. The report, released today, is available online at www.sba.gov/ombudsman/dsp_reports.html. **6**

7 "The ratings and the report are indicators of the government's relationship with the small business community," said SBA Administrator Hector V. Barreto. "Some regulations are necessary, but when enforcement is excessive or unfair, time and money is diverted from employee training, customer service, facility improvements, or healthcare benefits. As a result of the Congressional authority granted the ombudsman's office and the direction provided by President Bush's agenda for small business, the creative energy of the nation's entrepreneurs is where it belongs – helping the economy expand and grow by putting more Americans to work."

8 As required by the 1996 Small Business Regulatory Enforcement Fairness Act, Barrera's office reports annually to Congress on federal regulatory enforcement activities. Agencies are evaluated on how quickly they respond and resolve concerns from small businesses and the quality of those responses; representation by the agencies at regulatory fairness hearings held around the country; regulatory compliance assistance provided by agencies; and adoption and enforcement of non-retaliation policies by the agencies.

Barrera said the report provides valuable feedback to federal agencies on the federal regulatory enforcement environment for small business. "It is our hope that federal agencies will use the report as a tool to improve compliance assistance and move further from a 'gotcha' to a 'help you' attitude. This report also provides some of the best practices by federal agencies in their efforts to improve the overall enforcement environment," he said. **9**

For more information about the office, where hearings will be conducted, or to file a comment or concern, go to www.sba.gov/ombudsman, or call 1-888-REG-FAIR.

For more information about SBA's programs for small businesses, call the SBA Answer Desk at 1-800 U ASK SBA or TDD 704-344-6640 or visit the SBA's extensive Web site at www.sba.gov. The SBA, in co-sponsorship with Staples, has introduced an online newsletter, **SBA Solutions***. For a free subscription, go to http://web.sba.gov/list and select New* **SBA Solutions** *Newsletter.*

10

1. Release date always in upper left section of release, under letterhead.
2. Contact information should include phone number, possibly email address.
3. Headline should be short, fitting on one line, if possible. If sub-headline is used, place it in italics.
4. Dateline—include the location source of the release in large capital letters.
5. Lead is short, often one sentence. Try to keep this to four lines.

6. Include additional information in links in all releases.
7. First quote should be short, so that the principal can be identified quickly. Follow with longer quote capturing the essence of the release's message.
8. Paragraph after quote often includes more details on release's subject.
9. Final quote often ends release.
10. Conclude releases with either "###" or "-30-".

Try to avoid the trite, boring, overdone quote that sounds like it was written by the press secretary. "I'm pleased to accept this award from the Four Tipped Fern Growers of America. Their contribution to democracy and ferns everywhere is important." When writing a quote, if you start with the phrase, "I'm pleased . . . ," start over. Unfortunately, negative emotional quotes are often more attractive to reporters than positive ones. Starting a quote with, "I'm outraged . . ." or "I demand . . . ," is often more likely to encourage the reporter to read on. Some cautious organizations and federal agencies may not have the option of blasting away at a policy or group to get reporters' or bloggers' attention; but if you're looking to get noticed, it often works. It would be nice to think we could get in the local papers with positive stories, but regrettably the media's culture is biased toward the negative.

The remainder of the release should flow with the most important facts to the least important. Be sure you answer the basic journalistic questions of the Five W's and H: Who, What, Where, When, Why, and How. (Some public relations professionals and teachers feel that the Five W's and H should be in the lead—and that is sometimes the case. However, this is a constraining rule that can overburden a good lead.) When writing your outline, the flow of facts should indicate a clear connection from one paragraph to the other. Always include one or two more quotes—often saving the last paragraph for a concluding quote.

Ideally, the release should be on one page, but a two-page release can often be a very persuasive document, especially on the meatier subjects, such as the release of a report or survey. Since any data related to the release will be posted on your organization's web site, be certain to include URLs for more information. (For more information, see § 2.5, Email Press Releases.) Finally, all press releases should end with either "# # #" or "- 30 -" centered on the page.

One concluding note on press release writing. There is a debate in the public relations community over whether releases should be brimming with praise for the principal or organization, or whether they should be objective, sounding more like actual news stories. Reporters often will say they'd rather have an objective release—but then cover the member of Congress who writes a bombastic, self-congratulatory release.

Much of your judgment on what kind of release to write depends on the content of the story you have to tell. For example, federal agencies often write releases to convey straight policy information, and press release writers should strive for neutral-sounding dispatches. Weaker subjects might require a bit more work—a great quote, the specter of possible danger or ill consequences if some action isn't taken, or a broader connection to a greater social trend. However you write it, make sure that every word is true and defensible. The quickest way to get in trouble with the media is to put something out that isn't true. That's a sure-fire way to make certain all future releases will end up in the circular filing cabinet or the "deleted" subdirectory of a reporter's computer.

§2.7 Press Advisory

Another standard tool to attract media attention to an event is a press advisory. This differs from the press release in both goal and format. The advisory's goal is to notify the media of an event or occurrence that you wish them to cover. They can be issued as much in advance of an event as necessary, depending upon the event. However, keep in mind the barrage of events you're competing with in the minds of assignment editors and newspaper editors. The key is to get them to put the event on their calendar, or what is sometimes called a "futures file," so they can plan accordingly. If you issue an advisory more than a week in advance, you probably should do a follow-up advisory a day or two before the event.

The format is simpler than a press release. Advisories should have clear headlines, be no more than two paragraphs in length, and repeat relevant information in a clear and readable format. The key information should be spelled out in summary form, including: event, time and place, content or subject of event. The challenge is to provide enough information to entice coverage, but not so much so that you end up scooping yourself.

§2.9 Backgrounders

The "backgrounder" or "fact sheet" is an in-depth memo, more detailed than a press release. As its name implies, the backgrounder provides detailed background information on a particular topic.

Backgrounders often provide statistical information, chronologies of events, or contact information and sources, which may help reporters fill out a story. If done particularly well and in an objective voice, small newspapers will print pieces of backgrounders verbatim as part of a story or as sidebar pieces. (The ultimate thrill of a public relations professional is to see your words in print attributed to someone else.)

These tools can be one-page summaries, or longer report-like documents. A backgrounder that is more than three or four pages should probably be

§2.8 Sample Press Advisory

CSPI CENTER
FOR SCIENCE
IN THE
PUBLIC INTEREST
Publisher of *Nutrition Action Healthletter*

| ADVISORY | 2 |

FOR PLANNING PURPOSES:
Monday, June 2, 2003

FOR MORE INFORMATION:
Jeff Cronin: 202-777-8370

1   News Conference 12:00 p.m. Wednesday, June 4
CSPI to Urge Limits on Acrylamide in Processed Foods

3   The nation's leading food-safety and nutrition watchdog group, the Center for Science in the Public Interest (CSPI), will call on the Food and Drug Administration (FDA) to set limits on the amounts of acrylamide in processed foods. Acrylamide, a known carcinogen and neurotoxin, was discovered by Swedish scientists in certain fried and baked foods last year—a finding confirmed by the FDA. CSPI 4 will announce the filing of a petition with the FDA at a news conference at the National Press Club in Washington on Wednesday, June 4, 2003 at 12:00 p.m. ET (noon).

5   **Who:**   Michael F. Jacobson, Ph.D., CSPI executive director
                   Dale B. Hattis, Ph.D., Research Professor, Clark University

What: News conference announcing CSPI's petition to FDA asking for the agency
              to set limits on the amounts of acrylamide allowed in processed foods.
              Acrylamide levels of various packaged foods will be presented; several of
              those foods will be on display.

When: 12:00 p.m. ET (noon) on Wednesday, June 4, 2003

Where: National Press Club (Lisagor Room)
              529 14th Street, NW, Washington DC

6   The information in this news advisory is strictly for media planning purposes only and is embargoed until 12:00 p.m. on Wednesday, June 4.

–30–

7   *The Center for Science in the Public Interest (CSPI) is a nonprofit health-advocacy group based in Washington, D.C., that focuses on nutrition and food safety. CSPI is supported largely by the 800,000 U.S. and Canadian subscribers to its* **Nutrition Action Healthletter** *and by foundation grants.*

8   1875 Connecticut Avenue, N.W. / Suite 300 / Washington, DC 20009-5728 / (202) 332-9110 / FAX (202) 265-4954
on the Internet at *www.cspinet.org* • Executive Director: Michael F. Jacobson, Ph.D.

1. Include in headline both content information and possibly some logistics.
2. Note that this is an advisory, not a release.
3. Provide information on what reporters can expect if they attend the event.
4. Include basic information in the body of the advisory.
5. Break down information in sections covering: who, what, when, and where.
6. It is valuable to note that information in the advisory is not to be released.
7. When appropriate, provide background information on the credibility of the organization staging the event.
8. Provide additional information on web site related to the topic and organization.

labeled something else, such as a "report" or "analysis." It's best to create them with bullets or headings to separate the facts and make them easier for reporters to scan the information. When possible, identify sources of all material at the end of an important point, statistic, or bullet. Avoid using quotes, unless the quotes are absolutely necessary and are not provided in any other form, such as a press release. And, just like any other document provided to reporters, remember that backgrounders can be quoted and will be used by the media in any way they see fit.

Finally, the tone should be very objective. In a public affairs environment, this tool is meant to convey straight facts. Campaigns and other partisan or political groups will use backgrounders to support their views. Reporters see them for what they are—biased propaganda, advocating one opinion and ignoring other ideas. The most successful backgrounders appear as complete objective reference tools that reporters sometimes will use without attribution.

§2.10 Op-eds

Op-ed pieces (called such since they are "opposite" the "editorial" page) can be one of the most effective and persuasive tools in a press secretary's toolbox. At their zenith, they can sway hearts on an issue, determine the outcome of vital legislation, and bring grown men to tears. At their nadir, they are boring pap, created to inflate the writer's over-inflated ego, forcing the readers to ask themselves, "Why the hell did I waste my time reading that crap?"

An op-ed can be used for many purposes. It can be a policy pronouncement by a public official and make news all by itself. It can be a defensive piece to explain a policy position, offering the writer much more time and space to explain a rationale than an eight-second television sound bite will allow. Or, it can be a persuasive piece, meant to move public opinion and change public policy. They should strive to be timely and to add value to the debate or controversy.

Whatever the goal, op-eds are judged by the same standards as any other piece of journalism in the newspaper. If they appear in the Podunk Chronicle, it's likely that the competition won't be too fierce in the accompanying column. However, when writing for *The New York Times*, your boss—the "author"—will be lined up next to the best columnists in the world, and comparisons will be inevitable, since the writings will be side-by-side.

Although writers for decades have tried and failed to determine a formula for good op-eds, there are some characteristics that are common to the best ones. At the heart of a good op-ed are the author's credentials: has the writer earned the right to speak about this topic? Many policy-makers feel they have every right to comment on anything happening in the realm of public affairs. But, unless they are brilliant writers, their scribblings probably will go unnoticed. Newspaper editors usually do a good job of weeding out those who don't have credibility on certain topics, and will often only seek out authors because of their unique perspective.

In determining whether to write an op-ed, the author should ask more than, "Do I have something to say?" Rather, she should ask, "Why am I uniquely qualified to contribute to this debate?" Answering that question usually provides the communication specialist with ample ammunition to pitch editorial-page editors, and may form the basis of the piece. Also, often a persuasive op-ed has a statistic or two to back up any particular viewpoint. Like it or not, people believe statistics and numbers—there is comfort in numbers.

Despite the lack of an accepted formula, there is one device that can be helpful for the occasional op-ed writer: tell someone's story and wrap the policy argument inside it. *The Wall Street Journal* perfected this method for straight news stories, and for years it seemed that every article on its front page started with an anecdote, followed by a discussion of the broader implications embedded in this one story. President Reagan seemed to have a pocketful of letters that he'd whip out at any public event to convince his audience that one of his policies was correct because some seven-year-old in Topeka was urging him to do it.

Whether it be a standard news article, political speech, or op-ed piece, policy arguments without tangible people connected to them are distant and often weak. Everyone in the public policy arena is in this business to make people's lives better. Surely, the underlying purpose and cause of the op-ed will benefit *someone*. Tell a person's story up-front, convey the important facts of the policy, and then return to her story at the end.

Occasionally, the principal for an organization writes his own op-ed pieces. Senator Daniel Patrick Moynihan was legendary for writing his own op-eds, which were often erudite and thought-provoking explanations of public policy. Some senior principals possess the writing skills to create such work, but most rely on their public relations or policy staff to write some or all of their pieces.

Like speeches, the drafting process of an op-ed is particular to whose name is going to appear as the writer. It may start with the author conveying to the public relations professional broad outlines of ideas, with some suggested language, and asking her to fill in the blanks. Others may take a more collaborative approach. Sometimes these processes can be quite rewarding, but often they are tortuous. Draft after draft is sent into the boss' office, with each one sent back with miles of red ink scribbled throughout the margins.

That's why it's so important to have a solid "idea meeting" at the start of the process. Know what your boss wants to say, what her goals are, what points does she want to emphasize—and add your judgment at that time. If possible, agree on a broad outline so that you don't waste your time going through the whole drafting process only to find out you missed the most important points.

An op-ed should be a seamless flow, like a casual ride the reader climbs aboard for the three-to-five minutes it takes to read the piece. There should be no opportunity to get off the ride, nothing jarring or inappropriate; just a short journey from the land of "I don't have an opinion on this" to the palace of "she's right." People form opinions about public policy in a variety of ways, and certainly television and photographs are paramount in building the foundation for changing someone's mind. But op-ed pieces can close the deal. They have a finality and intelligence about them that no other public relations vehicle possesses. They are the *complete* argument in the court of public opinion, not just a snippet or portion. For these reasons, op-eds need to be cogent, powerful messages that are the sum of the best arguments an individual or organization can muster.

§2.11 Letters to the Editor

Letters to the editor are used in public affairs for a variety of purposes. They are used to respond to criticism, correct an inaccuracy, complain about the slant of coverage, point out a missing fact in a story, or amplify an element of the story in an interesting way.

A newspaper or magazine has a variety of motives in publishing letters to the editor from public figures. The letters may be well-written; the author is connected to the debate in some way; the author has important credentials worthy of inclusion in the publication; or, the publication feels an obligation of fairness to a public figure who may feel ill-treated by recent coverage.

In drafting a letter to the editor keep in mind a few rules:

- **Keep the letter short.** No more than two to three paragraphs, about a hundred words.
- **Focus on the facts, not the messenger.** Letters to the editor that whine about bias in coverage are usually useless unless backed up by provable facts demonstrating significant errors on the part of the

publication. Newspapers sometimes will print a rebuttal to the charge accompanying the letter—giving the exchange a juvenile "did too, did not" tone.

- **Try to make the letter self-contained.** Readers may not be familiar with the piece that generated the letter. Include at least one line that explains the previous article the letter is referring to.

- **Send letters quickly—the same day, if possible.** Publications like to keep things current, even criticism of their own coverage.

- **Use letters to correct inaccuracies.** If an incorrect fact has been placed into the public record, letters to the editor are important clarification tools that may be useful in the future. Especially in politics, a charge unanswered, even if inaccurate, eventually becomes fact in the public's mind.

§2.12 Speeches

Entire courses are given on speechwriting, and if you find yourself as a full-time speechwriter, you should take one. If you're not a full-time speechwriter, but still want a quick run-down on the basics, here are three extremely helpful speechwriting books: *Speak Like Churchill, Stand Like Lincoln: 21 Power Secrets of History's Great Speakers*, by James C. Humes, ISBN 0761563512 (Prima Publishing 2002); *The Lost Art of the Great Speech: How to Write One—How to Deliver It*, by Richard Dowis, ISBN 0814470548 (AMACOM 1999); and *The 7 Principles of Public Speaking: Proven Methods from a PR Professional*, by Richard Zeoli, ISBN 1602392838 (Skyhorse 2008). Speechwriters often recommend that those new to the craft not read speechwriting books, but read great speeches. William Safire's *Lend Me Your Ears: Great Speeches in History* (W.W. Norton 2004) is a great read, whether you're a speechwriter or just an aficionado of wonderful rhetoric.

For most public relations professionals, writing speeches is an intermittent responsibility, usually requiring one to do workmanlike projects of limited rhetorical flourish. Press secretaries are usually called upon to draft the garden-variety speeches, such as the ribbon-cutting ceremony of a new bridge, the remarks to company employees at the annual meeting, or the brief after-dinner speech at a fund-raising event.

Like op-ed pieces, each principal will have her own system for writing speeches. Some will do most of the outlining and writing themselves, others will have staff write the entire speech. As you get to know your principal, learn about her speaking requirements, how best to fulfill them, and what other people on your staff you can draw on to help you. People are usually more particular about what they say than what they write. This is because they are often *looking* at the audience, and have to endure their reaction if things don't go well.

One of the greatest challenges is to learn how to craft a speech in the "speaker's voice." Do they like lots of statistics in a speech? Do they like to start every speech with a joke? Are they scholarly, or do they prefer to speak in a common person's cadence? Only through trial and error can you learn the unique aspects of a principal's speaking style, and public relations professionals who only spend 10 percent to 20 percent of their time on the task often don't find a groove until months into the job. Yet, it's important to try to find that groove, and add this communication merit badge to your list of skills.

The first task in crafting a speech is to determine audience needs and desires. Who are they? What do they want to hear from us? What are they expecting? How long should the speech be? When working for a major official, public relations practitioners can often negotiate the speech topics based on resources available in the office and previously written speeches. More than once I've convinced an environmental group that a speech on the Clean Water Act would be terrific—only because I knew I already had a speech on that topic in the can that only needed slight modifications to sound fresh. For the more infrequent speaker, or for the really important speeches, it's very important to understand your audience and tailor the remarks to fulfill their needs.

Like other public relations tools, your principal or organization should have goals for the speech. The most basic goal often is to impress an audience and gain their support. However, you might also want to obtain additional media coverage, or to win over a group of reluctant supporters with a surprising offer of assistance, or move the audience with "red meat" to motivate them to action.

Whatever your goals, know them before you begin writing and keep them in your mind throughout the process. As you work with the person giving the speech, clarify in advance the goals and general outline of the remarks. Make sure you're aware of key points the speaker wants to make, and exactly the phrases she'd like to use in making them. In essence, act like a reporter, taking careful notes during the planning session. This will reduce the number of drafts you have to create.

§2.13 Press Conferences/Events

Planning a press conference or a press event is a little like staging a play, and you're the director. In the lead, hopefully, is your principal. In supporting roles are characters who enhance the story and make it more likely to earn media coverage. The production can be as simple as a one-man act in front of a podium, or include a cast of hundreds.

Like all good plays, your event must start with a compelling story. The content must attract a reporter to the event. Politicians standing behind podiums and talking are boring. Events involving kids or animals are fun and engaging. The People for the Ethical Treatment of Animals (PETA) came up with a novel way to encourage lawmakers to avoid eating meat: in July 2009 PETA stationed two Playboy Playmates outside a congressional office building to pass out vegetarian hot dogs to members of Congress and staff. The ladies were clad in fashionable bikinis made of lettuce, virtually guaranteeing a photograph placement in Capitol Hill newspapers. The event or press conference must stem from your message, but it also must add a new twist or dimension in order to get coverage.

A key component of any event or press conference is visuals. All media want to tell a story with pictures—even if it's a radio reporter describing an exciting scene. One U.S. senator plans all of his events in the state backwards. Before they even consider the content, his staff asks themselves, "What do we want the newspaper picture to be," and backward-plan the event based on that image. Consider any props that could help tell your story.

During his presentation to the United Nations about the potential dangers of Saddam Hussein, Secretary of State Colin Powell held a vial purporting to contain anthrax to emphasize his point that the Iraqi dictator could attack the United States with a small amount of the biotoxin. (It was later reported that the vial did not contain anthrax.) Needless to say, those present paid very close attention to Secretary Powell's presentation and his handling of the glass vial.

Carefully consider the venue. Will there be enough room for video camera crews? Are the lighting and acoustics suitable for radio and television? Think of what the reporters will need, and any way you can make it easier for them do so. It will ensure their likely attendance at future events when you think like a journalist and anticipate their needs.

Where you can, work to control the environment in which the press conference will take place. Depending on the situation, you may want to be able to control access to avoid unnecessary disturbances. If you can, provide light-

§2.14 Press Conference Checklist

Below is a checklist for preparing for a press conference or press event. This list covers the logistics of a press conference after the topic and message have been determined. These tasks should not be performed by just one person, and do not all need to be done by public relations staff. However, a public relations specialist should at least oversee all aspects of the planning, preparation, execution, and follow-up of the event.

Planning
- Determine target media list
- Draft advisory
- Vet advisory with policy staff
- List possible locations
- Scout possible locations
- Select location (include alternative rain location if outdoors)
- List possible guest speakers
- Vet possible guest speakers
- Select guest speakers and determine speaking lineup

Preparation
- Issue press advisory
- Conduct follow-up phone calls to media and pitch event
- Prepare and review principal's talking points or remarks
- Draft press release and other media kit materials
- Vet materials with policy staff
- Review media kit materials
- Print and collate media kits
- Coordinate preparation of any additional props or tools (charts, PowerPoint, etc.)
- Confirm attendance and talking points of guest speakers
- Review event/room set-up
- Arrange/review media monitoring procedures
- Coordinate in-office photography

Execution
- Collect list of all press attendees
- Identify special needs of reporters (post-event interviews, post-event information requests)
- Distribute press release to target media list (done simultaneously as event occurs)

Immediate Follow-Up (Same Day)
- Post photos and press release on web site
- Post video on YouTube and create link on web site
- Respond to reporters' requests for additional information
- Conduct follow-up interviews
- Draft initial summary of coverage, including names and organizations of attending reporters

Long-Term Follow-Up
- Collect clips and video of event
- Prepare report summarizing coverage

ing and power to camera crews, and have a mult-box, a box into which micro-phones may be connected, to ensure sound quality for the reporters' equip-ment, reduce the tripping hazard and the tangle of microphones in front of the speaker.

Also, give careful consideration to having your own crew cover the con-ference as well. Having your own copy of the event provides you with resourc-es for those journalists who, for whatever reason, could not make it but still want to cover it. This also provides material for your web site and web publications.

Like any production, it's best to "script" your cast to the greatest extent possible. In addition to writing talking points for your boss, you'll want to spend a great deal of time coaching other people sharing the podium. In some cases you'll need to enter into careful negotiations on who says what and when. The less public speaking experience a person has, the more time you'll want to spend preparing and rehearsing him for the event.

Coaxing reporters to attend your press conference is always nerve-rack-ing. It's a little like throwing a party, and then waiting to see if the guests will arrive. Try to get reporters to commit whether they'll attend in order to pro-vide your principal with an estimate on coverage. In many cases, you should provide all the key details of what reporters can expect to cover if they attend. Few public figures have the gravitas to compel reporters' attendance without revealing the key components of the story.

Executing the press conference can be the toughest part, depending on the topic and the number of journalists who show up. Rather than trying to keep order, work to manage the chaos. Be sure you collect a list of all press attendees and also a list of those who want to follow up with a post-event interview. Also make sure during the conference that someone on your team notes when the speaker replies: "I'll have my staff follow up with you on that" and then do it. It is another good reason to have your own copy of the event.

Following up is one of the most important things you can do for both your and your boss' reputation. Following up in general is just good business; fol-lowing up on specific elements and promises is what your and your boss' cred-ibility hangs on. For more information, see § 2.14, Press Conference Checklist.

§2.15 Photography and Video

Like journalists, public relations professionals can use photographs to tell a story. Unlike photojournalists, communication specialists often have very little training in photography—a fact that we come to realize when we review our first digital photos after taking a new job. Yet, photos are essential to internal and external newsletters, web sites, and even for smaller newspapers. With a little practice, you'll be surprised at how quickly your photos take on a professional look.

The key to simple public relations photography is framing the shot. The image you want to save is usually the principal involved in some activity—speaking to a group, meeting with people, shaking hands with a dignitary. Unless your market audience is a very small weekly newspaper or specialized trade publication, you should avoid the smiling-at-the-camera-hand-shaking shot.

Public relations professionals need to put themselves in the perfect position to get the right photo. You may even have the flexibility to move people around to get it just right. Don't worry about ruffling feathers or appearing as though you're staging the event. When the photo appears in the local paper or trade publication, your boss won't care that you made him stand too close to some visiting luminary just to make a photo look good.

Be liberal about taking many shots. This isn't a class trip and you don't have to worry about looking like a goofy shutterbug. Take three to four shots from a variety of angles—you never know which one is going to catch your subjects in just the right way. Photos can be instantly transferred to web sites, and smaller newspapers and trade publications often have no problem using them.

Just as taking photos at an event is a valuable tool, so is getting video. In the age of ubiquitous Internet video, a good video can bypass the media filter and reach your audience directly. Additionally, members of the media often welcome videos to include on a blog or their web site. (Note: this is apart from providing videos via satellite feed to TV stations. For more on that topic, see § 2.20, Television Feed.) While the more "high tech" the video camera, the better the quality, even a simple video camera or phone video can record your principal's remarks at an event or his interaction with constituents. The same rules of photography apply to videography—get in a good position and frame your shot. For video recording, get good sound quality as well.

Once you record the video, you may want to post the video in its entirety, especially if it's under five minutes. If longer, edit down to the best parts. Once it's ready to share, decide how to distribute it. For blogs, Facebook, and Twitter, post the video on YouTube and link or embed from there.

Of course, not every video will get picked up, much less go viral. Consider the videos that you see posted on blogs and linked to on Twitter: they resonate emotionally, are powerful, feature strong words, and may be quirky. Be creative in your pitch and hope that your principal has given you good material.

§2.16 Direct Mail

Some public relations tools, such as op-eds, speeches, and web sites, bypass the filter of the media. Direct-mail pieces and newsletters also fall into this category. Direct-mail pieces take many forms: they can be simple one-page letters, brief 5" by 8" postcards, or glossy multicolored brochures. Like all public relations, their goal is often to persuade the reader to take action—win her vote in an election, get her donation to a cause, or encourage her participation in some grassroots campaign. Even so-called "informative" pieces usually have ulterior motives, or have some additional request for action attached.

Generalists in the communication field often don't do the sophisticated writing, graphics, and layout work that some direct-mail pieces require. However, they are often called upon to draft or write copy, especially for simpler pieces, such as letters. There are some basic principles that apply to all forms of this written communication.

As with all communication, consider the audience. The best direct-mail pieces are targeted to a specific audience, with content tailored to their interests. An email from Lady Gaga to college students alerting them to a pending bill in Congress that may affect them is going to attract the targeted audience's attention. A letter from a congressman to 250,000 constituents that starts with an opening line, "Let me tell you about some of the things I'm doing in Congress," is likely to be tossed away.

Targeting also means clearly identifying the audience member *by name*. People are much more likely to open an envelope with their name on it than one addressed to "Occupant." From your own experience receiving direct-mail pieces, you know including a name is still not a sure method to get your message read, but omitting any personal connection to the audience is just another reason to have your piece discarded.

The receiver of a communication also makes a clear distinction in his mind on whether to read the message based on the identification of the sender. A person is much more likely to open a letter from the president of the United States than Pete's Bicycle Shop. Envelopes and letterhead that identify the sender are powerful communication packaging tools. There are people who frame letters from members of Congress that may have actually been written by an eighteen-year-old intern. Never underestimate the power of official-sounding organizations.

§2.17 How NOT to Do Congressional Direct-Mail Pieces

For decades, members of Congress have sent constituents newsletters touting their work for "the people." Some House members spend $300,000 a year on newsletters and direct mail, frustrating anti-spending groups. Some of these pieces are very effective, but many are not. General newsletters that summarize *everything* the member of Congress has done recently—photos of a tree-planting with kids, bill signing with the president, charts on the impact of tax legislation—all violate the basic rules of communication. Simple, targeted, single-issue direct-mail newsletters are much more effective than generic overviews of accomplishments. The only piece of mail people will read that covers a multitude of topics is an Ikea or Pottery Barn catalog. Unfortunately, the activities of a member of Congress are often less interesting than a new coffee table. Communicating one idea to hundreds of thousands of people is a lot better than communicating many ideas to just a few.

When writing any kind of direct-mail communication, keep the topic simple, directed, and limited to a single idea. Messages that start, "There are a few issues I'd like to discuss," often lead nowhere and will fail to motivate the reader to action.

The tone of a message can be very different, depending upon the goal. A letter from a member of Congress on a recent environmental vote is a lot different than a fund-raising pitch from the Sierra Club. The common elements are:

- **Make the opening line sharp.** It's the most important line in the message and will determine whether the piece will be read.
- **Make use of bullets, sub-headlines, underline, and italics.** Even the most official letter can include lists in easily readable, bulleted forms.
- **Make ample use of "P.S."** Next to the first line, this is the most-read part of any communication.

Finally, all direct-mail pieces should include some kind of call to action. It may be just a request to visit your web site. Or, it may be something much more significant, such as a financial contribution. If you've captured the readers' attention, informed them of some important issue, and convinced them that you've got something to say—they're waiting for you to tell them what to do. Don't miss this golden opportunity.

§2.18 Newsletters

Like direct-mail pieces, newsletters can vary wildly in structure, cost, and design. Like direct-mail pieces, the best newsletters are targeted to a specific audience. Unlike direct-mail pieces, newsletters are often sent to a group that already has somehow agreed to receive the newsletter. People who have joined clubs, contributed to nonprofit organizations, or requested information through a web site are often not surprised when they receive a newsletter in the mail, and are more apt to read it.

Writing a newsletter is like writing a small newspaper. You want to identify what the reader's interests are, the most newsworthy items that occurred since the last newsletter was written, and present it in an interesting way. The writing style should be journalistic, using the inverted pyramid to guide story construction. Good headline writing is paramount, as that is likely to be the only part of the newsletter most people will read. And, be sure to load the newsletter with lots of photos and graphics, with less emphasis on the text. Most people scan newsletters and don't read them cover-to-cover.

Finally, like any direct-mail piece, include a call for action. If the newsletter is not in an envelope, which is often the case, this request should be on an outside cover. For most of your target audience, they will only look at the front and back covers of the newsletter, so consider these sections the most important parts when crafting the message. For more information on the electronic versions of newsletters, see § 6.41, Tips for E-newsletters.

§2.19 Radio Feed

The radio feed or "actuality" is a brief audio recording of the principal's comments on some topic. These recordings are captured by a recording device, usually a broadcast-quality audio recorder, and transferred or saved in a format that can be transmitted to radio stations. For smaller radio stations with few news reporters, actualities are essential to collecting good sound bites to accompany their stories. Larger radio stations shun radio feeds and often insist on having their reporters interview the principal (where she repeats everything that she would have said in a radio feed, and nothing more). Therefore, the audience for the radio feed is often the station with a one- or two-person newsroom, scraping together wire copy, national news feeds, and rewrites of the local paper to put together a respectable newscast—every hour, on the hour.

The basic equipment needed to do a radio feed starts with the same tools a radio reporter would possess: a good broadcast-quality audio recorder and microphone. If you're a public relations professional in a small shop and are expected to produce radio feeds without good equipment, you'll need to explain to your boss that he needs to spend a few hundred dollars for a new audio recorder, or the local station will probably broadcast the latest update on wheat futures instead of his comments on agricultural policy.

To produce a radio feed, the public affairs officer interviews the principal as if he were a radio reporter. The advantage to this set-up is that, unlike the real news media, you can tell the person you're interviewing what you're going to ask and coach him on the correct answer (which is another reason why some radio stations don't take radio feeds). Interviewing your boss should be the simple part. You're giving him the question, coaching him on the response—this isn't exactly the *60 Minutes* treatment, right? Despite these advantages, principals often have difficulty with this format. Perhaps it's the flexibility to adjust the message, perhaps it's the annoying feeling we all get when we hear our voice on tape. Whatever the cause, you may have to do some additional coaching to get through the process.

If necessary, write out talking points so your boss has some ideas to use. You could even suggest exact wording, *but don't have them read a script.* Unless you work with an actor, reading a script is often very detectable. When this sound bite is heard on the radio, you want it to sound natural, as if your principal was being interviewed by a reporter. "Canned" sound bites can be detected by reporters, who already are squeamish about accepting your pre-packaged sound bite. Get the principal to respond to questions naturally. If he doesn't say it right the first time, have him do it again until he's comfortable with the statement.

When selecting sound bites, remember you don't have to—and should not—produce a full radio story. You want to give radio stations "raw" sound that they can edit into a 10- to 20-second sound bite. Ideally, your boss will give a good 90- to 120-second answer to the most important question, and that will be your feed. Radio feeds should be no longer than three minutes. Also, it's okay if your voice is on the tape asking the question, even if it breaks up the feed. It demonstrates that the principal was acting "naturally" and answering an honest question. The more you can make yourself sound like a real reporter, the more comfortable the radio station will be in using the sound bite on the air.

The Internet and digital recording have simplified the transmission of radio feeds to stations. Gone are the days of using tape recorders and answering machine-like devices to send the recording over a phone line. Today, offices record audio feeds using digital recording devices and place the recordings on their web sites, where radio stations can take the recording and use it on the air. After you place the digital recording on your web site, send a notice to radio station news directors in a brief email or a formal advisory.

§2.20 Television Feed

The television feed operates on the same principle as the radio feed: create raw footage of the boss commenting on some aspect of public policy and provide it to television stations. The hope is that they'll take this footage and create a television story. However, the complexity of the television medium makes this vehicle more difficult to use.

Most importantly, using television technology is much more expensive than radio. A television feed requires technical personnel, a television studio with satellite uplink capabilities, and the purchasing of satellite time to send the feed. Because of these added expenses, public relations professionals often want to test the market to see if television stations will really be interested in running a story. Some public relations organizations are fortunate enough not to have to worry about expenses and simply produce feeds on a regular basis in the hopes that they'll be picked up by stations. But many want some assurance their expense and work isn't wasted, and will pitch the story to television station assignment editors (the air traffic controllers of a newsroom who manage the assignment of reporters) to determine if the station will use the feed to create a story.

Once stations are prepped to accept the feed, all you have to do is produce it. Unlike a radio feed, which is usually just straight sound from one person, a good television feed should include most of the components of a television story—interviews, video to accompany the story, and "cutaways" (broader, medium- and wide-angle shots of the interviewer). In essence, the public relations professional is acting like a television field producer—conducting the interviews, directing the camera crew to get certain shots, and determining the raw components of the story that later will be edited.

In producing the story, take all the steps a television reporter would take. The television interview with a principal is much like the radio interview, with the public relations professional acting as a reporter asking the questions. Remember that the average television sound bite is about ten seconds. Make sure you collect other raw footage from the location (coverage of the press conference, wide-angle shots of the event, background shots related to the interview). When editing the feed, keep the material raw so that it can be easily edited into a television story. You're not creating a full story, you're providing the raw material so someone else can. Give the stations some editorial license to create real news from your video.

§2.21 Video News Release (VNR)

Producing a video news release (VNR) is exactly like producing a television story. It is a complete story that public relations professionals hope stations will take and put on the air, just as if it was a real story. To write or produce a VNR, you must have some television experience, as a novice's work will be quickly spotted by television producers. If your organization or company has the resources to produce a VNR, it's likely that a former reporter will be involved in the process.

While there are many steps to this process that are more journalistic than public relations in nature, there is one rule for the communication specialist involved in these projects: do not oversell the story. VNRs must look like real stories, so they must appear objective. Trying to put a political spin on a VNR will just result in the piece being ignored by stations. The most successful VNRs are technical in nature, often using scientific or medical experts that small local TV stations don't have access to.

§2.22 Public Service Announcements

Under the Federal Communications Act of 1934, radio and television stations have a responsibility to serve the public in addition to their overt goal of making money. One way stations fulfill this responsibility is by running public service announcements, or PSAs. These thirty- and sixty-second pleas for some cause are excellent ways for communication professionals to completely control their broadcast message and advance an altruistic goal of the principal or organization.

At the heart of the PSA should be some societal goal. Think about the PSAs that you actually watch. They raise awareness to a problem, inform viewers of a community in need, and appeal to the audience's conscience. PSAs can be magnificently produced television spots costing hundreds of thousands of dollars, or one person sitting looking at a camera asking for help.

The first key component to a successful PSA is that it be well-written. Sloppy, long verbiage is an instant snoozer, and an invitation for the viewer or listener to change the channel. With thirty seconds or less to convey a message, the selection of each syllable is vital. Another key component is the spokesperson. Celebrities are often the best people to deliver PSAs, if they are

§2.23 Tracking and Filing Systems

The one public relations component that public affairs professionals often ignore is *evaluation*. Private-sector public relations professionals routinely produce reports for their clients, in part to justify their fees. Public relations practitioners in the public or nonprofit sector usually have fewer resources, and are focused on tomorrow's story—failing to spend the time to evaluate yesterday's work. However, the only way to improve on your work is to carefully evaluate past performance.

Create a tracking system to monitor all coverage. Use a database that can break down the coverage by date, publication, medium, placement, reporter, and category. If possible, scan all clips into an accompanying database and have them catalogued for easy retrieval. Or, create two hard-copy filing systems that store clips chronologically and categorically. It may seem difficult at first; but creating these systems will provide you with a great library of data and will likely be invaluable for preparing future public relations strategies or defending against attacks.

credible representatives for the cause. Members of Congress and public officials can sometimes be good spokespeople, and as a public relations professional you may have no choice but to put the boss on camera or on audiotape. Hopefully, she has enough charisma to carry it off.

Another helpful component is additional footage. If you're making a plea for more donations to a charity that is seeking a cure for a childhood illness, it's probably a good idea to show pictures of kids in a hospital.

Finally, the PSA must look professional. Many PSAs that are relegated to the slot before the 3:00 a.m. informercial look like they were shot in someone's basement with Uncle Fred's video camera. Obviously, budgets will dictate what's available. But creative planning can make up for a lack of funds. If the studio looks junky, shoot the PSA outside on a sunny day to improve the lighting. PSAs don't have to be boring.

§2.24 Teleconferences and "Telephone Town Halls"

More and more associations, nonprofits, and congressional offices are taking advantage of teleconferences. Teleconferences, also called "telephone town halls," are a convenient way to reach stakeholders, who can talk to the principal without having to leave their homes. Association leaders can reach their membership with new initiatives, nonprofits can advise supporters of upcoming advocacy campaigns, and elected officials can use the technology to avoid the direct constituent contact and messy personal interaction that accompanies in-person public forums.

Many firms and vendors now specialize in teleconferences. They will work with you to select a list of potential participants to call (anywhere from 1,000 to 40,000 outbound calls), send out the robo-calls to encourage attendance, and set up a user-friendly computer-based system to screen questions and put stakeholders on the line—just like a live radio call-in show. Fees are often based on the number of target audience recruited for the call.

A typical teleconference requires a moderator (usually the public relations professional), three-to-four "screeners" (generally other office staff), and someone to serve as a liaison with the moderator and principal. Based on the screening system, you can identify questions that reflect timely issues and messages you wish to discuss during the teleconference. Even though you select who gets on with the principal, by no means should you limit yourself to taking "favorable" or "softball" questions. As with an in-person town hall, the goal is to show your principal to be accessible to stakeholders and knowledgeable and dedicated to their concerns. Throughout the teleconference, you can also ask participants to vote in an interactive poll. It can be as simple as "Do you want Congress to raise the debt limit? Press 1 for yes and 2 for no." Another advantage of the teleconference is that you can make it as special ized and as targeted as you want. You can hold a teleconference that targets seniors, veterans, or single women who could be potential supporters.

You also should consider inviting media to listen in on the call, while making clear they will not have an opportunity to ask questions. If they can't attend, most firms will provide recordings of the teleconference, which you can post on your web site and send to reporters.

§2.99 Chapter Summary

- Press releases are the fundamental tools to persuade reporters to cover stories. They need to have strong leads, one- to two-sentences long, use the inverted pyramid for overall structure, and include quotes that emphasize emotions, not facts. Many reporters today prefer email releases. (§§ 2.4 and 2.5)
- Press advisories are used to alert the media to upcoming events, and should include just basic information, such as the topic, time, and place. (§ 2.7)

- Backgrounders are in-depth memos written in objective style to convey straight facts in an objective tone. (§ 2.9)
- Op-ed pieces should strive to be timely and to add value to the debate. The best are written by those who have some unique qualifications to comment on the subject, or are excellent writers. (§ 2.10)
- Press conferences or events are like staging a play, with the public relations professional as the director. Create engaging events based on visuals available, and script the participants as much as possible. (§ 2.13)
- When photographing a principal, position yourself and your subjects correctly, get action shots (not "smiling-at-the-camera" shots), and take many photos. (§ 2.15)
- Direct-mail pieces should target specific audiences with clear topics, have sharp opening lines, use bullets and a P.S., and include some request for action by the receiver. (§ 2.16)
- Radio feeds should be created with broadcast-quality equipment. Public relations professionals should interview the principal like a journalist and create a 90- to 120-second feed to deliver to stations. (§ 2.19)
- Television feeds often should be pitched to stations before incurring the expense of creating them. They should be created like radio feeds, with raw material sent to stations that can be repackaged into a finished product. (§ 2.20)

Chapter Three:
Developing a Message
and Communication Plan

> *"Without publicity, a terrible thing happens . . . nothing."*
>
> P.T. Barnum

Developing a Message and Communication Plan

§3.1 Introduction

As public relations has become more sophisticated, the strategies and terms that previously were only discussed in boardrooms and in campaign headquarters have now worked their way into mainstream media. The word "spin" was considered an insider term fifteen years ago—now it's part of our common language.

Similarly, "message"—a term and concept formerly only used by professional public relations and marketing practitioners—is now a regular staple on CNN. We now accept the notion that all public figures and organizations must have a message, whether they sell soap, candidates, or ideas.

Developing a message is one of the most difficult aspects of a public relations professional's job because it's not just journeyman work—it requires savvy political skills, coordination among the diverse interests within an organization, and, above all else, creativity. This chapter addresses the components of a message and how to integrate it into a practical communication plan. In the public affairs arena, that often means marrying policy ideas with public relations tactics. Developing a message and communication plan is the tangible beginning of that partnership.

§3.2 The Message

A message is a succinct articulation of a vision designed to convey a broad theme or to motivate people to a specific action. It must be a clear, concise, value-based image or statement that connects with a targeted audience in a meaningful way. In the marketplace, a product's message is summed up in the advertising or slogan. Candidates are often associated with creating a message, which usually includes an aspect that contrasts them with their opponent. The political campaign community is often the most sophisticated in the public affairs environment in defining their messages. Paul Tully, the late political director of the Democratic National Committee said, "A message is a limited body of truthful information which is consistently conveyed by a candidate and an organization in order to provide the persuasive reasons for an audience to choose and act on behalf of their choice of our candidate."

Yet in the communication-rich environment of the twenty-first century, message is more than an image tool used to motivate people to perform a single act, such as voting for a candidate or buying a product. Message is an umbrella of images, words, and actions that combine to define a person, agency, or organization in the minds of people. It is the public cloak you wear every day of your life in the public affairs arena, the script that dictates your every public utterance, and the reasoning behind your game plan that directs your every public move. In the world of public affairs, a man, woman, or organization without a coherent message appears weak, equivocal, and is unlikely to achieve their strategic goals.

Message development can vary based on the type of organization crafting the message. For example, political candidates, who are crafting messages to contrast themselves with opponents, use different processes than federal agencies, who often craft messages to alter social behavior. Yet, all messages fall into two general categories: *strategic* messages and *campaign* messages.

A strategic message is a broad theme, an overarching set of principles or ideas that guides and shapes all communication. It is composed of general ideas and its goals may or may not fit into a limited time period or have a clearly measurable outcome. In a commercial environment, a strategic message is similar to company marketing or branding. In a public affairs environment, the strategic message is tied to the overall, long-term mission of the organization or principal.

A campaign message is a subset of a strategic message. It is composed of specific ideas, has a time limit or a particular practical result, such as the passage of legislation, and usually has a measurable outcome. The word "campaign" is not merely useful for political candidates—it represents a process and a way of thinking, planning, and execution that is helpful in any public affairs setting.

For example, the Sierra Club's strategic message is to define the organization as a prominent advocate of environmental protection. Yet the organization's leaders will often create campaign messages around measurable goals, such as the passage of a clean water bill. President Reagan built an image around the strategic message of less government, support for conservative social causes, and a strong national defense. Yet he and his advisors would create campaign messages for specific goals, such as passing a major tax cut bill.

> ## §3.3 How the Word "Campaign" Is Used in This Chapter
>
> The word "campaign" is often associated with an election campaign. But a campaign can also refer to any coordinated public affairs effort of a time-limited or goal-specific nature, such as a public relations campaign. Election campaigns fit into this category, but so do campaigns by nonprofits to enact legislation, campaigns by federal agencies to raise awareness about drug abuse, and public relations campaigns to announce a new association initiative on health care.

§3.4 Strategic Message Development

An organization's strategic message flows from its strategic goals. Developing a strategic message is inextricably linked to crafting strategic goals themselves, and the two processes occur simultaneously to be most effective.

Members of Congress, companies, organizations, federal agencies—all benefit from a clear strategic message. It helps define their roles in the marketplace of ideas and allows citizens to frame the organization in their own mind. The simplest messages can sometimes be boiled down to slogans. For example, 7-Up nailed its niche in the marketplace by declaring itself "The Un-Cola," perfectly separating itself from Coke and Pepsi. In 2008, Barack Obama defined himself as a candidate of "hope" and "change" and emphasized upbeat, optimistic messages.

In the extraordinary competition for citizens' attention, it is important to understand and plot your position in the target audience's mind, which is already cluttered with their own value system, worries about family and the office, and the more than 5,000 advertising images they receive on a daily basis. Al Ries and Jack Trout, in their breakthrough book *Positioning* (Warner

Books 1993), argued that Americans have to put all "new" products and ideas into an already existing context—a process they called "positioning." "The basic approach of positioning is not to create something new and different," Ries and Trout wrote, "but to manipulate what's already up there in the mind, to retie the connections that already exist."

In public affairs, developing a strategic message is all about positioning your principal or organization in the context of the audience's priorities, interests, desires, value system, and beliefs. For many organizations, this stems from a pre-existing mission. For example, the Transportation Security Administration's "position" in the "marketplace of ideas" is to protect airline passengers from terrorists. When considering that agency's strategic message, all images and communication emanate from that mission.

Often, organizations or individuals have flexibility in defining both the mission and the strategic message. Sometimes it's as simple as naming the organization. People who work for Citizens Against Government Waste or Defenders of Wildlife have absolutely no need to offer a second sentence of explanation of their message when they introduce themselves. Acronyms are an added boost to strategic message. The most brilliantly named organization in history is Mothers Against Drunk Driving, which adopted the acronym MADD. The name conveys the organization's precise strategic goal (it is "against drunk driving"); it contains a complete value system (motherhood) that is instantly recognizable to the audience; and its acronym embodies the emotional force behind both the strategic goal and the value system in one word. It's no accident that one of the most successful grassroots public policy campaigns in the twentieth century—raising the drinking age and strengthening drunk-driving laws—has a perfectly clear strategic message tied to its name and acronym.

To develop a strategic message, one must first start with the organization's strategic goals. When a public relations professional starts a new job, he is usually in one of two positions: either the organization has clear strategic goals and it's his job to develop a strategic message around those goals (easy), or the organization has unclear strategic goals and it's his job to create some semblance of purpose using public relations as a means (hard). In the latter case, the process of crafting a strategic message actually can be extremely helpful to an organization or public official who seems adrift. The communication process requires difficult questions to be answered in order to craft a message—difficult questions the principal may have avoided during the strategic planning process.

Whatever the state of affairs on Day One of the job, the first step in identifying and clarifying the strategic goals is with the leadership. The principal is the first and last voice in creating an organizational strategic message. He is the genesis of the goals of the organization and is usually the primary spokesman. A long informal meeting may clarify matters, where the public relations professional can ask:

- What is our core mission?
- What are the values that underpin our organization's mission?
- Who are our stakeholders and what are their needs and interests?
- In previous outreach efforts, what has garnered the most attention from our stakeholders and the media?

Asking other key employees is also valuable, especially if they have different answers to the questions above. Depending on where employees sit on the organizational chart, they may share the same goals, but differ on prioritization of those goals.

After gaining a good understanding of the principal's and organization's goals, certain clear themes should be apparent. Again, you might just be adopting the strategic message that already exists. But you'll have to at least shape it with your own perspective, if only to add your value to the work done by your predecessor.

§3.5 Campaign Message Development

A campaign message is a subset of the strategic message. At any given time an organization can have one or many campaign messages, and may be executing them independently or in concert with allies. There are many ways to create a campaign message, but here is a four-step method that will make the process go more smoothly.

Step 1—Agree on Goals. The first step in developing a campaign message is to make certain that everyone in the organization agrees on the message goals. If it's something clear—such as supporting an effort to get a bill passed by Congress—there is no need for a long debate. But sometimes the campaign message may be more amorphous and hard to measure, such as encouraging abstinence to reduce unwanted pregnancies. In those cases, an organization must agree on the specific goals of the public relations campaign, the role the public relations component will play in that success, and ensure there is an evaluation component at the conclusion of the campaign.

Step 2—Identify Target Audience(s). A basic element of any public relations campaign is to identify the target audience. Who is the message intended for? What are their needs, interests, and aspirations? What are their

§3.6 The Message Box

Political and advocacy communication professionals continue to benefit from a tool known as the "message box." Often credited to the late Democratic strategist Paul Tully, the message box is useful in any communication setting where you will be competing against another group's or person's ideas and messages.

This tool can be used to create campaign messages and communication plans. It also helps prepare you for any potential attack. The four quadrants of the box should be filled with specific ideas or phrases to help you build your message and prepare for future debates.

The box below uses the debate over President Obama's health insurance reform plan—to his opponents, "ObamaCare"—as an example.

What We Say about Us	What Opponents Say about Themselves
• Reform ensures that all Americans have access to quality, affordable health care, and significantly reduces long-term health-care costs • Health insurance reform puts you—not the health insurance companies—back in charge of your health care	• We want to make quality health-care coverage affordable and accessible for every American, and let those who like their current health-care coverage to keep it. • Instead of a government takeover of health care, we believe the American people deserve the freedom to choose the health care that is best for their families.
What We Say about Our Opponents	**What Opponents Say about Us**
• They are defending a failed status quo that benefits Big Insurance, while hard-working Americans struggle to get the health insurance they need and deserve.	• They are pushing for a government takeover of health care that would have devastating consequences for families and small businesses. • A government takeover of health care will raise taxes, ration care, kill jobs, and let government bureaucrats make decisions that should be made by families and their doctors.

values and how do those values relate to our organization or principal? When identifying an audience, it's helpful to be as specific as possible and consider communication networks and vehicles that the audience uses to get its information. For example, when marketing experts match a product to a target audience, this can be very narrow. If you sell a laxative that is most likely used by people over sixty, you might buy advertising in an AARP periodical. In public affairs, the goals and audiences are not always as easily narrowed. Yet, narrowing the goals and audiences will greatly enhance the likelihood that a campaign message will be successful and will be very helpful when determining which communication vehicles to use.

Step 3—Develop and Clarify Language. Words are the building blocks of any public relations campaign. Boiling down the campaign to a simple slogan or phrase sometimes means the difference between success and failure. In 1991, long-shot candidate Harris Wofford was running against the apparently unbeatable sitting Attorney General Richard Thornburgh for a Senate seat in Pennsylvania. Wofford was serving an interim Senate appointment as a result of the death of the incumbent, John Heinz. He and his political team, led by two little-known consultants, James Carville and Paul Begala (who in 1992 led Bill Clinton's successful presidential campaign), focused on health care as an issue. That alone might not have struck a chord with voters, if it hadn't been for a simple phrase that Wofford said over and over again throughout the campaign: "If criminals have a right to a lawyer, working Americans have a right to a doctor." It was a difficult statement to refute and helped lead Wofford to an upset victory and a seat in the U.S. Senate.

This is one part of the process that cannot be done by communication professionals alone. It is crucial that development of the message language be an inclusive process within the organization and draw on all key personnel. The principal and close policy advisors must be comfortable with the language the group will repeatedly use. The choice of words has policy implications, and reporters will parse every syllable a public figure utters to find an error or inconsistency. The message language must mesh seamlessly with actual policy and have full buy-in from every individual in the organization.

Also, consider your target audiences. What language will resonate with your target audiences? Do values held by your audience give you clues to potential phrases or language? Research is an essential component to a successful campaign. To settle on the best phrases, talking points, and slogans, it's helpful to test potential messages with target audiences. See Chapter Ten, § 10.5, Polls and Policy Positions, for more on use of polls in language development.

Step 4—Get Creative. Creativity is an important element through the message development, planning, and implementation process. A boring message, formulated with garden-variety plans, delivered through an unimaginative vehicle, such as a simple press conference, *deserves* to fail. The competition for the media's and public's attention is growing more fierce and is increasing on an hourly basis. Editors and assignment editors are bombarded with story ideas stemming from a myriad of public relations campaigns. What will make your message stand out? What phrases or images are most likely to connect with the audience? How can you tailor a sharp message that enables you to reach your audience directly through social media, including Facebook and Twitter? What supporting material should you meld together to create the most persuasive package?

Your message must have a clear narrative with visuals. Psychological research shows that human beings are not really analytical creatures, but "feel" their way to a decision. In 2011, House Budget Committee Chairman Paul Ryan advanced a budget plan to cut spending and alter Medicare. His PowerPoint presentations were filled with charts and graphs. Yet, his message might have been more powerful if he showed a picture of his son's elementary school class—then superimposed a headline: "The Government of the United States has saddled each of these children with a debt of $250,000. Do you think a lemonade stand will cover that?"

§3.7 The Limits of Message

Despite the reputation some public relations experts have for spinning straw into gold, no matter how good a message is, it cannot mask a truly bad idea. When Newt Gingrich and the GOP took over the House in 1994, one of their legislative goals was to alter the funding mechanism of many federal programs and shift them to block grants, eliminate accompanying federal regulations, and turn the money over to states (at a lower rate). The concept won big votes in the Congress with welfare reform legislation (which had no powerful constituency), but when Republicans tried to transplant the idea to other popular programs, opposition mounted. One of the candidates for the block grant concept was the national school lunch program. When block grant proponents ran into opposition from school superintendents, teachers, and parents, they said they had a "message problem." But the best spin doctor in the world could not put a good face on a proposal to literally take food from the mouths of children. The proposal was eventually killed by a congressional committee.

Similarly, the 1993 Clinton health-care plan sought to win supporters in Congress and the public through its appeal for universal health care. But the plan itself never caught on. The complexity of the proposal was too much for even members of Congress to totally comprehend. Opponents devastated the initiative with huge charts that purported to outline the new bureaucracy that would be created as a result of the legislation. And an ad campaign sponsored by the health care insurance industry featuring two "real" Americans, Harry and Louise, focused on simple values and beliefs (the public's suspicion of government-run programs) to destroy the proposal.

A public relations campaign message in a public affairs environment must be connected in a meaningful way to the values of the audience. Specific measures have some attraction—for example, everybody wants a tax cut. But it is much more persuasive to connect with an audience member on an emotional level, as opposed to a practical one, and emotions are evoked by touching our values. The policy *and* the public relations message must both connect with those values or the effort is not likely to succeed.

§3.8 Developing a Communication Plan

The development of a campaign message and a communication plan should overlap. As the process of creating a message unfolds, ideas on how to communicate the message should naturally bubble to the surface. Nonetheless, the final crafting of a communication plan requires a great degree of detail. The promulgation of various ideas must be connected to specific timelines, with available resources and tasks assigned. The scope and detail of the plan depends upon the magnitude of the campaign goal and size of the organization. This planning process follows the same guidelines as most action planning processes. In general, communication plans address these questions: what will be done, when it will be done, how it will be done, and who will do it.

Throughout the communication planning process, ask yourself basic questions designed to evoke ideas that will capture the attention of the media and public:

* How does what we do affect people's lives?
* What is the average person interested in?
* What would make the front page of the paper or the top TV story?

Unless you're dealing with an extremely narrow audience with a unique background, you'll want to keep these questions and answers as broad as possible. Even people of a particular audience subset react to good ideas the same way, and are subjected to the same degree of message assault that we all encounter every time we turn on the radio, TV, or iPad. Your job is to create a message and plan that will break through that enormous clutter and make a TV assignment editor say, "I want that story on tonight's newscast."

Step 1—Identify and Clarify Objectives. In strategic planning parlance, objectives are different from goals. You may have a series of objectives that are components of reaching one particular goal, using your message as an umbrella under which everything operates. For example, your campaign *goal* may be to defeat proposed changes to the national school lunch program. Your campaign *message* is that every child in public schools deserves at least one hot meal a day, connecting to the charitable values in the audience. Therefore, your *objective* is to use teachers, administrators, and parents as spokespersons to advocate against the school lunch cuts. Identifying the objectives may evolve from the message development process, but the objectives must be clarified and put in writing.

Step 2—Establish Milestones and Timelines. Any communication plan is a compilation of subset plans all built toward the same goal. As you construct the overall plan, identify the key milestones that will represent the building blocks of your plan. These milestones may be attached to dates or events that are outside of your control. For example, if you're waging a campaign to convince the video game industry to increase the use of warning labels on their more violent video games, you may want to peg certain events around the holiday shopping season, when there is more attention on these types of products.

If you're involved in a time-limited campaign, perhaps tied to the congressional session, use the same planning technique that political campaigns use: engage in backward planning from the anticipated date that the targeted legislation will be voted on, recognizing that the media's attention will increase as the actual vote date approaches. Or you may want to create your own milestone event, such as a major rally or march, that involves logistical planning and coordination with other groups.

However you map out these events on a calendar, make certain that you have the resources to fulfill your objectives. In any planning process, the difficulty lies in making trade-offs, and every individual and organization in the public affairs process has to give up something that they may want to do, but don't have the resources or time to undertake.

Step 3—Identify and Organize Allies. Most campaigns are not solo efforts, especially in Washington. Working with coalitions is one of the best ways to increase your resources, enhance your voice, and expand your political power.

The best allies are natural and consistent ones who have a long-standing relationship with your organization. In those cases, your job is to participate in pre-existing coalitions. But each campaign is also unique, and has the potential of garnering new friends who support your cause. Consider who shares a

§3.9 How to Do Everything Right and Still Fail— or, Getting "O.J.'ed"

One of the unusual things about public relations is that you get blamed for things that aren't your fault and credit for things you didn't do. Such are the vagaries of the industry. This rule means that you can do everything perfectly right, and still not get any coverage.

On June 17, 1994, I was working for a U.S. senator from Wisconsin, and was having difficulty getting television coverage in Green Bay. The rule in Green Bay was, if the story didn't have something to do with the Packers, you were out of luck. Somehow we managed to get all three network affiliates and both newspapers to cover a juvenile crime event with the senator at 11:00 a.m. This was our first success with the Green Bay media in a while, and we were all set to watch the evening newscasts and reap the rewards of our labors.

All this work was smashed to bits at 4:00 p.m., when the world stopped and began watching a live television feed from Los Angeles. A national story was unfolding before us, involving hovering television helicopters, about a hundred police cars traveling down a highway, and a slow-moving white Ford Bronco containing an ex-superstar football player accused of killing his wife. Every story on every newscast in America that night was ALL about O.J. Simpson. Green Bay televisions devoted their entire newscasts to this story (with a quick sidebar on a potential trade for the Packers), and, as far as my senator was concerned, he was the tree that fell in the forest while everyone was watching a murder mystery, not hearing a sound.

The moral of this story is: In public relations, you can do everything right— make every phone call, prepare every backgrounder perfectly, get the best location—but if major news happens someplace else that captures the audience's and media's attention, there's not a thing you can do about it. You have been "O.J.'ed."

similar interest and who might have resources to assist in your effort. Remember that "politics makes strange bedfellows."

Step 4—Develop an Action Plan. The action plan is where the rubber meets the road in public relations. It must include:

- tasks to be performed;
- person or organization assigned to the task; and
- timeline or deadline for the assignment.

The planning document also may include other details, such as resources

§3.10 How to Connect Your Message with Your Audience? S-E-D-A-T-E Them

When developing a communication plan, you want to draw on a diverse series of persuasive tools to get your message across. There's one word that captures all the tools: S-E-D-A-T-E. (Please forgive the accidental association with brainwashing—it just happens to be a word with the right letters and is easy to remember.)

- **Statistics:** Numbers are one of the most persuasive tools in a public relations professional's arsenal. Proponents of America's foreign aid budget defend it by pointing out that it only represents 1.3 percent of the federal budget and helps millions of starving people. Opponents point out that the $25 billion spent annually on other countries could be used to repair and renovate every crumbling school in America over the next five years.

- **Example:** Convey to an audience specific examples to illustrate how something works in the real world. The cell phone industry has created a beneficent image for their merchandise by running newspaper ads telling how people saved lives by having a cell phone in the right place at the right time.

- **Demonstration:** Demonstrations are often persuasive in anything related to science or technology, among other things. Walking reporters through a new web site or software is much better than trying to put that experience into words.

- **Analogy:** An analogy can be extremely powerful (such as Harris Wofford's analogy comparing criminals and lawyers to "working Americans" and doctors).

- **Testimonials:** Wheeling out a real person who can tell a real story is always more persuasive than a politician, expert, or some other talking head. It's one thing to tell people that the nationwide nursing shortage is hurting patient care. It's an entirely different thing to hear the same message from a compassionate-looking woman in a white nurse's outfit, or from an ailing patient.

- **Experience:** Draw on an audience's own memories and lives to win them over. Much of the public relations efforts to help pass a Patients' Bill of Rights (legislation to provide patients with additional powers when dealing with health insurance companies) was built on people's own experience with HMOs.

to be used or how alliances will be forged. The complexity of the plan depends on the scope and nature of the objectives.

In communication action planning, you must keep in mind the relation of your event or public relations effort to everything else that might be occurring in your environment that could compete for the media's attention. It is the rare public relations specialist who can command the high ground of a reporter's attention. Especially in Washington, leading members of Congress or the president can take over the pages of a publication with just a mere utterance, and most media outlets will only budget so much space for public affairs-related stories. Timing is everything. A news peg to a particular event or issue (like an historical anniversary) can make your story fly. Similarly, you can get completely ignored if something else is capturing the news (see § 3.9, How to Do Everything Right and Still Fail—or, Getting "O.J.'ed"). This means that you often have to "counter-program" by considering what else is going on and planning around it.

Step 5—Conduct Contingency Planning. Every communication plan should include two other elements: 1) What if something goes wrong? and 2) What else can I do if I have additional resources? This does not mean you need to create a complete alternative plan. Having add-on's or back-up plans is good insurance. Events can fall through, principals can change their minds, or other stories can overpower yours. In order to achieve your objectives, it's prudent to have multiple methods to get there. For example, your plan may include emailing a hundred press releases and doing follow-up phone calls to 25 percent of the list. A contingency plan may include doubling that to 50 percent if some tasks get done more quickly than anticipated. Or, you may have as an add-on the possibility of writing an op-ed, but only if a statement written by the policy staff is easily adapted to an op-ed format. Contingency planning helps provide some assurance in a public relations world where there are very few sure things.

§3.11 Taking Advantage of Opportunities

Most of this chapter has made it seem as though message development and communication planning is like producing a play—you create a theme, get policy experts to draft a script, cast principals as actors, and get the media to serve as an adoring audience. In reality, a lot of public relations work is more unpredictable and *reactive*. A lot of members of Congress figure out their message and strategy by opening the newspaper every day, and then saying to their press secretary, "We should do something on that issue."

Most often, ideas hatched over the morning coffee are worth about as much time and effort as went into wolfing down that second doughnut. But that doesn't mean that you must rigidly stick to your plans. The best public relations professionals not only create great plans, they adapt them to fit changing circumstances.

The best way to take advantage of opportunities is to prepare for them in advance. Each sphere of Washington public relations has its own set of potential circumstances that dictate the best preparation methods. In general, though, one all-purpose way to prepare for opportunities is to ensure that you have good contacts and resources so that you can capitalize upon them when the need arises. This means reaching out to reporters who may not be on your regular call list, or putting together press contact lists on topics that may not be your primary subject areas, but which may emerge as crucial if conditions change.

For example, one of the missions of your association may be to promote affordable housing, so you've developed a press list of reporters who cover housing issues. However, you're also aware that Congress is considering bankruptcy reform legislation, and, while there are no housing provisions in the bill that passed committee, you're not sure what will happen on the Senate floor. Therefore, you might want to create a press contact list of all reporters who have covered the bankruptcy bill when it passed committee, just in case some senator unexpectedly offers a housing-related amendment.

You must use good judgment in recognizing the parameters of your message and allow some opportunities to pass by. The organization's and principal's personality will dictate whether your operation is too cautious or too haphazard. Some members of Congress tend to be too opportunistic, grasping at so many issues that their constituents never get a clear idea of what the member stands for or has accomplished. Nonprofit organizations tend to be too wary of opportunities, seeking to keep to their safe ground, thereby missing chances to enhance their influence. Agencies are often too slow to react and even a perfect public relations product at the wrong time is perfectly useless.

Recognizing which opportunities are worth pursuing is the mark of a good public relations specialist—and you're probably one of the few people in the organization who will spot them. Ask yourself: Is this opportunity close to our mission? Does it warrant changing our plans to pursue it? What are the costs to the organization of pursuing the opportunity? Can we effectively take advantage of the opportunity during the short time-frame the news cycle offers? What is the likelihood we'll get positive media coverage as a result of our work?

§3.12 Connecting the Message to the Meaningful

The message cannot be an island; it must be connected to a tangible goal that excites the audience and is framed in such a way that gives that goal meaning. When John F. Kennedy made his famous speech announcing his intention to launch the Apollo program, he made that connection. "We must go to the moon and do the other things that need to be done, not because they are easy, but because they are hard."

His message wasn't that we needed to put a piece of hardware on a rock millions of miles away. He was saying that a manned moon landing represented the advancement of human achievement, and that this incredible scientific endeavor would mean something more important than the task itself—we would be *better* as a people because of it.

That message connected the space program to every American, indeed to every person on the planet, and therefore gave us all a stake in its success or failure. The message pulls together the routine activities of an organization and gives them a broader meaning through an association with the audience's values and beliefs. Use a great message to make that connection with your audience, and you'll have the power to put a man on the moon.

§3.99 Chapter Summary

- A message is a succinct articulation of a vision designed to convey a broad theme or to motivate people to a specific action. There are two types of messages: strategic and campaign. (§ 3.2)
- A strategic message is a broad theme, an overarching set of principles or ideas that guide and shape all communication. It is composed of general ideas and its goals may or may not fit into a limited time period or have a clearly measurable outcome. A strategic message flows from an organization's strategic goals and helps define its role in the marketplace of ideas, allowing citizens to frame the organization in their own minds, based on their own desires, interests, and value systems. (§ 3.4)
- A campaign message is a subset of a strategic message. It is composed of specific ideas, has a time limit or a particular practical result, such as the passage of legislation, and usually has a measurable outcome. To develop a campaign message, an organization should (§ 3.5):

1. Agree on goals;
2. Identify target audiences;
3. Develop and clarify language; and
4. Get creative—develop novel strategies that help the message stand out.

- There are limits to a message. No matter how good a message is, it cannot mask a truly bad idea. (§ 3.7)
- To develop a communication plan (§ 3.8):
    1. Identify and clarify objectives;
    2. Establish milestones and timelines;
    3. Identify and organize allies;
    4. Develop an action plan; and
    5. Conduct contingency planning.
- Be prepared to take advantage of emerging opportunities. The best public relations professionals not only create great plans— they adapt them to fit changing circumstances. (§ 3.11)

Chapter Four:
Interacting with Reporters

Interacting with Reporters

§4.1 Introduction

The most important aspect of day-to-day public relations work is interacting with reporters. The one-on-one contact that a communication specialist has with a representative of the media is crucial in defining how successful that person is in his job. How the message is portrayed; the placement of the principal or organization in the story; the quotes the reporter uses—all depend on successfully communicating with another individual, the reporter.

However, you're not communicating with an individual—you're also talking to the thousands, maybe millions, of his audience as well. When I was preparing a member of Congress for an important interview, he balked at the detail I pressed upon him. "Come on, Brad, I'm only talking to Tom," a reporter he had a long-standing and relatively good relationship with.

I replied, "You're not just talking to Tom, you're talking to everyone who reads his paper."

It's as if you're giving an extemporaneous speech to 100,000 people at a stadium. As the words come from your mouth, they are instantly displayed on the scoreboard for all to scrutinize. Then, they are taken down and chiseled into marble outside the stadium to be used against you for all time in the court of public opinion.

Reporters are not just employees of one news organization; they view themselves as representatives of the people and the most important defenders of the First Amendment. As such, they believe they have a license to ask

§4.3 Steps to Pitching a Story

1. Narrow the topic.
2. Organize and compile documents.
3. Develop talking points.
4. Determine if principal can be interviewed.
5. Call reporters.

any question of any individual, especially public figures. And they believe it is the responsibility of anyone in the public eye to answer those questions. This may not seem fair to the person being questioned, and the reporters' motives are often not as altruistic as they would like to believe. Nonetheless, their role is an extremely important part of the democratic process, and the first rule in dealing with a reporter is to respect that role and understand the power that a reporter possesses.

§4.2 Pitching a Story

Whether you're a presidential press secretary or deputy press assistant for a small nonprofit organization, you will have an agenda and want news organizations to promote your message. Some public relations jobs seem more reactive than proactive, but if you want to advance your organization's goals, you must spend a fair amount of time pitching story ideas to reporters.

Before you call up twenty reporters and try to interest them in a story idea, you need to get organized. The extent of this preparation depends on the complexity of the story. Press officers can find themselves coordinating with policy staff for months on the release of a major new report. Other times an idea is developed in the morning staff meeting and someone urges the press office to call a few reporters to see if anyone is interested. Regardless, preparation is the key to a good pitch. You should:

- Organize and compile documents that may be necessary to augment the story; be prepared to fax or email them to reporters.
- Develop talking points on the most newsworthy aspects of the story; write them out in advance and check them with the relevant experts in the office.
- If appropriate, discuss the possibility of media interviews with the principal in case you want to offer an interview during your story pitch.

When developing your pitch, consider the audience of the reporter. Ask yourself, "If I were in her shoes, what would I want to write about?" When dealing with local reporters, identifying a local or regional angle is always a plus, if not essential. Or, dovetail off a developing national story and find a

§4.4 How to Determine a Reporter's Interest

The key to identifying the level of a reporter's interest in your story is to listen very carefully to her initial response. Her first reaction is always very telling, and indicates whether you've got her hooked, or whether she's not anywhere near the bait. Here's what you want to listen for:

- **Silence, or the Indication They're Doing Something Else:** If you get absolutely no reaction to your pitch, it either means the reporter is completely spellbound with your story, or bored out of her socks. Regrettably, it often means the latter, because if she were interested, you'd get some reaction.

- **"Uh-Huh":** You've barely got her attention, but will lose it if she gets an email, her cell phone rings, or she gets a mild urge for some M&Ms from the office vending machine.

- **"Really":** You've got her on the hook, but not solidly. She's indicating that there might be something to report about in your pitch, and she wants to hear more.

- **"Wow":** This is a sure-fire indication that you're going to get something written. It may not make Page One, but you've got her totally hooked and should start thinking about when to line up the interview with your principal.

- **"Holy Shit":** This is the brass ring, the top award in pitch-dom of stories, the mother of all reactions that every press secretary yearns to hear. You can start planning on the Page One story. (And, believe it or not, for some inexplicable reason, nearly every reporter uses this exact phrase when responding to a great story.)

new or local twist. Longtime *New York Times* columnist Russell Baker said his business is misnamed. They shouldn't call it "news," he said, they should call it "olds," since reporters always gravitate to what has already been reported upon.

You also must identify the universe of reporters who might be interested in the story. If the logical media audience is more than a hundred outlets, you'll probably have to create an email or fax pitch to tease them into calling you. If it's a manageable number, organize your phone list and start dialing. Research past stories on your topic and develop a list of reporters who are most likely to cover it. If the story idea is more appropriate for a select audience, consider a tailored pitch targeted to a few reporters. It can often produce better results than a mass email campaign or cattle call on the phone.

The time of day you begin pitching also is important. Even with our

24-hour news cycle, unless you're the White House press secretary, most of your reporters go to work at around 9:00 a.m. and want to be home with the kids by 6:00 p.m. or 7:00 p.m. This means that pitching them a great story at 4:00 p.m. does two things: it diminishes the likelihood you'll get covered, and it annoys the reporter, who has to stay at the office until 8:00 p.m. to write up your news. Unless you're dealing with a story you expect reporters to sit on for a few days, the calmest part of the day (and that's a relative term) is between 10:00 a.m. and noon.

Keep your initial story pitch to thirty seconds or less. After you've gotten across the key points, ask if this is something the reporter might be interested in. Rarely can a public relations professional browbeat reporters into covering a story that they find boring, so it's a waste of your time and theirs to continue pitching. Once you get past the first level, continue to draw them in with other salient facts. You'll know whether you've got them hooked and if they'll want to pursue it. Reporters are remarkably blunt and sometimes downright rude. Don't take it personally—they're usually on deadline and have an editor breathing down their necks.

If you're dealing with reporters outside the Washington area, appreciate the fact that they don't eat, sleep, and breathe politics and government. It's not necessary to talk down to local reporters, but it is necessary to be more explanatory. Avoid the alphabet soup of acronyms that dominate our nation's capital, and be sure to explain any term that might not be familiar outside the Beltway. For more on pitching print reporters, see § 5.2, Print Medium.

When dealing with television, all these principles apply, even more so. Your pitch must be *very* brief. And the prejudice against public policy stories will be stronger. The old adage, "if it bleeds, it leads," is a common criticism of local television news, and often true. Local crime and basic day-to-day existence stories, like weather and transportation, always trump complicated policy stories. You have to know going into the pitch that policy stories have a higher hurdle to overcome and compete for attention with some cute little kid who just won the regional hopscotch championship.

Also, create the complete story in the television producer's mind. Tell him other video that might accompany the story that you can help provide, and suggest possible local contacts who could be interviewed. Make it easy for him to determine that this is a worthy candidate for his newscast. You have a lot of competition vying for limited time on the air—make your story more attractive by making it newsworthy, visual, and easy to produce. For more on pitching television reporters, see § 5.6, Television Medium.

Even as you pitch newspaper and television reporters, consider bloggers who may be interested in the story, including political bloggers and bloggers who write on specific issues such as health care, the environment, or civil liberties. A story that starts on a blog can receive widespread pick-up, including in newspapers and on television. Generally, bloggers are averse to receiving a press release that has been blasted to other reporters. Instead, consider what issues bloggers write about most and why they would care about your pitch. A blogger also has no "deadline"—she can post when she wants, so consider bloggers when you want to get out time-sensitive information.

Finally, it never hurts to follow up with a reporter who has been pitched a story via email or fax. However, don't just contact the reporter to see if he got the advisory or written pitch—try to have new information. Even if it's just a quote from the principal, or a new detail about an upcoming press conference, make the call worthy of the reporter's time.

§4.5 Handling Reporter Calls

When a person in the office who doesn't usually deal with the press gets a call from the media, often his first reaction is to run to the press office and in a panic-stricken voice say, "We're in trouble . . . I got a call from a reporter." The victim of this call makes it sound as if he were just bitten by a snake, and he'd like you to begin removing the venom.

Despite the overblown belief that reporters are inherently dangerous creatures, taking press calls can be one of the most interesting, challenging, and rewarding parts of a public relations job. The relationship between the reporters and those they cover is not adversarial per se, it just seems that way sometimes. Most of the time, reporters ask innocuous, very simple questions. And, helping them do their job is a straightforward and easy way to advance your principal's and organization's goals.

When a reporter calls, his requests fall into two categories: *access* (to a principal or an expert in the organization) and *information*. It is the communication specialist's job to provide them both. How you provide these commodities will determine, in part, how successful you are at the job.

The first task in fielding reporter calls is information gathering. You can't determine how to help the reporter or coordinate the response without understanding the basics of the story.

A public relations professional needs to ask the reporter:

- What are you writing about?
- What sort of information do you want from me?

§4.6 Tips on Talking to a Reporter

- **Always ask questions before providing answers.** Public relations professionals can't determine how to respond if they don't know what the story is.

- **Plan your interactions with reporters, when possible.** Use the resources of the office to research talking points, test the statements, and rehearse the interviews.

- **Talk in short sentences and be disciplined in your speech.** Don't ramble, it gives reporters too much flexibility to choose which part of the conversation to use.

- **Debate, but never argue.** Reporters get the last word in every argument, and spread it to 500,000 of their readers.

- **Know your message and stick to it.**

- What information or interviews have you already compiled?
- How big a story will this be?
- Do you want an interview with my boss or someone else in my organization?
- Do you have any documents related to this story that you can send me?
- What's your deadline?

Most reporters will answer some or all of these questions in the initial call. They understand that they need your cooperation to do their job, and the best way to get that is to cooperate with you. When handling negative stories, discussed later in § 4.7, or in handling a crisis or scandal, discussed in Chapter Twelve, the rules are a little different. But, the basic principle remains: don't say anything until you know what you're dealing with.

After collecting basic information when dealing with a new topic, your response should usually be, "I'll get back to you." Unless the reporter's question is simple, or one that you've answered before, public relations professionals rarely should give detailed answers on the first call. You have resources within your organization, perhaps including other people who deal with the media. Take advantage of those resources and treat every call as an opportunity to shine or as a potential disaster. Further, "I don't know" is a perfectly acceptable answer. Reporters need the information by the time of their deadline—not when they pose the initial questions.

Next, you should begin developing a plan for how to deal with the call. It may just be a simple question that requires you to check with a source in the office and return the call to the reporter. Or, it may have the potential to be a great press hit or a negative story, in which case you may want to assemble a variety of documents, do further research, and prepare your principal for an interview.

Reporter calls usually change the priorities and schedule of your day, force you to perform work to help them, and interrupt your planned activities. If you view these "interruptions" as annoyances rather than opportunities and an integral part of your job, it's time to start considering another profession.

There are many different ways to develop a response strategy and reply to reporters' questions. Yet, the overall rule is that it rarely hurts to be responsive. People outside the public relations profession usually are suspicious of reporters' motives when there are no ulterior motives present. If this is a garden-variety inquiry, treat the questions appropriately and simply respond in a timely manner.

Some public figures employ a strategy of not returning reporter phone calls. This is almost always a poor policy and a sure-fire way to get on the bad side of a reporter. Ask any member of the media what advice they give to public relations professionals, and often the first suggestion is, "return all phone calls, even if you don't have anything to say." Ninety-nine percent of the time, this is a good rule. It demonstrates respect to the reporter and the responsiveness of your organization.

However, 1 percent of the time a public relations professional may want to avoid talking to a reporter. You know the story will be negative, and anything in quotation marks will only add to the pain of an already damaging story. These instances are extremely rare, and those in the public eye should only avoid a reporter call when they are absolutely certain that nothing can be gained from an interaction, and when they are willing to accept some short-term damage to the relationship with the reporter and seeing "unavailable for comment" in the story.

§4.7 Handling Negative Stories

As a young Senate press secretary for New Jersey Senator Harrison Williams, Mike McCurry got a call from a reporter asking for a comment on a scandal that was brewing in Washington. The reporter said that Senator Williams was being investigated by the FBI for allegedly taking bribes in exchange for official favors from agents posing as representatives of an Arab sheik. Supposedly, the FBI had evidence of the senator taking bribes on videotape.

McCurry collected all the information he could, agreed to look into it, and called the senator. When he got Senator Williams on the phone, he heard the words that would change his life and influence his thinking when another future boss was accused of wrongdoing. "Ah, Mike, there may be something to that," Senator Williams said. McCurry weathered the scandal storm known as "Abscam" that resulted in his boss' resignation and conviction on bribery charges (along with four House members), and went on to one of the most prominent careers in recent public relations history.

How press secretaries handle negative stories defines both the principal's reputation and the public relations professional's reputation. We will discuss some of the rules of crisis communication in Chapter Twelve, but not all negative stories rise to the level of crisis. They often may just be a run-of-the-mill, one-day bad story. Yet, handling a single negative story well can significantly reduce the likelihood that it will mushroom into a full-blown crisis and impact the reputation of the principal, the organization, and the public relations professional.

Most negative stories are one-time hits. It may be a congressman who voted in committee for a bill that will play poorly back home. Or an agency that inconsistently enforced a regulation in a small town. Or an organization that staked out a position its board of directors thought was principled, but some editorial writer thought was extremist. Good public relations professionals recognize these stories before they occur, raise their potential for problems in the staff meeting when the policy is being discussed, or point out that a particular line in a speech could be quoted out of context. The occasional blind-side will occur, but many negative stories are foreseeable.

The first important challenge is to identify that you're dealing with a potentially negative story. Reporters rarely feel the need to announce at the beginning of a phone conversation, "Bill, I'm calling because I really want to nail your boss in tomorrow's paper and I'd like to get your reaction to this dirt someone just passed on to me." The clever reporter will try to lull you into a false sense of security and pounce when you don't have your guard up.

Listening between the lines is the important first step. When you're not sure what a reporter is driving at, be suspicious. If he's evasive, he's probably got something that could turn into a problem for you. Most reporters will be up-front and tell you the purpose of their call. If you think this is going to be a negative story for your boss or the organization, you have more questions to ask yourself.

While gathering information is important for all reporter calls, it is even more important with negative stories, because the reporter likely will have more information than the public relations professional. As you're asking the questions noted in § 4.5, internally ask yourself these additional questions:

- Is the reporter telling me everything?
- Is there someone behind this and what's her motivation?
- What tone should I take that best portrays our position?
- What is our liability (did we make a mistake)?

It's very hard to make sure you get every scrap of information, come off as non-defensive, and consider possible response strategies, all while someone is telling you something that has certainly ruined your day and will most probably ruin a good part of your week as well. The important point is: stay calm and don't say anything that could be quoted. The occasional uninitiated public official will be caught with the "Oh my God" reaction to a reporter's question. Be sure that the only thing the reporter can quote you as saying is a completely non-committal "uh-huh."

Immediately after you've gotten off the phone, it's time to spring into action. Begin developing your strategy as to how to respond. This means you may need to marshal other forces in your organization to assist in this effort. Press relations folks are accustomed to having their days wrecked by annoying reporter questions—policy people are not. You need to convince your colleagues that this story poses a serious problem and that they must rearrange their schedules to assist you in playing defense.

As you plot strategy, try to visualize the story. What is the lead? What is the most negative thing that will be said? Who are possible accusers that the reporter may not have told me about? And, most important, what is our liability (in other words, did we do something worthy of criticism)?

Sometimes, reporters just get the story plain wrong. They've collected incorrect data, an enemy of your principal or organization has misrepresented information, or the reporter is just stringing a series of honest facts into a conclusion that is wholly insupportable. In rare cases, public relations professionals can kill a story by appealing to the reporter or his editor. If a reporter is way off base, and there is evidence to disprove the allegations or accusations, he may actually drop the story.

Communication professionals can also cast doubt on a story by damaging the credibility of the accuser. But, that usually just excites the reporter more, offering the potential of a good public fight—always an attractive newspaper seller. The reality is, once a reporter has put time into a piece, sees the poten-

§4.8 Issuing Written Statements versus Doing Interviews—Sometimes Less Is More

Sometimes offering a written statement is preferable to allowing one's principal to do a full, "on the record" interview. Below is an analysis of the pro's and con's of the two approaches. Ultimately, it helps to know the reporter when determining what to provide. Some reporters are more than happy—or even prefer—to receive a written statement, and will print it as "so-and-so said" without noting it was a prepared statement. Other reporters will never take a statement, especially after they've asked for an interview first. Increasingly, reporters are comfortable taking a written statement via email—but don't assume that will be the case.

Written Statements

Pro's

- Limits the reporters' choices as to what she can quote.
- Increases the likelihood that your message will get across.
- Requires less time of the principal and no preparation time for the interview.
- Avoids the possibility that the principal will have to face uncomfortable questions.

Con's

- Reporter might be offended that he is not provided access to the principal, hurting the coverage and possibly your relationship.
- Could reduce the role of the principal or organization in the story and eliminate any chance of your principal being quoted— reporters sometimes give preference to those they interview.
- Sometimes can be viewed as a way for the guilty to hide.
- Sometimes sound "canned" or non-conversational.

"On the Record" Interviews

Pro's

- Sounds genuine and sincere.
- Possibly enhances the role of the principal or organization in the story.
- Improves the long-term relationship with the reporter.

Con's

- Principal may say something unexpected or inappropriate.
- Gives the reporter more choices as to what quote to use and message to cover.
- If no major quote results, wastes the principal's time.

Issues to Address in Determining Which to Use

- When a quote is more likely to be used or essential to a reporter's story, statements can be safer routes. If a reporter must use a quote, and doesn't require much verbiage, the statement is often easier for the public relations professional and the reporter.

(Continued on page 77)

> ### §4.8 Issuing Written Statements versus Doing Interviews—Sometimes Less Is More (continued)
>
> - When dealing with a negative story, statements reduce the variables of how your organization will be portrayed.
> - If a principal has weak interview skills, statements use the resources of the office to articulate policy. However, written statements are not permanent substitutes for a live person. Principals, especially when they are high-ranking, have a "charisma factor" that can work wonders with reporters.
> - If a principal is absolutely unavailable, statements are the last resort.

tial for front-page coverage, and has the added bonus of getting a few hits on a public figure, it's hard to get him to drop it.

As you craft a response strategy, consider how each piece fits into the story. News stories are like puzzles that fit nicely together. The media tend to favor stories that mimic morality plays. They like to tell stories that have heroes, villains, innocent victims, broad social consequences, and clear moral themes. Life is rarely that simple, and there are probably a lot of facts that will complicate a black-and-white story and won't fit into ten column inches or a ninety-second TV story. It's the press secretary's job to convey those complicated facts in a way that ensures they get into the story. If your principal or organization is being cast in the role of the villain, you need to find a way to tell your story without sounding defensive.

One way to handle negative stories is by giving the reporter very little information or no information at all. Sometimes the office will come to the conclusion, "They're going to hit us, why give them a bigger bat by talking to them." The occasional "unavailable for comment" may have its place, but it's often viewed as the last resort of a guilty party. If at all possible, a response must be crafted to accompany a coordinated strategy to deal with the negative story. Often only a brief, written statement will suffice. The pro's and con's of a written statement versus an interview are discussed in § 4.8, Issuing Written Statements versus Doing Interviews—Sometimes Less is More.

The best way to defend yourself in a negative story is to have someone do it for you. Independent, third-party surrogates are the best defenders, since they can appear to have no bias. For example, if a public official is accused of ethical misconduct, the best exonerating evidence is an ethics attorney or professor who will go on the record saying no wrong was committed. Often, you cannot develop these friendships quickly, so you must rely on those in your Rolodex with whom you have a pre-existing relationship. However, in this age when it seems everyone wants to see his name in print or face on the air, reporters can usually find "experts" to say almost anything without much difficulty. If you use a surrogate, seek one who has a unique status, who has little connection to your principal or organization, and who has a reputation for offering a balanced perspective.

In larger organizations, you may have experts on staff who can "de-bunk" stories, or at least serve as a credible defense against an attack. One wonky expert pitted against another wonky expert often results in a public relations draw in the reader's or viewer's mind. Be cautious on the legal implications of an immediate response. While lawyers are poor public relations advisors, they're usually good legal advisors. Some negative stories have long-term implications for organizations, and plotting a response with those implications in mind can prevent you from compounding the problem.

The one thing you definitely do not want attributed to you or your principal is, "No comment." This is the public relations equivalent of saying, "I'm guilty." Over the years, it has been translated as being an admission of wrongdoing by the public, and a declaration of stupidity in dealing with the media by public relations professionals. Basically, it's an excuse for not thinking by those who are not trained in the art of public relations. There is even a rumor in the public relations field that the Philip Morris public relations department has a "no 'no comment'" commandment enforced on every spokesman (and those are folks who know about negative stories).

Anything is better than "No comment": "I was unaware of those charges." "The organization is developing a strategy to deal with this particular situation." "We need to consult with our board to address this matter." Basically, anything that conveys activity, as opposed to ignoring the problem, is better than "No comment."

§4.9 Arguing with the Media

Disagreements with reporters are inevitable. They'll ask you to research things at inconvenient times, force you to ask your principal embarrassing questions, and sometimes write articles that get you in trouble. The relationship between the public relations professional and the reporter is rarely equal. Either the press secretary is some senior guru and the reporter is just hoping to grab some crumbs from her table; or the communication specialist is a junior assistant at a nonprofit organization, hoping to curry favor with a *Washington Post* reporter. In either case, if combat occurs, it's usually not an even playing field.

In most cases, the public relations person is at a disadvantage because of the first rule of public relations: never get in a pissing contest with someone who buys ink by the barrel. Reporters, editors, news directors, and anchors *always* get the last word because they ultimately control the medium. For this reason, disagreements are to be avoided if at all possible.

When one does need to debate a reporter, make it a polite debate. Most reporters are open-minded and susceptible to persuasion. Sometimes they'll play devil's advocate just to get an emotional reaction from you, hoping it might coax out a better quote. Keep the discussion civil and to the point. When possible, refute all negative points with documentation. You'll likely have some degree of success in influencing the story if you're genuinely in the right.

After a story is run, arguing with the media is not very productive. Letters to the editor may make the principal feel good, but the damage has already been done. If you do write a letter to the editor, impugn the facts of the story, not the messenger. Attacking the credibility of a news organization usually appears undignified and downright whiny.

Another strategy may be to get another story run on the topic that favors your perspective. But, as discussed in Chapter Twelve, Crisis Communication in Public Affairs, a second-day story is risky because it inevitably will include the negative information from the first day's story, and there's no guarantee you'll get a better play on day two.

Finally, *never* get angry with a reporter. Anger is inappropriate in all professional settings, and in this one your behavior could be rebroadcast to thousands of readers or viewers.

§4.10 Common Reporter Problems

Most reporters are smart, hard-working, ethical individuals, who feel fortunate to have interesting and important jobs in our society. They deal forthrightly with the people they interview and try to convey the facts in a fair and balanced way. However, not all reporters fall into this category. Moreover, the pressures of the modern media industry force well-intentioned reporters to do some fairly outrageous things—all for the good of "informing the public."

Public relations professionals have to deal with the shortcomings of reporters and their industry on a daily basis, and should be prepared for the occasional less-than-ideal contact with a member of the Fourth Estate.

Often the biggest challenge is working with a reporter who has a clear bias. It is very hard to change a reporter's mind about a story once he has it made up, and it can be infuriating when you have information that you believe legitimately belongs in the story that the reporter dismisses. Despite the prominence that fairness and objectivity are given in the journalistic profession, reporters are human beings, and their experiences, values, and opinions are often reflected in a story.

Getting information from reporters can sometimes be a problem. Despite the need that reporters have for public relations professionals to provide information to them, reporters are sometimes extremely miserly with information they possess. Simple questions from press secretaries, such as, "What's your story on?" can be met by evasive or even downright untruthful answers.

But the First Amendment is a two-way street. The freedom to speak is also the freedom *not* to speak. If you're dealing with a reporter who won't provide you with basic information about the story or give you a hint as to what he might be interested in, he has no right to expect your full cooperation. Certainly, elected officials and federal agencies have basic ethical and, in some cases, legal requirements to provide information to the press and the public. Yet, you have some discretion as to the degree of that cooperation, and you can base it on the level of candor and openness of the person asking the questions.

Reporters are also often limited by the deadlines imposed on them by their profession. The advent of the 24-hour news cycle has placed extraordinary pressure on journalists to produce massive amounts of content for the news behemoths that pay their salaries. This often requires reporters to transfer that pressure onto the people they seek information from. It might seem unfair to have less than an hour to develop a seven-second answer to a complicated policy question, but the show must go on, and the reporter will likely run the story with or without your comment.

Unreasonable deadlines often put people in the public affairs arena in a difficult position. You often have to change everything you're doing, assemble a team to deal with the media question, and rush to a decision—or else you won't get covered in the story. Since public relations usually is the linchpin to any successful public affairs strategy, this is a difficult dilemma. However, don't be afraid to let those stories slip by. Once a policy is made, it's etched in the permanence of the "public record" forever. Never let a news organization's deadline force you to make a decision that you wouldn't otherwise make, if given a little more time.

Then there is the occasional intelligence problem. Sometimes public relations professionals have to deal with a reporter who does not have enough

§4.11 Minnesota—Land of 10,000 Lakes and News "Justice"—for Forty-One Years

Perhaps it's the cold that keeps people indoors too long looking for something to do, but this northern region for a time was the only state in the United States that dispensed "justice" to wayward news organizations. The Minnesota News Council <www.news-council.org> was founded in 1970, and in its forty-one years of existence meted out decisions in more than 150 cases related to biased coverage, discriminatory advertising policy, and conflicts of interest. Twelve media representatives, twelve citizens, and one chair reviewed cases and, most notably, "lawyers are not allowed to speak at hearings," according to the group's web site. News organizations in the homeland of Paul Bunyan took the decisions seriously, and often responded to the rulings by printing or broadcasting the decision and offering an apology.

However, due to the dwindling revenues in the print media business model that funded the council and the recession of 2008, on February 1, 2011, the Minnesota News Council closed its doors. In his last posting, Board Chair Tony Carideo also noted how the council's role had been supplanted by new media. "The proliferation of blogs, which allowed news consumers their own distinct voices, email and comment sections to online news stories, provided an instantaneous outlet for complaints, concerns and commentary on the news. Our hearing process, which was both thorough and, as a result, time-consuming, couldn't measure up to the instant access allowed by electronic media."

background or is struggling with understanding elements of the story he is assigned to write.

A reporter who is having tough time with the job and the story will appreciate a source who spends a little extra time explaining the background, walks him through the history of a topic, and provides some extra information. From a public relations point of view, you sometimes have the best chance of significantly influencing the coverage if you're the most helpful source with a helpless reporter.

Finally, television offers a unique set of challenges to any public relations professional. Since television is still the number-one medium to reach almost any audience, it's usually worth the trouble. Interacting with television is discussed in Chapter Five, but there are certain limitations with the medium that are wise to keep in mind.

First, television reporters often can't or won't do certain stories. Public policy stories usually are discouraged in local television since they are hard to translate into people's day-to-day lives, unless they have very good pictures to go with the story. Anything dealing with numbers—budgets, economics, sociological trends—are deadly unless they have pretty pictures to accompany them. (The exception to this rule is polls in political campaigns, which television stations usually favor in place of substance or issue pieces, because they're easier to do.) If there aren't visuals to accompany the story, it's a weak candidate for the television medium.

Second, television has extraordinary time restrictions. The average local newscast has eleven to fourteen minutes of hard news in a thirty-minute newscast, in addition to sports and weather. Each story is fifty to ninety seconds in length. Written out, a ninety-second story comes out to about one page of double-spaced paper. Try telling a complicated story on terrorism using one page of paper and you'll understand the challenge broadcast reporters face.

Third, because of the time restrictions, television necessarily "dumbs down" stories. Television news has to be quickly digestible for the viewing public. This requires a degree of simplicity in writing that can overlook important details and context.

Finally, the medium often does a poor job of telling "big" stories or the whole view of a particular topic. Journalistic legend Edward R. Murrow described broadcasting as a searching spotlight that focuses the public's attention on a small spot of a large object for a few seconds, only to move away moments later. This is why it is so crucial in public relations to have people available who symbolize a larger story. If the spotlight is only going to be on one thing for a few seconds, make sure it's trained on something or someone that conveys the information, values, and emotion of a story in a short period of time.

§4.12 "Off the Record"

Some people in Washington believe there is no such thing as "off the record." The credo is: "If you don't want to read about it in *The Washington Post*, don't say or write it, and avoid thinking it, if possible." While it's true that reporters have sometimes burned sources they promised to protect, using "off the record" is a useful tool in any communication specialist's toolbox.

They teach in journalism school that "off the record" means that the information will be known only to the reporter (and possibly her editor), and cannot be used in the story. Before you say these magic three words, everything you say to a reporter is fair game and "on the record." This "rule" has sometimes been broken—enough to make any source a little leery when sharing sensitive information with a member of the press corps.

Going "off the record" is one way to communicate to the media without being quoted. Your decision to employ this tactic often is based on your level of trust with the reporter. You are much more likely to go "off the record" with a reporter who has covered you for years than someone with whom you're dealing for the first time. Also, you must negotiate in advance what "off the record" means to this particular reporter; not everyone took the same journalism class at the same university and there are different interpretations of its meaning.

§4.13 Off the Record— Glossary

"Off the Record"
Information is not to be used publicly or shared with any other person, except possibly the reporter's editor.

"On Background"
Information may be used, but the source may not be specifically identified. The source may be identified generally, using a description mutually agreed upon.

"On Deep Background"
Information may be used, but the source may not be identified in any manner.

Despite the potential for mischief, going "off the record" is a valuable tactic for public relations professionals. Press secretaries most often go "off the record" to help shape a story and create a more comfortable atmosphere to convey a broader message. When talking to a reporter "on the record," a seasoned public relations professional engages a part of the brain that censors everything. It tries to visualize every sentence and run it through an instant check system asking, "How will this look in print?" "Is this the right way to convey my message?" "Can this be taken out of context?" "Will this cost me my job?"

When the spokesperson goes "off the record," that part of the brain relaxes a little (although the check system should never be completely turned off). You can tell the story in a more conversational way, and say things that might not serve your communication goals if they were seen in print. For example, public relations professionals sometimes go "off the record" to give information that might damage the credibility of an accuser, or to embellish the reputation of the principal or organization. An "on the record" quote in these cases could make the public relations professional look self-serving, but an "off the record" comment will influence the reporter and increase the likelihood of a more favorable story.

"Off the record" comments often are used to enhance credibility by providing background information. Public relations professionals will provide detailed background information about a story leading up to today's news, but the quote in the paper should be about *today's* news, not the background information. The best way to limit a reporter's choice of quotes to today's message is to give all background information "off the record" or "on background."

"On background" means that the official will be quoted, or paraphrased, but that his name will not be used. Instead, he'll be known as a "high-ranking State Department official" or some other generic term. The use of anonymous sources has grown dramatically in the last thirty years, and previously was only used when identifying the source would cause some significant harm to him. Now, "background" status is used with abandon to hurl insults and accusations against enemies, with the comforting knowledge that the media will convey the attack and that it is unlikely harm will come from it. In court, all accused have a right to face their accuser; this principle does not exist in public relations.

Another term sometimes used is "deep background." This is less commonly known and the interpretation usually needs to be negotiated with the reporter. "Deep background" means that the reporter will use the information and could convey that information to another person, including someone else involved in the story. Reporters also use "deep background" information in stories with no attribution at all. In the old days, this information was often preceded with the ego-boosting phrase, "This reporter has learned . . . ". However, "deep background" information is usually not used in a story without additional confirmation. After getting some juicy tidbits on "deep background," the reporter may ask a potential victim an ambush question: "I understand you used the slush fund to buy a new boat."

The line between "deep background" and "off the record" is very thin. When walking this line, the best advice is to negotiate with the reporter. Clearly spell out how the information will be used and whom it will be conveyed to. This must be done *before* any information is conveyed—there is no such thing as a retroactive "off the record."

Sources and reporters also are now using a stranger practice of agreeing to do an interview, then allowing the source to approve quotes that will appear in the story. This allows the source to feel less constricted in his comments. The reporter will ask afterwards, "Okay, can I use this quote?" However, this is a dangerous game and can lead to major conflicts of interest. If a source says something juicy to a reporter, the reporter has an obligation to his news orga-

§4.14 Using Embargoes

An embargo is used by public relations professionals to provide information to the media and to restrict its public release until a specified date and time. The information can be a report, the introduction of a bill, the announcement of a new official in an organization—anything that the public relations specialist deems necessary to be temporarily withheld.

Embargoes are commonly used in a few ways. Often, public relations specialists place an embargo on information in order to have it hit the public at a particularly advantageous time. For example, a press secretary may release information to one or two news organizations regarding the announcement by a congressman of a bill he intends to introduce. The press secretary will provide the information to the reporters on a Thursday, but stipulate that the information is not to be released until Sunday's paper, maximizing the number of people who will read about it. Reporters sometimes agree to these restrictions on the promise they'll receive an exclusive, or an exclusive for their market or medium.

Embargoes can also be used with information that is especially complex, and the reporter may need time to review it and interview other sources. For example, the release of a major hundred-page report is a good candidate for an embargo so that reporters can spend a few days reading the data and determining how best to present it.

Embargoes should be used sparingly, as they invite problems and go against the instincts of the media to spread the news once they get it. Usually it's best to keep an embargo to one or two news organizations and for no more than one or two days. Trying to keep an embargo with ten to twenty reporters is like telling a juicy tidbit of gossip in the high school lunch room and expecting no one to tell their classmates. Reporters live to tell good stories, and you're playing with fire when you give them a great piece of news they'll be itching to tell. Moreover, reporters and editors know they have an opportunity to scoop the competition if they come up with some "ethical" way to break an embargo.

With all embargoes, make certain that the restricted information is provided in written form and with the time and date of the release clearly noted on the documents.

nization and the public to convey relevant facts. If he determines this obligation outweighs the pledge to you, there's nothing you can do about it—other than not talk to the reporter again, which may or may not be possible for you or even relevant to the reporter.

In rare cases, if a news organization determines it has a good enough reason for violating its pledge of confidentiality to a source, it'll break that pledge. A political consultant in Minnesota actually sued the *Minneapolis Star Tribune* for "breach of contract" for identifying him as the source in an "off the record" context. The consultant was not exactly playing above board himself—he leaked damaging information about his client's opponent to the paper and wanted to stay anonymous. The paper determined that revealing the source of the information was a more important principle than its promise to the consultant, and burned him in the process. The consultant lost both his job and—after a lengthy legal battle—the lawsuit.

Most of the stories about reporters burning sources are less well-known. Many sources are embarrassed about their gullibility. Suffice it to say, when going "off the record," always consider the consequences if the information makes it into the public domain.

§4.15 Dealing with Trade or Specialty Press

The news media universe is increasingly becoming specialized in the audiences they seek. The audience for *Asian Petroleum News* is not the same as for *The New York Times*. Thousands of publications and web sites now exist to communicate to targeted audiences interested in narrow topics. The specialty or trade press offers unique challenges and opportunities for public relations professionals, and must be dealt with somewhat differently than the mainstream media.

First, there is an unfortunate tendency among some communication specialists to treat specialty reporters with less respect because they have smaller audiences than major dailies, television stations, and radio stations. This is a huge mistake and ignores the value of these niche reporters. Specialty reporters often have more time and space to delve into a topic, providing public relations professionals opportunities to tell more of their story. These reporters often are steeped in their topic, requiring less background and education than mainstream reporters. But, this also means that the public relations specialist must provide specific, detailed information for a highly versed audience.

Specialty press reporters often are less likely to write negative stories as well. Their interest is to tell a story in detail to a targeted audience, not criticize or embarrass a public figure. In addition, they are much more dependent on their sources, as they often have fewer of them. Reporters are much less likely to burn a public official if they know they cannot do their job without that official's assistance.

Finally, a media strategy that incorporates the use of smaller, niche publications can lead to broader coverage. It is much easier to pitch *The New York Times* on a story that your nonprofit organization is a leader on environmental clean-ups if you can send the reporter an in-depth story in *Waste Water Treatment Monthly*. Trade publications are often reviewed by the major media outlets, and the story that you thought would only hit 10,000 readers may end up on a network newscast or in a major daily newspaper, reaching an audience that will learn about an issue for the first time and, possibly, key decision-makers.

Food Safety News, Energy and Environment News, and the *Chronicle of Higher Education* may not be household names and likely aren't found in your dentist's office, but if you are trying to affect FDA policy, reform the way we consume energy, or make college more affordable, then you should be working to get coverage in these specialty publications.

§4.16 Becoming Friends

Veteran ABC News reporter James Wooten was covering the vice presidential campaign of Spiro Agnew in 1972 when the campaign staff and the press corps attended a joint cocktail party. A press aide, Victor Gold, started nudging reporters toward the vice president. Gold wanted to introduce the influential reporter to his boss, but Wooten resisted. Apparently, the idea of mixing with the subject of his stories in a social setting was not consistent with the reporter's values and practices. "No, I don't want to meet him," Wooten said. "I'll meet him, but not at a party. I'm here to cover the vice president, not to be his buddy." (Timothy Crouse, *Boys on the Bus* (Random House, 1972).)

Washington is filled with friendships between reporters and those they cover, and more than a few mixed marriages. In a town where the average workday starts before 8:00 a.m. and ends after 8:00 p.m., it's logical that the people you socialize with are the people you come in contact with on the job. There are no hard-and-fast rules about becoming friends with reporters (some of my best friends are reporters), but there are some cautionary thoughts to keep in mind.

Reporters who cover a beat have a responsibility to their news organizations, society, and to their own sense of fairness. Friendships and relationships don't fit neatly into that ethical hierarchy and often present difficult decisions for reporters. This doesn't mean socializing with reporters is inappropriate—quite the opposite. Meeting in casual settings is often the best way to prove to one another that the other person is not pure evil and doesn't have horns and a tail. It does mean that sometimes obligations to friends and loved ones come into conflict with professional responsibilities. If you're prepared for that conflict, facing it will be easier and less painful.

As with all "off the record" settings, people who interact with the media must be careful to remember that what is said could end up on the front page. Reporters get some of their best material after the third beer, and loose lips sink more than ships. In mixing social settings and the media, it's best to strike a healthy balance between letting your hair down a little and not baring your soul.

Finally, never forget that reporters are people just like you, often interested in the same topics, with the same type of education, and filled with the same sense of public service as those in the public affairs arena. They demonstrate their patriotism by serving as a link in the chain of communication between the governing and the governed. They consider it their constitutional right and responsibility to ask, probe, question, sneak up on, criticize, cajole, press, and sometimes annoy the public figures they are assigned to cover.

Some take relish in the pain they cause, but most journalists recoil and are disgusted by the darker sides of their profession. They seek inspiration and guidance from their historic roots. They've chosen a calling pioneered by Murrow and Cronkite, Woodward and Bernstein, Koppel and Walters. And, they consider their role just as important today as the veterans who paved the way. Like public relations professionals, some days they want to chuck it all—the deadlines, the editors, and annoying press secretaries, who often call umpteen times begging for a minute in the news or a few inches in the local paper—and find something that pays better with shorter hours (which some mistakenly believe is the public relations profession).

But most of them stick with it, get back in the game, and grind out another story for another day. When you deal with a reporter, recognize that the sacrifice he's making to do a job is not much different from your sacrifice, appreciate the parallels to public relations, and recognize that this cousin in the world of communication has many of the same goals and ideals as we do—he's just going about accomplishing them in a different way.

§4.99 Chapter Summary

- Develop a strategy and talking points for pitching stories. Keep the pitches short (thirty seconds), and make sure they address the question, "If I were in her shoes, what would I want to write about?" (§ 4.2)
- Reporters want two things from public relations professionals: access and information. When handling reporter calls, ask key questions and respond

only after you have researched the answers and have a clear command of the facts. (§ 4.5)

- When handling reporter calls on potentially negative stories, listen "between the lines" for potential details that could be strategically crucial. Never respond immediately—craft a response using all office resources and experts. And never say, "No comment." (§ 4.7)
- Never argue with a reporter. Debate the facts, not the person. (§ 4.9)
- The most common problems in dealing with the media are: clear bias, getting them to share information, and short deadlines. (§ 4.10)
- Go "off the record" to shape a story, attack an opponent, or enhance credibility—all in ways in which you wouldn't want to be quoted. Always confirm what "off the record" means to the reporter. (§ 4.12)
- Take advantage of trade or specialty press. They are more likely to cover your topic, and it may result in broader coverage. (§ 4.15)
- Get to know reporters in social settings. But never forget that their obligation to their news organization may conflict with their personal relationship with you. (§ 4.16)

Chapter Five:
Overview of the Media:
Print, Radio, TV,
and the Internet

> *"Television news is to journalism as bumper stickers are to philosophy."*
>
> Richard Nixon

Overview of the Media: Print, Radio, TV, and the Internet

§5.1 Introduction

Interacting with the various forms of media and reporters is a little like the herpetologist who grabs rattlesnakes, wrestles alligators, and picks up big spiders. You need to know how to deal with each species, or you'll get stung, bit, or badly chewed up.

Each form of media—print, radio, TV, and the Internet—has unique characteristics and must be dealt with differently. Knowing the differences helps public relations professionals correctly develop strategies, pitch stories, and handle potentially negative news.

This chapter will provide for each medium:

- an overview of the value and impact;
- an overview of the structure and decision-making;
- distinctive pitching and response techniques;
- relevant deadlines; and
- unique aspects.

§5.2 Print Medium

Overview of Value and Impact

Despite the dominance of television in shaping public opinion through the impact of video, the print medium is still considered the reigning king of the

Fourth Estate in Washington through its ability to influence opinion leaders and other forms of media. The print medium has an extraordinary and positive history, is valued by elected officials (presidents are more likely to read *The Washington Post* than watch *The CBS Evening News*), and spends large amounts of time and resources to cover public affairs.

The prominence of the print media largely gives it top bragging rights in driving much of the public affairs agenda. This should not be misconstrued to imply that television isn't the most influential medium in setting public opinion—the printed word conceded that high ground to the moving picture in the 1960s and 1970s. Yet, because television networks, producers, and reporters still are greatly influenced by morning newspapers, and a large percentage of the public relies on print media as their primary sources of news, recognizing the formative role that newspapers play in setting the agenda is a basic first step in considering public relations strategies.

Equally important, television will follow print stories, but rarely follow other television stories. It's common for all three network affiliates in a local market to cover the lead story in the morning paper; but it's very unusual for them to run a story on their 11:00 p.m. news because the competition had it on at 6:00 p.m.

Print is also the target for the stories that are difficult to tell on television, such as any story dealing with numbers, policy or "think pieces," studies that don't have logical or easy accompanying visuals, or long-term trends that don't have obvious symbols to convey the general facts. Print media will often cover the complicated stories that the broadcast media will ignore.

Overview of Structure and Decision-Making

Newspapers in the twenty-first century are usually part of large corporate machines. The image of Orson Welles in *Citizen Kane*, using his printing press to illuminate public wrongs and decry injustice, has given way to consolidation, media mergers, and profit margins. The first thing to understand about newspapers is that they are businesses and must make money to survive.

This doesn't mean that the print medium and those who work in it are not noble and enormously constructive forces in our society. It just means that their structure and operations are designed to sell advertising and subscriptions, and the decisionmaking process in determining what appears on the front page is sometimes driven by business, not journalistic motives.

Newspapers devote more personnel to the gathering, reporting, and writing of the news than any other media. Their hierarchy starts with a strong

§5.3 Where Americans Get Their News

2002

"Where do you get your news?" (Respondents were given the option to say "yes" to more than one medium.)

- **Local Television News:** 57 percent
- **Newspaper:** 41 percent
- **Radio:** 41 percent
- **Cable Television News:** 33 percent
- **Network Television News:** 32 percent
- **Online News:** 25 percent

(Source: Pew Research Center for People and the Press, April 2002 Survey)

2010

"Where do you get most of your news about national and international issues?" (Respondents were given option to say "yes" to more than one medium)

- **Television News:** 66 percent
- **Internet:** 41 percent
- **Newspaper:** 31 percent
- **Radio:** 16 percent

(Source: Pew Research Center for People and the Press, December 2010 Survey)

leader, complemented by various lieutenants in different decisionmaking capacities. In major papers, the leader is the editor. In smaller papers, the publisher may take an active role in the news production process.

The key players are:

- **Publisher:** Sometimes the owner of the paper;
- **Editor:** Top decision-maker who often guides key stories or front page;
- **City Editor:** Top decision-maker for local section of paper;
- **National or "A" Section Editor:** Top decision-maker for national or "A" section of paper;
- **Section Editor:** Top or influential decision-maker for various sections such as sports, lifestyle or style, local/metro, and business;
- **Assistant Editor (sometimes referred to as Assignment Editor):** Assistants to the section editors who make editing, news, and assignment decisions; they are often the only decision-makers at a newspaper after normal business hours; and
- **Reporter:** Primary author of the story.

Decision-making in newspapers varies, depending on the size of the paper and the established system within that particular news organization. Smaller papers may have one person selecting the stories to run each day. But most newspapers allow individual department heads to select the content for their sections. For public relations professionals, this means it's often just as valuable to establish a relationship with the editor of the local section as it is to establish one with the reporter who covers you. Reporters are still the main point of contact for print media, and are the most influential in determining whether your story will get covered. But if you only get to know the reporter covering your beat, you're closing off a gateway into the news organization that could be useful in the future.

Distinctive Pitching and Response Techniques

Because most Americans primarily rely on television for their news, it's often said that the best reason to get your story placed in the newspapers is so that television assignment editors will read it and decide to do a story. This is, of course, an exaggeration, since millions of people read newspapers every day. Ideally, public relations professionals want all forms of media to simultaneously cover any story, event, or announcement. But, sometimes there is a progression from print to broadcast stories; and, therefore, this medium should be central to any pitching strategy.

Usually the reporter who covers the beat is the right person to pitch a story. Newspaper reporters are told to get to know their sources and subjects, and papers like to have the stories developed from the ground up, at the reporter level. Print reporters do not have the same time pressures as broadcast reporters, so the public relations professional can develop longer pitches and provide extensive background when discussing a story idea. One must still get a reporter's interest quickly, or lose the chance of getting covered. If a reporter is interested, she will likely want to discuss the topic more broadly, so be prepared with background information.

When reacting to a question from a print reporter, you must understand that *everything* you say is on the record unless you and the reporter agree otherwise. From the second you pick up the phone, any utterance, laugh, sigh, cough—or any other sound that can communicate emotion or fact—will be written down by the reporter and possibly conveyed to her readers. Because of this, it's usually wise to not say anything on the record when initially approached on a new topic by a reporter. For more general advice, see § 4.5, Handling Reporter Calls.

Relevant Deadlines

Daily newspapers have their entire world set up on a 24-hour cycle. Reporters usually don't have to produce a story every day, except in very small papers, but they have strict deadlines that drive their story production. For morning

§5.4 The Constantly Updated Newspaper Web Site

In an episode of the HBO show "The Wire," a fictional character who is breaking into the newspaper industry as a cub reporter for the *Baltimore Sun* can't sleep as she anxiously awaits her first byline running in the newspaper. After a fitful night of sleep, at the break of dawn, she leaves her apartment and walks to a nearby convenience store to pick up the first edition of the paper. "The Wire" is praised for its realistic portrayal of Baltimore and its interconnected institutions, yet this outdated scene would be more appropriate if the show were made in 1988, not 2008.

In reality, if this fictional reporter wanted to see her article, she would go to the newspaper's web site, where the story would have been posted online earlier in the day, possibly as soon as her editors "put the story to bed." And long before she went to the convenience store to get the hard copy of the paper, *Sun* readers would have commented on it, shared it with friends and family members, and maybe even contacted the reporter with praise or criticism.

As newspaper circulation numbers decline, print publications understand that their web sites must be constantly updated with fresh content. Breaking news stories are posted when they are ready and updated throughout the day with new information, quotes, and reaction. "Instant analysis" is posted less than thirty minutes after a big speech or event. Inaccuracies can be updated within minutes of the original post.

As a communication professional, you must understand the nature of print-related web sites and use the dynamic to your advantage. Most press secretaries set up Google News alerts to receive a story as soon as it "goes live." You can set up news alerts for stories that mention your principal, issues your principal cares about, or even specific reporters you work with. As soon as a story comes to your in-box, you scan the story and see if there is an opportunity for follow-up. If there is a factual error or if you believe your principal was misquoted, it is your duty to contact the reporter immediately. If a story is posted without mentioning your principal, you can try to contact the reporter with a quote or other content that could be included. At some newspapers, the web site is the crucible in which stories are placed to determine if there is enough energy in them to make the morning hard-copy edition.

Do not wait to pick up the print edition in the morning from the local convenience store—or you risk missing the news cycle.

papers, most reporters have to submit their copy at around 6:00 p.m. Reporters will sometimes tell public relations professionals that the deadline is earlier because they want the extra time to work on the story. But the actual deadline is usually at the end of the business day.

§5.5 Daybooks

A daybook is a listing of the major events in a state or city. The most popular and well-used are run by the Associated Press and Reuters. But others are operated by online public relations services (such as PR Newswire and Business Wire), many major newspapers, and Washington publications. Press-event notifications should be emailed and faxed to daybooks at least a week before the event to be included in weekly listings, and no later than noon the day before for daily listings. To determine the best method to send material to a daybook editor, simply call the bureau and ask for the most convenient procedure.

Changes can still be made in a story even after it has been submitted by contacting an editor (see § 5.4, The Constantly Updated Newspaper Web Site). Perhaps a principal wasn't ready to provide a quote, or new information is available. When trying to get new information added to a story after the reporter's deadline has passed, it's always best to go through a reporter and get him to change the story. But, if the reporter is unavailable, editors usually will insert short components or quotes to make sure the story is complete and accurate.

While a reporter's deadlines may be slightly fungible, it's usually a good idea to reach the reporter earlier, when he is still building the story. Principals who wait until the last minute to do an interview have lost the opportunity to shape the story, and will merely see their quotes plugged into available spaces. However, the public figure who talks to the reporter early in the day has the potential to influence the framework for the story, forcing all others to respond to her benchmark.

Wire Services

In some respects, the most influential spectrum of the news media is wire services. An article written by the Associated Press (AP) national service has the potential of reaching as many people as a piece on *The NBC Nightly News*. In addition, the wire services' Washington bureaus have vast staffs of highly specialized reporters whose beats are either geographic, often covering a congressional delegation, or by topic, such as covering the Department of Agriculture. Their stories are picked up by any kind of news organization that subscribes to the service—print, television, radio, and Internet—and are sometimes used to complement local reporting or fill in the blanks of national stories.

There are two major wire services, AP and Reuters. United Press International (UPI) formerly was the major competition to AP, but now only has a fraction of the subscribers it once had. Other news services have developed niche expertise, such as Bloomberg News and Dow Jones Newswires. All of these services have slightly different decisionmaking structures than newspapers. The directors or "heads" of the bureaus often play the role of managing editor of the product that is put on the wire.

Because of the constant need to file stories, technically there are no set deadlines for wire services. However, this news medium seeks to be responsive to its customers—other news media. So, they'll seek to file stories in accordance with print and broadcast deadlines, usually aiming to meet print deadlines close to 6:00 p.m. each day.

Public relations professionals also must not forget that getting a story on the wires doesn't guarantee it will be read by a single person, other than reporters. You may want to employ a follow-up strategy after a story is on the wires, contacting key media outlets that might want to run it. Assignment editors and desk editors have multiple demands for their attention. A call from you pointing out that a great story is all done and ready to run is a lot easier pitch than asking them to devote precious resources to cover something.

Finally, wire service stories are the easiest to correct. After a reporter files a story on your topic, *always* review it online immediately to check for errors. Other news media rarely will pick up a story in the first few minutes—this is your time to correct any inaccuracy, complain about significant bias, even add a quote from a principal that you didn't have available earlier. As with all reporters, raising minor points about slant usually falls on deaf ears. But, if there's a major problem with the story, the wire service reporter and his boss will want it corrected before it runs in one of their clients' newspapers.

§5.6 Television Medium
Overview of Value and Impact

Television has been the dominant medium in America since the 1960s. Public policy in the last quarter-century has often followed the pictures emanating from this box in our living rooms. The U.S. government's policies related to the Vietnam War, the civil rights movement, and NASA's moon exploration program were largely influenced by television pictures.

While newspapers may lay the foundation of the battlefield upon which the public relations wars are waged, the primary weapons are the television camera, the picture, and the sound bite. While total viewership of network television news has steadily declined over the last decade, millions of Americans still get their news from network television newscasts. Cable news networks and the Internet have made inroads, but the anchormen and women who became fixtures since the 1950s are still our favorite people to turn to for what's going on in our communities, nation, and the world.

During the 1992 presidential campaign, candidate Bill Clinton frequently referenced television pictures in his criticism of the Bush administration for not intervening to alleviate the growing hunger crisis in Somalia. (President Bush eventually ordered troops into Somalia in December 1992.) Similarly, when American soldiers were ambushed in the capital of Mogadishu, and pictures were broadcast of the body of a dead soldier being dragged through the streets, Clinton administration and public support for the humanitarian mission withered quickly. Bill Clinton seemed eager to please public opinion—both to enter Somalia and to get out—and television pictures drove public opinion.

While getting a story placed in network television news is like bagging the great white whale, most communication specialists focus their time and energy on trying to influence local television newscasts. Since this is where the vast majority of public relations professionals spend time spinning their wheels, the rest of this section will be devoted to local television news.

Overview of Structure and Decision-Making

The first thing to remember about the difference between standard television newscasts (not the 24-hour cable networks) and daily newspapers is the gap between the sheer amount of news product they create. Omitting weather and sports (the main reasons why people watch television news), local newscasts are lucky if they can cover ten to fifteen stories effectively in a thirty-minute newscast. Local newspapers can cover a hundred stories on a daily basis, not counting all the detailed sections such as obituaries and movie listings. *Time* is one major difference between the print and broadcast media. Broadcasters have less time to find the story, research the story, and tell the story. These time pressures account for huge differences in decision-making between media using the written and the spoken word.

The second major difference between the print media and television is the dominance of the picture. Visuals are the driving force in most major decisions in television news. If you don't have good pictures, you probably don't have a story the producers will accept. This point was hammered home to an NBC News Washington correspondent in 1980.

Political opponents were criticizing President Carter for being "soft" on defense. In an apparent attempt to counter the charge, the Pentagon leaked the news to NBC correspondent Bob Hager that the United States had secretly developed a remarkable bomber that could fly from the United States to the Soviet Union, drop its bombs and fly out undetected. This was an astounding weapon and had the potential to shift the strategic balance of power in this sector of combat. When told of the story, the NBC producers in New York headquarters for *NBC Nightly News*, instead of accepting the news as presented, asked for pictures. "This is top secret," the Washington desk explained, "there are no pictures, but we can do a damn good story." "Without pictures," said New York, "we can give you only a few seconds."

Washington Bureau Chief Sid Davis negotiated with New York for more time. Hager went to work with the bureau's graphics department and came up with a drawing of what the secret bomber might look like. The New York producers, having a picture now, gave Hager a few more seconds, a total of twenty seconds. NBC News televised the drawing, with the disclaimer, "artist's conception." It was an honest attempt but it bore no resemblance to what was later revealed as the B-2 Stealth Bomber—first reported in the middle of a newscast for less than half a minute.

Unlike newspapers, many television news stories are not generated through reporters. Off-air personnel, such as assignment editors and producers, are often important decision-makers in allocating the scarce resources of a TV station. Also unlike newspapers, where one or two senior people determine what goes on the front page, television station newsrooms often work like committee meetings, with four to eight people making the final calls.

The key players in television are:

- **News Director:** Leader of the news department. Often this person makes final budgetary and personnel decisions. In larger stations this person usually avoids the day-to-day management of the newsroom. In smaller stations, he could be the final arbiter of what leads the newscast.
- **Executive Producer:** Overseer of all news content. (Very small stations may merge this position with news director.)
- **Assignment Editor:** Air traffic controller of television news. She manages and directs all the assets in the newsroom, assigning reporters, camera crews, and satellite trucks. Often, this person, or the individual show's producer, is the primary target audience for pitches.
- **Producer:** Responsible for overseeing the gathering, writing, and production of an individual newscast. The producer also determines

§5.7 How to Understand Television Ratings

The television ratings systems commonly use two terms to explain how many people watched a television program: "rating" and "share."

- **Rating:** Measures the number of households in a market—out of the total number of households that have a TV set—watching a particular program. For example, if Peoria has 100,000 households with TV sets, and 20 percent of them are watching the WMBD-TV newscast at 6:00 p.m., then the program has a rating of a 20. Another way to say this is that one rating point is worth 1,000 households.

- **Share:** Measures the number of households with a television set turned on that are watching a particular program. For example, if, of the 100,000 households with TV in Peoria, 50,000 of them are turned on, and 50 percent of those are watching the WMBD-TV newscast, then the program has a share of 50.

story length and sometimes the video for parts of the newscast not prepared by individual reporters. This title is also used in larger stations for people who work with individual reporters, often on specialty stories, such as consumer issues or investigative pieces. These producers often have a large hand in writing the stories, in addition to setting up the pieces.

- **Assistant Producer:** As the title implies, the person who assists the producer. Larger stations will have this second position to help with the production duties—smaller stations may not.

- **Reporter:** Primary author of the story.

- **Photographer or "Photog"/Cameraman:** The man or woman with the camera. In many operations, they often have more of an interest in the technical aspect of the job than in the content of the news.

- **Editor:** Edits the story. This is the person who performs the technical work to fit the components of the story together. Often this may be the photographer, but many medium-to-large stations have full-time editors who do not leave the station to cover stories.

This cast of characters has to pull hours of television production together in what would appear to a layman as a hurricane of information and chaos. Watching television professionals in a newsroom, one can only marvel at the ability of the human brain to process information, make decisions, and create something coherent, all while a storm of data bits, personnel struggles, and technical foul-ups muck up the process. It's like an orchestra trying to put on a symphony while an erratic side crew throws additional notes onto their music sheets.

Most television story ideas are not generated through the research of their reporters. Television reporters often don't get the time or resources to develop relationships with sources like newspaper reporters; they are spread thin, and have the burden of a photographer and equipment to lug to any potential interview—not quite as simple as picking up the phone for a quote. Stations in larger markets often give reporters more time and resources to develop sources on beats.

Television stations heavily rely on the local newspaper, and the morning and noon newscasts are often dominated by the front page headlines. Assignment editors also track upcoming local events, such as city council meetings, important public meetings, or community festivals, which are provided either through press releases or from a regular schedule. The "daybook" will provide a run-down of many of the important political and official activities of a day or week. (See § 5.5 for a description of daybooks.)

Story assignments usually are made two times a day. The first time is in the early morning (between 8:30 a.m. and 10:00 a.m.) to plan the 5:00 p.m. and 6:00 p.m. newscast lineup. The second time is in the afternoon (between 2:00 p.m. and 3:30 p m.) to review the morning decisions and make assignments for the 11:00 p.m. newscast. These meetings often include the executive producer, producers of the daily shows, assignment editor, and maybe the news director. These meetings are often not attended by reporters, so it is important that public relations professionals interact directly with assignment editors and producers to ensure that their story idea is brought into the meetings.

One final note about decision-making in local television news. Several times a year, the priorities, logic, and some of the integrity of the news process change for the sake of ratings. These are called "sweeps weeks," periods primarily focused in February, May, July, and November when the ACNielsen Company comprehensively tracks the ratings of all the television shows in the nation. Advertising rates are largely set based on these ratings, so there is a strong incentive to show good numbers during these times. News personnel often get promoted or fired based on these numbers, forcing the decision-makers to create any content that will grab viewers.

During sweeps weeks you'll see investigative reports on consumer scandals, lengthy how-to stories on life's financial decisions, and every topic imag-

§5.8 Live TV/TV Talk Shows/24-Hour Cable Networks

Getting on a 24-cable network is like surfing—watch for the great wave and when it hits, paddle like crazy to catch it. Cable television has become the medium of the single story, and the networks want to cover that story and all possible angles. Whether it's health-care reform, debt ceiling, presidential debates, war, or some celebrity's difficulties—whatever the current hot topic, the major cable news television networks—CNN, Fox News, MSNBC, and CNBC—will cover it 24/7. The cable news networks have shed the diverse ways of their stodgy brethren in the over-the-air medium, and strive for concentrated coverage of single events. The key to getting their attention is to be quickly connected to the event.

Ideally, it's best to develop relationships in advance with cable television contacts so there is no need for a frantic pitch when a story breaks. But, if you work for a more obscure nonprofit organization, or a rarely called-upon federal agency, there's no telling what catastrophe will strike that demands your input before a national audience.

Even if there is no relationship, if your principal has a connection to a story in the news and it is attractive to cable news networks, pitch it anyway. The basic pitching techniques to television stations discussed in Chapter Four and this chapter apply. But, networks get more attention from public relations professionals than local stations, and more pitches. Press secretaries have to be a little better prepared, a little faster, and maybe even a little more aggressive.

Be ready to email quick biographical information and relevance to the story to the network contact. Follow up with a phone call to provide additional information. And, most important, if you get "no" for an answer, knock on another door at the network. Each show may have its own booker; try to find out the other shows' producers. Another booker with a different perspective may find your principal worthy of putting on the air. Also see § 8.7, Tips to the Principal for Appearing on Television.

inable related to sex. News personnel often cringe at the base stories they must run during sweeps weeks, designing their news content to scintillate our senses rather than enlighten us. Yet, they'll acknowledge with the same breath, "this is what pays the bills to let us cover you the rest of the year."

Distinctive Pitching and Response Techniques

When talking to someone in a television newsroom, you will be struck by how incredibly busy they are and wonder how they can think to themselves. Assignment editors are the ultimate multi-taskers. They have an uncanny ability to simultaneously carry on two telephone conversations, read an online publication, keep an ear up for anything unusual emanating from the police scanner—all while fixing themselves their eighth cup of coffee for the day. With all that competing for their attention, a public relations professional has about fifteen seconds to sell a story. After those fifteen seconds, the assignment editor has either seen something more interesting online, heard about a fire on the scanner, or spilled her coffee.

In addition to being fast, the best pitch usually has a connection to something that already has been covered, either by the station, a broadcast competitor or, mostly likely, the local newspaper. Television stations are always looking for ways they can "advance" the story from the morning papers. They know that the audience has a knowledge of the print story— they want to build on that interest and find a new angle to capture the viewers' attention. If you start your pitch with, "I've got a great new angle on the lead story in today's paper and have some incredible video to accompany it . . . ," you'll usually get an additional fifteen seconds for your pitch.

When responding to a TV reporter's call, you don't need the same instant game-face as when dealing with print reporters. Usually, the reporter or assignment editor is sizing up your principal to see if she would be a good interview for the story. The key to getting covered is: 1) having a message that fits into their preconceived hole in the story; 2) being available to do the interview on the timetable they lay out; and 3) having or suggesting good pictures to accompany the story. Try to convey to the reporter what the principal would say in the interview—even using the same words if possible. Demonstrate that your principal is the best person for the interview, as there will be competition. And be prepared to adjust the principal's schedule to accommodate the television reporter.

§5.9 When to Pitch a TV Station

It rarely hurts to double-check with a TV station to remind them of an event. If you've laid the groundwork with a good release, a reference in the AP Daybook, and maybe even a short conversation the day before, a follow-up call the day of the event will help. Find out in advance when the story meeting is (usually sometime between 8:00 a.m. and 9:30 a.m.). Call about thirty minutes before the meeting and make contact with the assignment editor. It may be that only one out of five times this results in an extra camera showing up at your event, but that extra camera may just be the trick to connecting with your audience and impressing the boss or client.

Relevant Deadlines

Because of the nature of the medium, television deadlines can vary, depending upon the size of the market, the significance of the news, and the skill of the news personnel at turning raw facts into a television story. Even "live, breaking news" requires extensive preparation. In general, because of the technical requirements surrounding the production of a newscast, anything that happens closer than two to three hours before a newscast is going to have to be pretty important to bump what's already in the lineup.

The content of the most-watched newscasts, at 6:00 p.m. and 11:00 p.m., is set during the meetings discussed earlier. If it's not a live story, producers will want their reporters and editors back in the studio and putting together their stories at least two hours before the broadcast. This means if you're aiming to get your story on the 6:00 p.m. newscast, anything that happens after 3:00 p.m. is not going to make it.

Relevant information can still be conveyed to stations an hour or even minutes before the newscast. But the closer it gets to show time, the harder it is for a producer to alter the content. Each newscast is timed to the exact second, and any change to that timing has a domino effect that requires the rest of the show to be altered.

Selecting the Television Interview Location

As a public relations professional, you'll have some input—perhaps complete control—of where a television interview with your principal will be conducted. Obviously, you want to select a setting that puts your boss in the best light—literally and figuratively. You'll probably have some degree of restrictions on what you choose from, based on where you work. Here are some tips for selecting an interview location.

Pick a spot that reflects the nature of the story. If you're releasing a numbers-based report and have to set up the interview quickly, then the principal's office with bookshelves in the background will suffice. If you're releasing a report on protecting wetlands, and can talk the reporter into a few minutes' extra travel, then an outdoor interview with a marsh in the background is ideal.

Outside interviews in decent light are usually better than inside. Indoor lighting for television is an art form, and cameramen often do not have the time to set it up perfectly. Help the cameraman and the reporter set up the shot. Move furniture, take down glass-framed photos that could reflect the lights, even clean up the office before the television crew arrives. Regardless

§5.10 The Growing Partisanship of "News"

In 1996, Rupert Murdoch and former Republican consultant Roger Ailes launched Fox News, joining CNN and MSNBC in the cable news universe. In 1999, Fox averaged 500,000 prime-time viewers on an average day in late December. Ten years later, the network averaged more than 2.5 million viewers during the same period, a 500 percent increase. Meanwhile, MSNBC's prime-time ratings went from approximately 250,000 viewers to 1 million viewers in the same period, a 400 percent increase. In contrast, CNN's prime-time viewership grew much less—from 800,000 average viewers to 1 million, a 25 percent increase.

What does this mean? It means that agenda-driven coverage has proven to be a successful business model. Putting aside Fox's "Fair and Balanced" slogan, few would deny that Fox presents for the most part a conservative perspective. In 2010, MSNBC re-branded itself with the tagline "Lean Forward" and featured in prime-time left-leaning programs hosted by Keith Olbermann, Rachel Maddow, and Ed Schultz. In contrast, CNN has attempted to avoid blatant "agenda-driven" coverage, but lags far behind Fox and MSNBC in the ratings.

Cable news is not the only place where news has become fragmented. Online, consumers can now get their news and opinions on web sites that reinforce their beliefs. In May 2011, the left-leaning *Huffington Post* surpassed the *New York Times* web site in unique visitors, making *HuffPo* the top U.S. Internet news provider. Conservative readers can bypass either of these sites and solely visit the *Drudge Report* or *RedState.com*.

The days of the "general public" getting the same news from Walter Cronkite or the local newspaper seem to be fading. This presents a challenge for a communication professional. While many members of your audience may still get news from a national newscast or a "mainstream" newspaper, many more are getting their information from agenda-driven media. Every principal must decide how engaged they want to be with these media outlets. Some members of Congress will use conservative or liberal outlets to "rally their base," while others like "mixing it up" along the ideological spectrum. You must analyze agenda-driven media sources and determine if there is any benefit—or significant downside—to engaging with them.

of the nature of the interview or how biased you may feel the station is against you, the cameraman and you both have the same objective here—making the picture look good.

Tips for PIOs

When a dramatic event happens always look for the best vantage point from which the TV viewing public can watch. That is what the TV cameramen will want.

As an example, on April 19, 1995, Oklahoma City Fire Chief Jon Hansen was one of the first to arrive on the scene of the Murrah Building bombing. Because his number-one priority was public safety, and knowing the best way to keep the public safe was to keep them informed, Chief Hansen surveyed the scene and one of his first commands was to designate the area for the press. It was the perfect vantage point for TV, slightly elevated to show the entire scene, far enough away to not interfere with his command post, and close enough so he would not have to travel far for his press briefings, which began about fifteen minutes after his arrival and continued every fifteen to twenty minutes thereafter for the first few hours.

This location remained the primary site for television coverage for several weeks as the event moved through the rescue, recovery, clean-up, and final demolition phases at the Murrah Building.

A final thought on the television news, and the relationship between the spoken word and the picture. Despite all the work that you and your policy people might put into ensuring that the message is perfect, never forget that the picture *is* the story. This is best illustrated by a recounting that CBS White House correspondent Lesley Stahl told in her book *Reporting Live* (Simon & Schuster, 1999). During the 1984 campaign she did what she believed was a blistering five-minute piece exposing the Reagan administration's hypocrisy in framing perfect photo opportunities while glossing over his policies. "President Reagan is accused of running a campaign in which he highlights the images and hides from the issues," she told millions of viewers.

The story showed beautifully crafted pictures—the president at the Special Olympics, or an opening ceremony for a retirement center. "No hint that he tried to cut the budgets for the disabled or for federally subsidized housing for the elderly," she reported. American flags, big bands, worshipping crowds. She expected a negative reaction from the White House, but was shocked at the call from Reagan aide Dick Darman, who had watched the lengthy piece with the president's top communication strategist, Michael Deaver.

"Way to go, kiddo," Darman said. "What a great story, we loved it."

Stahl was dumbstruck. "Why are you so happy? Didn't you hear what I said?"

Darman responded with a lesson the network correspondent would never forget. "Nobody heard what you said," Darman said. "You guys in Television-land haven't figured it, have you? When the pictures are powerful and emotional, they override if not completely drown out the sound. Lesley, I mean it, nobody heard you."

§5.11 Radio Medium
Overview of Value and Impact

Radio, the first broadcast medium invented, is the most esoteric of the three mainstream media. However, the most sophisticated public relations specialist will recognize the value of maximizing a radio strategy. Ignoring radio means leaving a potential source to public opinion untouched—or exposed to opponents to exploit unilaterally.

The most effective time to reach a radio audience is when most people are listening to the radio—"morning drive time," 6:00 a.m. to 10:00 a.m., with the best hours being 7:00 a.m. to 9:00 a.m. The second best time is "afternoon drive time," 4:00 p.m. to 7:00 p.m. The value of drive time depends upon the market size—the more time people have to spend in their cars commuting to work, the more likely they are to be listening to the radio, as opposed to watching a television network morning program at home. Most radio stations' audience size during the morning drive time is three times larger than other times of the day.

Radio is almost never a primary target for a public relations strategy. Rather, radio complements a strategy to extending a print and television strategy. If the same message that someone reads in her morning paper also is repeated on her drive to work, it's much more likely the message will settle in.

Some public relations professionals don't focus on radio because it doesn't have the glamour and impact of television or the permanence of print. However, local radio is often an easy target for coverage. The interviews can be very quick (often less than five minutes) and can be done over the phone. And, because radio reporters are so rushed for time, and often grateful just to get an interview, their questions are often straightforward and predictable.

Overview of Structure and Decision-Making

Radio station staff size varies depending upon the size of the market. A station in Grand Forks, ND, may have one full-time newsperson, who gets in before 5:00 a.m. to pull up wire stories, rewrite stories from the morning paper into broadcast style, and write one or two locally originated stories from interviews conducted the day before. In contrast, WTOP-AM, the news station in

§5.12 Radio Talk Shows

In the animal kingdom of media, radio talk show hosts fall into one of three categories: pussy cat, Tasmanian devil, or snarling lion. Before any public relations professional accepts an invitation for his boss to go on a live radio talk show, he should know what species of critter he's dealing with.

- **Pussy Cat:** Some radio talk show hosts are gentle interviewers, using their forum to draw out the personality of the individual they are interviewing, never thinking of offering the awkward or embarrassing question. Former talk show host Larry King of CNN was the epitome of the "softball" interviewer, interspersing lavish praise with easy questions; offering the subject an ample opportunity to spread a message and sound great. Public radio hosts also tend to be more gentle, but can surprise you with the erudite or complicated questions (sometimes meant to demonstrate to their audience what smart people they are and that they've done their homework). These can be the most fun interviews a principal ever does.

- **Tasmanian Devil:** The most difficult beast to predict in the talk radio kingdom is the Tasmanian devil. These are the erratic hosts who make their reputation doing strange or unexpected things. Don Imus is this type of radio host who may lean a little left, but can bounce to both sides of the political spectrum without warning—which is why so many politicians are uneasy about going on his program. One liberal radio talk show host in the Midwest can be counted on to support any lefty politician—until the issue of gun control comes up, which will result in his ranting about the sanctity of the Second Amendment.

    If you let your principal go on a show with someone who is prone to the unexpected, you better be darn sure your principal is quick-witted and spry on his feet. It only takes fifteen seconds to turn a boring one-hour interview into a disaster.

- **Snarling Lion:** In the 1980s, conservative talk radio flourished in America, led by Rush Limbaugh, who went from a few thousand to a few million listeners in a couple of years. Despite conservatives' cry of a biased liberal media, there is no denying that conservatives dominate talk radio.

    Many of them, like Limbaugh and Glenn Beck on the conservative side, and Keith Olbermann and Ed Schultz on the liberal side, made their

(Continued on page 109)

§5.12 Radio Talk Shows (continued)

reputations by being caustic, rough, and sometimes downright mean on their radio program.

If your principal has political beliefs in sync with this crowd, this is a great forum to expound views. If your principal does not agree with them, watch out. A lot of public figures believe if they could just "talk" to the opposition, they'd win them over with their rhetorical skills and persuasiveness. This is a myth. Many people who tune into these programs have a set political philosophy and if you try to challenge that philosophy, they will simply tune to another radio station. The only reason for a liberal to go on a conservative radio talk show or for a conservative to go on a liberal talk show is to be food for the lion. Unless your liberal principal is a brilliant debater, keep him away from this species of talk show host.

Washington, DC, has a news staff of fifty people and covers local news just like any TV station.

Most major markets have at least one all-news station, sometimes running talk radio during the midday and overnight hours. They'll cover all major news events, much like the TV stations in the market. The other radio stations in these markets will have a one-to-three-person news department. They'll do more of their reporting over the phone and use additional sources, such as national radio feeds, to build each newscast. Because of these vast differences in resources and structure, the decision-making varies widely.

In smaller stations, the person answering the phone in the news department is the reporter, writer, producer, and broadcaster of the newscast. There is no hierarchy, like newspapers; no committee, like television. If you get the reporter on the phone, and they have five minutes to do the interview, your principal will be on the air at the top of the hour. Even the larger radio stations are reporter-driven, giving the man or woman on the street with the microphone and tape recorder total flexibility to piece together the story as they see fit.

Distinctive Pitching and Response Techniques

Pitching stories to radio stations is quick and easy. Radio reporters often make decisions faster than television reporters—a habit developed in part because of their need to produce ten newscasts every morning within twenty-five minutes of each other. Even more than television, the best pitch to radio stations is to connect it to a story currently in the news. Unlike television, you don't usually have to advance the story with a new angle. All the radio reporter often wants is a sound bite to accompany the story he's already written. The interview will be very brief, the reporter gets what he needs, and the whole process from pitch to concluded interview could be less than five minutes. This means you often have to be prepared to do an interview yourself or have your principal ready when you're making the pitch.

Responding to inquiries requires the same degree of brevity and flexibility. Radio reporters usually aren't doing a ton of original reporting. They're following the story from the morning paper, trying to add a sound bite, and get it on the air as soon as possible. Being fast and available are the key elements to getting coverage.

Relevant Deadlines

Because radio newscasts run hourly, deadlines roll on throughout the day. While it's hard to find the perfect time to call a station, usually the safest time is just after a newscast (when they have another twenty-five minutes before the next one). Avoid calling radio stations between 6:00 a.m. and 10:00 a.m., or between 4:00 p.m. and 6:00 p.m., unless absolutely necessary, or it's a larger station with several people working in the newsroom. Reporters and producers are usually frantically trying to write and prepare newscasts during these times.

This means, if you're providing a radio actuality, one of the best times to call a station is before 6:00 a.m., when the reporter is putting together the morning drive-time newscasts and is looking for new material, or 2:00 p.m., when he is preparing the afternoon newscasts. The 2:00 p.m. requirement is easy. Getting into the office before 6:00 a.m. so you can feed an actuality to five or ten small radio stations requires a serious dedication to the profession, devoted loyalty to your principal, and several large pots of coffee. See § 2.19 for a description of radio actualities.

§5.13 The Internet Medium: Web Sites, Blogs, and Social Media

American journalists like to trace their heritage to the American Revolution, but the flack in a New York PR firm has more in common with the colonial muckracker James Callender than a *Washington Post* reporter. In 1776 American newspapers had no editorial check on content, no attention to balance of ideas, no common ethical standards for publishing information, and usually a pecuniary interest that could override anything. Content was usually determined by one man, based on his worldview or interests.

This is a good starting point to understanding blogs. In the twenty-first century, blogs are morphing into "normal" web sites that are updated regularly, with variations of tools, technology, opinion, and biases based on either the business model designed to make a profit or the political viewpoints of the creators—or both.

A communication professional in the world of public affairs should focus primarily on the types of blogs that are likely to interact with your organization and target audience. Each industry has its own niche blogs. As you survey the media outlets in your universe (either geographically or by issue), it's likely that one or more blogs may figure prominently. As you look to use the blogosphere to support a communication strategy, it is helpful to categorize the types and how to interact with them.

News Aggregators and Creators

Web sites such as *Huffington Post* and the *Drudge Report* pull in content from other news sources to create basic news aggregator sites. Often they will add their own content, sometimes with full-time journalists. In many cases there are opportunities for readers to comment. They will also often include a cadre of regular contributors (bloggers) who write short opinion snippets on current events.

Pitching these bloggers is similar to pitching a mainstream news organization. They're seeking solid content, fast turnaround, and access to individuals who can provide both.

Opinion Supplementers

Political blogs, like "FiveThirtyEight," use paragraphs taken from major news stories and commentary with bloggers' opinion grafted on. These bloggers see their mission as collectors and synthesizers of political and public policy information, and use their forum to pick and choose the stories they find interesting.

Communication professionals can't really "pitch" this community, but can feed them leads with a stream of relevant data and commentary. The bloggers usually rely on trusted sources, so you'll need to build a relationship with the blogger and gain a reputation with her as a supplier of content she can use.

Professional Columnists

Journalists who work in mainstream media outlets often find a place on the Internet to repurpose their content or create original content. These columnists add to the content from their print columns with online content. The only feature that differentiates this content from the printed version is its frequency and the ability of readers to comment.

When pitching a columnist who also writes a blog, a communication professional should remember the pressure the columnist is under to post to the blog on a regular, often daily, basis. Columnist-bloggers can't be as choosy as their print-only cousins, so they might be more open to your pitch.

Experts

Some individuals who are genuinely considered experts in their field choose to be active in the blogosphere. Entries are often longer (as these bloggers often actually know what they're talking about) and usually more intelligently written—much like a niche publication.

Niche and Issue-Specific Blogs

Many blogs have narrow topics, appealing to a target audience perfect for Internet marketing and communication. This is a safer target to pitch, as they often have a reputation for not bashing political figures. But the sloppy communication professional who doesn't prepare to interact with a blogger steeped in an issue might end up with a critical blog entry instead of a supportive one.

Like trade publications, niche, issue-specific blogs reach a more limited audience, but often it is a highly motivated and informed audience that cares deeply about that issue. Readers who care about specific issues, such as food safety or higher education or Social Security, can turn to blogs that delve deeply into those issues, providing both news updates and commentary.

A good rule of thumb for pitching all bloggers: understand that they often know their issues very well, possibly better than you and your principal. They probably don't want a press release full of platitudes and talking points. They care about substance. If you're setting up an interview, prepare your principal for tough, thoughtful questions and ask if a policy colleague can join the call. Instead of sending them a press release, send them a government report that your principal requested or give them an advance copy of an amendment your principal is introducing. Treat them as experts and they will treat your principal as a leader on the issue. Treat them poorly and they might use their blog to trash your principal and organization.

§5.14 What Blogs Do Well: Get People Fired

There is much chatter in the political community about the influence of blogs. And yet there is very little research to demonstrate their unique influence—except when you count the corpses.

Politicians and policy staff read blogs in much the same way they use other media, such as op-eds in newspapers. Blogs can influence decision-making in the same way as columnists, through the power of their ideas and the wide distribution of those ideas.

But as we consider the early "accomplishments" of blogs, the most noteworthy seem to be the scalps that bloggers proudly wear on their belts.

During the 2004 presidential campaign *60 Minutes Wednesday* ran a Dan Rather story based on documents that raised questions about President George W. Bush's service in the Air National Guard in 1972 and 1973 (see "Killian documents authenticity issues" on Wikipedia). Almost immediately bloggers spotted inconsistencies in the document. Most notably, the font system of proportionally spacing type did not exist on typewriters of the 1970s and could only be prepared on a word processor built after the documents were purportedly written. Rather and CBS foolishly defended the story—even after their own forensic expert disputed the story. Within months three senior executives and Dan Rather—a nationally recognized journalist with four decades of experience—were out on the street.

The second example of blogs helping topple the mighty was the downfall of Attorney General Alberto Gonzales in 2007. Gonzales fired six U.S. attorneys in December 2006. The firings failed to gain attention from national media, and interested only one blogger, Josh Marshall of "Talking Points Memo." Marshall and his team, with contributions from his readers, suggested that the firings were based on politics rather than the merits or skills of the individuals dismissed. Mainstream reporters began to pick up the scent of blood. Congressional hearings followed, which included Gonzales' lackadaisical performances before congressional committees. In September 2007, Gonzales resigned. The Justice Department Inspector General, Glenn Fine, later found no intentional or criminal wrongdoing by Gonzales.

The common theme here is the combination of interested people and an unfettered communication medium. These events should put all policy-makers, press secretaries—and journalists—on notice that no fact, utterance, story, press release, statement, or activity will go unnoticed and un-scrutinized in the blogosphere.

§5.15 Tips for PAOs and PIOs

The four major media discussed in this chapter each have their own strengths. Understanding these strengths is crucial in dealing with an emergency or crisis.

Radio = Speed
Radio is the quickest method to get information in circulation and should be your primary source for informing the public; for example, to inform the traveling public of response lanes and activities so as to avoid traffic jams and response delays.

Television = Impact
Video of a scene helps the viewing public understand the impact of an event and also carries emotional impact that can facilitate compliance with public safety instructions. Example: showing video and pictures of the aftermath of Hurricane Katrina will help emphasize the unpredictability of an approaching storm and remind the affected community that compliance with public safety instructions may be the difference between life and death.

Print = Longevity and Depth
Print publications have the ability to follow an intricate story over time. It is easily portable, shareable, and has the power of the archive that makes the historical perspective easily reachable and therefore very powerful.

Internet = Convergence
The Internet allows for the convergence of all these media, and with the proliferation of the mobile web via smartphones, makes them all portable and accessible on demand.

Successful bloggers typically operate under the basic rules of debate:
- The authority of your source
- The power of your ideas
- The strength of your argument

Most also have two requirements:
1. Access to the principal decision-makers and operators closest to the action
2. Making your information linkable

We are in the Networked Age with a digital economy and links are the currency. In many cases organizations now need to be their own news outlets, publishing news and information about their operations and issues on their web sites. Designing these web sites to be interactive by allowing blogs from the boss and comments on the posts is becoming a standard for both public and private organizations.

It is important to understand that for the communication professional this means working differently than we have traditionally. The enormous amount of data and information now available to an organization from their interested communities is staggering, making it both a blessing and a curse. However, those communities more and more are expecting the ability to interact. This means finding new ways to manage the workflows and respond to the community or be relegated to irrelevance.

Social media is also more of a community relations effort. You have control of your efforts on Facebook, Twitter, YouTube, LinkedIn, etc., but only at the consent of the community. Social media is NOT a place to pitch stories. It is, however, a place to TELL stories and have discussions about them—honesty, authenticity, and relevance are what matter. Depending on your community and your organization, social media may be a place to tell that story, to be picked up by bloggers and journalists.

§5.99 Chapter Summary

Print Medium (§ 5.2)

- Newspapers often set the public affairs agenda. Television reporters often follow the lead from daily newspapers, but newspapers rarely follow television stories.
- Reporters are the primary contacts; decision-making also rests with section editors.
- Most newspaper deadlines are at 6:00 p.m.
- Wire services can reach millions of readers and operate the primary daybooks that list upcoming events.

Television Medium (§ 5.6)

- Television is the dominant method to influence public opinion and convey a message.
- Television covers much less news than newspapers. The key decision-makers often are not reporters, but assignment editors and producers at the station. Local stations usually hold two decisionmaking meetings a day to determine newscast lineups: between 8:30 a.m. and 10:00 a.m., and 2:00 p.m. and 3:30 p.m.
- Pitches to television stations must be fast (fifteen to thirty seconds) and include recommendations for visual components to the story.

- Television interview locations should be selected by public relations professionals to make the principal look good or to illustrate an aspect of the story. Work with the cameraman to set up the best possible shot.

Radio Medium (§ 5.11)

- Radio can be very effective at reinforcing a message. The best time for radio coverage is morning drive time, 6:00 a.m. to 10:00 a.m.
- Radio news staffs are small, unless it is the top news station in a major market. Individual radio reporters work independently, deciding whether to cover a story, conducting interviews, and writing and editing the stories.
- Pitching to radio stations is fast. Reporters usually aren't interested in advancing the story or new angles—they just want sound bites to add to stories already written.
- Avoid calling radio stations during busy times (6:00 a.m. to 10:00 a.m., and 4:00 p.m. to 6:00 p.m.) while reporters are primarily delivering the news at thirty-minute intervals.

The Internet Medium: Web Sites, Blogs, and Social Media (§ 5.13)

- Blogs are generally divided into these categories: news creators and aggregators; opinion supplementers and professional columnists; and niche and issue-specific blogs.
- Blogs are a different medium than mainstream media. There are fewer checks on the content, either ethically or editorially, and require different pitching techniques.
- Organizational web sites can be designed to help in the connection to constituent communities and to develop the organization's presence in the blogosphere.
- Social media is a community relations effort. Consider it for telling a story rather than pitching one.

Chapter Six:
Online Communication

> *"I have now one ambition: to retire before it becomes essential to tweet."*
>
> Rep. Barney Frank (D-MA)

Online Communication

§6.1 Introduction

By the time you read this, much of what is written in this chapter will likely have changed. Authors, industry experts, and researchers frequently try to nail down global conclusions about the Internet, only to find that, before the ink is dry, someone has rewritten the rulebook, forcing us to rethink our assumptions about communication. Ubiquitous connectivity and the proliferation of connected devices including desktops, laptops, netbooks, pads, and phones have empowered individuals like never before. We are now in the Networked Age.

Since publishing the first edition of *Media Relations Handbook*, hundreds of millions of people have created Facebook accounts, Tweeted revolutionary activity in the Middle East, and provided grassroots fund-raising support for elected officals. The Internet is no longer an ancillary tool in communication strategy. The World Wide Web (web) is essential to all public relationships, communication campaigns, and community development.

This chapter offers guidance on how to integrate new media tools, practices, and strategies into media relations work. And yet, as stated above, the very nature of the developing medium makes it difficult to set any hard-and-fast rules. This new media environment offers professional communicators the opportunity to seize the Holy Grail of organizational communication: cost-effective mass communication with your constituents. E-newsletters, blogs, Twitter accounts, and Facebook pages, among other Internet tools, provide unprecedented access to our target markets, sometimes called Direct to Constituent Communication (DCC).

This chapter is not an exhaustive examination of this new media world. Such an exploration would require another book (or a web site that is updated daily). Rather, this chapter will seek to articulate those known best practices for online communication that relate to interacting with traditional media sources. The focus is on major components of online community action and how they play into other components of a media relations strategy.

§6.10 The Differences between Old Media and New Media

Despite the omnipresent nature of new media in our society, some principals view the Internet as a fad and some public relations practitioners still look at the web as merely a new technology to implement the same strategies and messages they delivered with traditional media (television, radio, and print). But in order to fully utilize the Internet and web capabilities one must first appreciate that they have some basic differences from other media.

For example, both television and the web can be viewed as revolutionary changes in communication—but in different ways. Radio changed the delivery system for information. Instead of paper-based, printed word communication, people got information through a broadcast audio medium. Television brought impact to the broadcast medium, making it an audio-visual medium. The web is more than a change in the delivery system—it changes the entire dynamic between an organization and its public. Online communication is an ongoing dialogue where the public relations expert must quickly respond to an audience's interests and needs, communicating core principles and messages.

Dr. Alan Rosenblatt's "3-D Model of Campaign Communication" best describes this effect. The model was created to describe the evolution of public affairs advocacy, yet it serves all communicators in understanding the web. Rosenblatt posits that the first iteration of the communication architecture of the Internet's web was "1 Dimensional." The communicator created a one-way communication pathway, merely substituting a new electronic vehicle to transmit the same communication effort sent via existing vehicles.

By 1998, a "2 Dimensional" world was evolving with the introduction of interactivity between audience and content creator. Online polls, responsive e-newsletters, and online chats dominated this brief era. The end of the first decade of the twenty-first century ushered in a "3 Dimensional" world, best epitomized by the development of social media. With social media, the com-

§6.11 Rosenblatt's 3-D Model of Internet Communication

1-D	2-D	3-D
Information	Action	Community
One-way Communication	Two-way Communication	All-way Communication
Campaign Talks to Activist	Campaign Mobilizes Activist to Action	Activists Mobilize and Talk to Each Other
Email Lists and Brochure Web Sites	Transactional Web Sites	Social Networks

Source: Dr. Alan Rosenblatt

municator relinquishes nearly all control of the communication platform and environment, allowing her audience to create their own content and conduct a dialogue with the audience the communicator helped to recruit. This audience is no longer merely an audience but now is a community and the focus is no longer "controlling the message" but "cultivating understanding."

Many communicators (especially those in a public affairs environment) view a web site or Facebook page as an online brochure—like a billboard that they post messages on for people to read. However, the interactive nature of the web is a much more intimate and powerful communication tool once a bond has been established with an audience. In order to develop the most effective and creative strategies for using the web, public relations professionals must go through a paradigm shift in thinking. They must appreciate that the web is more than an online bulletin board—it is a dynamic communication environment that converges with the characteristics and uses of television, radio, and print, creating greater communication potential than has ever been available before. The web changes the concept of mass communication from a broadcast paradigm to an interactive, interpersonal paradigm.

The mechanics for the internal creation of online content is discussed in § 6.13, Six Management Principles of Online Communication, but the central, guiding canon calls for an open process, allowing all segments of an organization or audience to contribute to the development and release of information—sometimes without the filter of a public relations expert. Indeed, the target audience itself becomes a co-creator of the message, building the community aspect of the relationship. This is contrary to traditional PR procedures, yet is essential to maximizing the potential of social media.

Also, traditional communication is less complex—the best strategies usually call for organizations to put forth a core message over and over again. Online communication in a public affairs environment can have a range of messages all targeted to various audiences. While certain core audiences should be catered to throughout a web site, a communicator should avoid message-like, repetitive themes or slogans and instead try to convey diverse information that meets the community needs while maintaining the core philosophy of the leadership of the organization. This is an exercise in leadership for your community.

Rather than hammer home the same message over and over again, online communication requires more subtlety. You can get your message across, but it must be contained within information the community wants.

In addition, unlike traditional communication that is filtered through a communication professional and then the media, social media reaches your audience unfiltered. This presents both a greater opportunity and a greater responsibility for security, accuracy, policy, and propriety on behalf of the organization. In this environment, strengthening an organization's internal communication strengthens its external communication reach and credibility.

A public relations specialist who creates a static web site with no interactivity for the visitor, or no social media strategy that invites dialogue, is today's equivalent of the politician who wouldn't do television in the 1960s, or who refused to install a telephone in his office in the 1930s. Trying to compete in today's communication environment using yesterday's strategies and tools is a formula for becoming irrelevant.

Another important concept is how new media strategies have become an organic part of the communication operations and processes. This is best demonstrated by the comparison of how presidential campaigns organized their online efforts between 2004 and 2008. In 2004 the Howard Dean campaign had an "Internet Division." This group organized their Meet-up efforts, contributed to the fund-raising operations, and delivered messages (crafted by other departments) to supporters via email. In 2008 the Obama campaign created no such distinction. Every division of the campaign had a web component—it was intertwined in every aspect of the organization.

As part of any strategic-planning process, an online strategy must be central to achieving goals. The benefits of using the web should be weighed *before* other media, as the tools are less costly, more efficient, and are more likely to reach a target audience than older media tools: building your community first. One cannot ignore print, radio, television, and the reporters who support those media, as they provide a validating and credible platform for authenticating a message. Yet the web requires public relations professionals to build a communication structure and strategy integrating old and new media so they complement each other.

§6.12 Al Gore Didn't Invent the Internet . . .

As a presidential candidate, Vice President Al Gore took a lot of grief for making the statement that he "invented" the Internet. In fact, his quote was, "During my service in the United States Congress, I took the initiative in creating the Internet." He was correct in claiming credit as one of a few members of Congress who saw the potential for this vast knowledge network back in the 1980s.

In 1962, J. C. R. Licklider wrote a memo discussing his concept of an "Intergalactic Computer Network." After he was appointed to a position at the Defense Department's Advanced Research Projects Agency (ARPA), he persuaded colleagues that the networked computer was important. One of these colleagues, Bob Taylor, was involved in the early development in the mid-1960s of what came to be known as ARPANET, the technical precursor to today's Internet.

On November 7, 1967, at the bill-signing ceremony establishing the Corporation for Public Broadcasting, President Lyndon Johnson spoke on the topic of information distribution.

"I think we must consider new ways to build a great network for knowledge—not just a broadcast system—but one that employs every means of sending and of storing information that the individual can use. The country doctor getting help from a distant laboratory or a teaching hospital; a scholar in Atlanta might draw instantly on a library in New York; a famous teacher could reach with ideas and inspiration into some far-off classroom, so that no child need be neglected. Eventually, I think this electronic knowledge bank could be as valuable as the Federal Reserve Bank, and such a system could involve other nations. It could involve them in a partnership to share knowledge and to thus enrich all mankind. A wild and visionary idea? Not at all. Yesterday's strangest dreams are today's headlines, and change is getting swifter every moment."

In late 1969, a few computer engineers, including Robert Taylor, Leonard Kleinrock, and Larry Roberts, connected four computers with a Department of Defense grant. The grant resulted in "ARPANET."

§6.13 Six Management Principles of Online Communication

Some people in public affairs think the biggest challenge of online communication is understanding the *technology*—and they are wrong. The biggest challenge is understanding the *management* of creating and maintaining online communication strategies. Despite many non-geeks' initial fears, getting a computer to do what you want is relatively simple and straightforward. Getting a social media strategy adopted in a risk-averse organization is much more difficult, because people are more complicated than machines.

Successful online strategies can only be built and maintained effectively through a management and execution scheme that touches an entire organization in some way. There are six key management principles for a successful online communication strategy.

1. Leadership—The communication professional works to support the leadership. Online communication strategies, just like off-line strategies, must have the support of that leadership. Managers must commit resources, ensure that all staff understands the importance of the strategy, and be involved in key strategic decisions. Leaders don't have to be involved in the day-to-day decisions, or create their own Twitter accounts; but if they're not behind the effort, it's likely to fail. One of the reasons that the federal government's portal, First.gov, is rated as one of the best web sites in the world is because two presidents, Bill Clinton and George W. Bush, devoted resources and support to using the Internet to make the federal government more accessible to citizens.

President Obama continued that support, issuing his Open and Transparent Government memorandum soon after entering office, and in 2010 the Department of Defense issued its Directive-type Memorandum 09-026 on the Responsible and Effective use of Internet-based Capabilities.

2. Internal Leadership—Behind most successful online strategies are one or two people inside the organization who drive the effort. They provide the creativity, knowledge, and basic hard work that result in great web sites, rich e-newsletters, and thoughtful social media efforts. It is their responsibility to push the thinking of leaders and colleagues about the value of the web to their organization, and translate those ideas into practical benefits.

§6.14 How to Get the Boss to Go Online

One moderating problem in the world of Washington public affairs is that there are many non-tech-oriented people in charge in Washington. The average age of an association leader is in the mid-50s, which means the web arrived in the middle, not the beginning, of their working lives. This is an unfortunate piece of math for the aggressive public relations professional trying to create a social media strategy for her group if the leadership is resisting updating media strategies. Here are a few tips to change the mind of most any hard-bitten old media lover.

- **Find examples or case studies from similar organizations.** Show your leaders that others have dipped their toe in the water of Internet innovation and it didn't get bitten off. Groups such as the Public Affairs Council and the American Society of Association Executives are great sources for successful case studies.

- **Go slow, build one success on another.** Leaders like pilot programs because they reduce risk. Identify something small to create a success. For example, instead of creating an entire social media strategy, build one around a single topic that your organization focuses on.

- **Lower expectations.** By definition the web is a medium of diffused interests. The days of big mainstream media splashes are dwindling. Online media coverage that reaches hundreds, not tens of thousands, of a targeted audience, is deemed successful. The trick is replicating those kinds of mini-successes over and over again.

- **Diversify tactics, but keep it safe.** One of the great things about the web is that it is inexpensive compared to mainstream media. Hire a PR shop to set up a press conference that bombs, and you've blown $15,000 in your budget. However, set up an online ad through Google or Blogads and you've lost pennies—unless it takes off and your targeted audience likes your message, in which case the investment is worth it. Try various strategies simultaneously, or at least proximate in timing to one another so you can compare results. A new adage: fail early, fail cheaply, fail often, keep learning.

- **Recruit allies within the organization.** The boss is going to feel more comfortable in uncharted waters if he's got other senior managers on board. The best path to innovative online strategies may not be directly to the top office, but rather through other senior managers who can benefit from your ideas.

§6.15 The Great Twitter Battle of 2010

Politicians are competitive beasts. So it wasn't shocking that soon after Twitter began being used to send out political communication that Democrats and Republicans would begin competing over who had the most and best "Tweets." Senator Claire McCaskill (D-MO) has distinguished herself early as a consistent Tweeter. Her comments are a good example of how to use the medium. She offers personal comments connected to her activities as a public official. "Excited to be meeting the Honor Flight of WWII vets from Franklin County in a few minutes. True heroes. My dad fought too, makes me miss him." Then there are the comments on policy: "I'm very frustrated at State Dept & Defnse Dep's inability to produce documents about their counter narcotics contracts. Billions spent."

Despite the Missouri Democrat's fame as a leading Tweeter, her party is already lagging in the competition. According to a study conducted by the public relations firm Fleishman-Hillard, House Republicans sent five times more Tweets than House Democrats in early 2010. This is not just an obscure statistic. In the 1990s Senate Democrats won an arms race with Senate Republicans in the competition over who could set up the most web sites. However, in public affairs, if you fall behind in online communication, it's very easy to catch up to the competition.

3. Internal Input and Cooperation—Occasionally, one challenge to creating online strategies is getting buy-in and participation from colleagues. Communication specialists cannot provide the content necessary for online communication without the full cooperation of fellow staff. In larger organizations, this can be a challenge; but it also can be a rich opportunity to bolster the organization's mission internally.

In many organizations in the public affairs arena, new strategies, tools, and tactics can face resistance. Risk-averse cultures thrive in Washington, DC, and state capitals, and strategic plans and policies often have as much to do with job retention of management as they do with sound communication practices. To achieve cooperation and collaboration, keep in mind these principles and questions:

- **Demonstrate the value of the contribution to the contributor.** Whether it is a policy statement that could better explain an issue, regular postings on an issue-oriented Facebook page, or YouTube video of a policy expert, the contributor and creator of the content must see value for his team and mission. Because these are all new strategies, some will fear unknown and potentially negative consequences. The payoff for the contributor could be greater recognition for their pet issue, or praise in an email sent from a senior communication staffer to the boss. Few of us take risks without potential rewards, so make rewards part of your communication plan.

- **Establish clear policies for online communication content and practices.** Because things happen fast on the web, professional communicators usually want to react quickly. But no public affairs organization likes making decisions under time pressures. Therefore, work must be done in advance with key stakeholders. Ask clear questions to get solid guidance. What content is it in our best interests to post online? What criteria will we use in selecting the content? Who will have access to online vehicles? Which online media (blogs, social media, e-newsletters) will we use and who will regularly update them?
- **Establish at least a two-person check on all online communication.** The fastest way to have your online strategy shot down is for someone in your organization to post something stupid. The Internet never forgets, with a memory that's backed up by servers all over the world. This is why you must have at least two people review everything that is posted online and to help keep watch over the organization's social media properties. It is true that one of the great values of social media is speed and authenticity to communicate. However, in the world of public affairs, words have policy implications. While it might delay content going online, a few minutes' delay is better than getting fired.

4. Catering to External Audiences—Because the web allows communicators and leaders to talk directly to audiences, anyone in the public affairs world must be prepared for a robust dialogue. Whether you like it or not, the dialogue on whatever is important to you and your organization will occur. The web has given hundreds of millions of people a platform to shout to the world. To many leaders, it may sound a lot like the television news anchor Howard Beale in the movie *Network*, who begins to lose his mind on live television and urges his viewing audience to go the window and yell, "I'm mad as hell and I'm not going to take it anymore!"

Yet, there is more than poisonous diatribe in most dialogues. There are thoughtful suggestions about the strategic direction of your organization, reaction to your latest public affairs agenda, and the opportunity to instantly gauge reaction to your tactics and policies. You can create a virtuous commu-

§6.16 Tips for PAOs and PIOs

When communicating with external audiences, be aware of what constitutes a "record" for your office. Records are generated every time someone transcribes a thought into a physical media whether it is a letter, email, web site, notepad or table napkin. Federal records are classified as temporary or permanent and have disposition schedules determining when they are destroyed or archived. Understand what constitutes a record for your office and consider records management options when communicating via social media or on web sites that are not governed by your agency. Check with your records manager and <*www.archives.gov/records-mgmt/*> to find out more.

nication cycle that feeds the needs of both your internal and external stakeholders. This does not mean that every VP for government affairs or congressman must respond to every comment. But by offering a forum and engaging your target audience, the thoughtful communication professional will establish an authentic, direct bond with the people you want to influence the most, gaining their trust and support: in effect, building a community. Most important, it sends the most powerful message an organizational leader can send to an audience: I'm listening.

5. Connection to a Strategic Vision—Your web-based communication should be a virtual representation of your organization. Your mission, strategic image, and the tone should reflect every aspect of your organization. This management principle is connected to the web site design principles discussed in § 6.22 and should be an underlying consideration in all online communication. In looking at online strategies, ask yourself: "Are all our goals reflected?" "Are we emphasizing the same messages online and off-line?" "Are we meeting the needs of all strategic stakeholders?"

6. Connection to the Physical, Off-Line World—Some communicators and managers perceive the web as a separate world, like the 1982 Disney movie *Tron* (and the 2010 sequel), where a computer expert is downloaded into a video game—a distinct environment not connected to reality. Connecting online and off-line strategies is probably the most important management principle of successful communication planning. Each environment has its own strengths and weaknesses, but linking them is essential.

More than any other category of online communication (such as commercial or news sites), many people go online to public affairs web sites because they are seeking connection to some part of government and public policy. They may want information or a service, but they are also inviting your organization to get them involved. During the summer of 2009, Tea Party Patriots used its network of 3 million supporters to collect and disseminate the locations of upcoming congressional town hall meetings. Tens of thousands of citizens took action, filling auditoriums throughout the nation. Most listened, some shouted, and the debate progressed, revolving around how and whether to reform America's health-care system. Here we had a communication technology spread a message throughout the land, and Americans responded in unprecedented numbers. Thomas Paine would be proud.

§6.17 How to Connect Off-line Activities with Online Assets

For public affairs organizations it is essential to connect off-line activities with online assets. People are often driven to your virtual office by something that happened in the real world, and that recognition will help you anticipate visitors' needs and interests. The obstacles for connecting these worlds are often internal, not external. Managers and colleagues may resist coordinating their work and goals with an online component. Here are a few ideas that have worked successfully with other public affairs organizations.

Directing People to Web Site with Off-line Media: The simplest way to connect online and off-line strategies is with an overt pitch to visit the web site. Use standard media—television, radio, print, direct mail—to explain to your audiences what they will find on your site. Some organizations have greater off-line tools to enhance their online traffic. CNN.com is one of the most popular web sites on the web because it has a television network promoting it. But there are other tools available. At any National Rifle Association press conference, viewers are saturated with large banners reading "nra.org" in almost every conceivable camera angle. A few members of Congress have sent direct-mail pieces to their constituents, with a cover stating, "Your Congressman Is Only a Few Clicks Away." One member who sent such a piece increased his web site traffic five-fold and added thousands of names to his e-newsletter list.

Collecting Email Addresses in Off-line Settings: As stated earlier, an email address is the most valuable gift (other than money) someone can bestow on your organization. You've seen the bumper sticker, "The Person with the Most Toys at the End of the Game . . . Wins." Well, when communicating on the web, the person with the most email addresses at the end of the game wins. Be a vacuum cleaner for email addresses, sucking them in through as many means as possible.

People phoning your organization should be asked for their email addresses (be certain staff making that request convey a strong privacy statement to ease callers' fears). Any event attended by the principal is another email collection opportunity. Online petition drives are extraordinarily successful times for broadening your email address database. The web site should make it easy to provide an email address, *without* requiring the visitor to provide a home address, phone number, or other information. (The exceptions to this rule are members of Congress, who need to confirm it is their constituents who are requesting information, by requiring a full address and zip code.) It should become second nature for every staff member to collect email addresses and communication staff should provide tools (forms, phone protocols, etc.) to make it simple for them to do so.

Grassroots Organizing: Probably the most effective and valuable connection of off-line activities through online tools is to use the web as a central part of a grassroots lobbying strategy.

The group that pioneered many of these tactics was Moveon.org. The group was formed in 1999 by Wes Boyd (the same guy who invented the flying toasters screen saver) as a sort of protest to Republican tactics during the impeachment of President Clinton over the Monica Lewinsky perjury affair. As the name and URL implied, organizers wanted Republicans to "move on" past impeachment to focus on other issues. The online movement caught fire and the group raised $1.5 million in two years, which they directed to Democratic congressional candidates who were running against members of Congress who served as "impeachment managers" in the House. After Clinton left office, Moveon.org used its database of millions of activists to mobilize for other efforts. The group threw its support to Barack Obama in the 2008 presidential campaign, bolstering his online efforts.

A significant Moveon.org campaign was its partnership with the Win Without War group to organize a "virtual march" on the Senate in February 2003 to oppose the impending war with Iraq. Organizers used their web sites and viral marketing techniques to coordinate tens of thousands of phone calls, faxes, and emails to the Senate. The Senate telephone switchboard was effectively shut down for the day because of the volume of calls.

While the effort cannot be credited with changing the vote of any member of Congress or the policy outcome, the campaign marked a more sophisticated level in grassroots lobbying tactics and demonstrated that small organizations (Moveon.org had a full-time staff of four people) can wield formidable clout in the public affairs arena. For those contemplating such a campaign, keep in mind that the strategy must be connected to a cause that genuinely excites some portion of the online public. For example, Moveon.org's campaign to oppose the Bush tax cuts generated fewer calls and faxes to Senate offices.

Adjust Web Site Based on Media Coverage: Many people visit an organization's web site after a representative or principal does a media interview. The sound bite they heard intrigued them and they want more. Be prepared for these instances with content that expands on the interview message, and, at least for a short time, make it prominent on the home page. Send out an email, text message or tweet to supporters alerting them of the "news" affecting an issue important to them. Have the interview captured and posted on YouTube. Television interviews are the greatest free media advertisements for your online media efforts—position yourself to take advantage of the attention that will follow.

Off-line Accomplishments and Ideas Drive Online Activity: Public affairs new media strategies are not completely virtual entities—they are connected to the real-world mission of the organization. One must never forget that most of your online interest will be derived from off-line activity. 2008 presidential candidate Barack Obama utilized many innovative web strategies, but his success wasn't due to the technology he and his team embraced—his message and personal narrative captured millions of Americans' attention . . . and they went to a web site to learn more.

This concept was best articulated by the advisor of another presidential candidate. It's ironic that the Obama new media team seemed to best the McCain new media team in the 2008 election because the Republican nominee was one of the early pioneers of using online media in political campaigns. During a Politics Online Conference sponsored by George Washington University, the creator of Senator John McCain's 2000 presidential site, Max Fose, was asked how others could re-create the incredible success the site experienced in the early days of the 2000 campaign. The site raised millions of dollars and registered thousands of volunteers in a matter of weeks. He answered: "Easy. First you start with a U.S. senator who will take on big tobacco, sponsors campaign finance reform legislation, and was held prisoner of war in Vietnam for seven years. Then you build a web site." Max's point was clear: people didn't come to the web site to visit the web site, they were interested in helping a person they wanted to be president. This was true eight years later for Barack Obama. The fastest computer and greatest web site can only accelerate and enhance a message; they can't create it. Don't expect technology by itself to invent interest in your mission. Start with your core beliefs and those shared values with a logical target audience, and build from there.

Crisis Management: One of a communication specialist's greatest assets in a crisis is the organization's web site. It is not a tool for putting out blandly positive material, ignoring the fact that the organization may be wrestling with a front-page disaster. It is a tool for instantly disseminating detailed information to both the public and reporters about the organization's position during a time when minutes can make or break a reputation. If you are in a crisis, and the web site is not a central part of your crisis management plan, go back to the drawing board and include it. (For more information on this topic, see § 12.8, How to Use Online Communication and Social Media in a Crisis.)

Get Creative: One of the coolest things about the web is that somebody comes up with a new way to use it every day. The most creative public affairs uses are not new gimmicks or special effects, but innovative strategies that advance an organization's cause or enhance its image. When something important is coming up, set aside time with staff to brainstorm how you can best integrate the web into your effort. Better yet, consider how you can best integrate your effort into the web. Think about how best to connect your organization to the audience you need in order to build a community to reach your objective. In the Networked Age, the effort is not about adapting the web for the organization, but adapting the organization for the web.

And, most important, *research* what other similar groups are doing. You may be able to adapt someone else's creativity for your use. A U.S. senator adapted the tactic used by grassroots lobbying groups to lobby Congress, and coordinated a petition drive to lobby the Bush administration. In the process, she collected more than 165,000 email addresses in a few months. Associations can extend the reach of their conventions by streaming video of key speeches on the web to members who can't attend. Nonprofit organizations can demonstrate the value of lobbying days on Capitol Hill by encouraging volunteers who meet with legislators to write up diaries of their meetings (and post them on the organization's web site), to both report back to other volunteers on the value of the work and recruit new volunteers.

The key to coming up with creative ideas is devoting the time and resources to developing them, instead of just handling the day-to-day activities. One technology trade association leader told his staff that their motto is: "Doing things today the same way we did them yesterday is just an excuse for not thinking."

§6.20 The Little Web Site that Could

Despite the lofty rhetoric of the potential of the Internet to change the nature of the political or governmental process, no online campaign has ever changed the outcome of a vote in Congress—except one. In 2001, a small nonprofit, the Environmental Working Group (EWG), wanted to influence a key section of the upcoming debate on the farm bill. The group's leader, Ken Cook, thought the current subsidy system was a travesty. The top 10 percent of the biggest farms (agri-businesses) annually received about two-thirds of the $125 billion in subsidies, according to the group. The data turned on its head the idea that farm subsidies were targeted to the proverbial family farmer; instead they were going to corporate conglomerates. They knew that with that much money at stake, a meagerly funded nonprofit couldn't take on the entrenched agri-business lobby with a traditional media campaign. So they tried something different.

The group invested its resources on research, identifying the names and addresses of every recipient in America of a farm subsidy. Some were low amounts—others were in the millions. The data was publicly available from the Department of Agriculture, but was organized in such a way to make it difficult to identify individual recipients, and it was not online. EWG created a user-friendly, sort-able database and put it on a simple web site. A list of recipients (mostly companies) that received more than $1 million annually was created; reporters identified the individuals and companies by state, county, and town; congressional staff created charts for congressional debate, and neighbors looked up neighbors, to see what the folks down the road were getting from Uncle Sam—all through the brilliant transparency of the web site that provided all the information online.

The group then engaged in an aggressive unpaid media ("earned media") effort to get the data into the hands of reporters. The effect was remarkable. As the Senate debate unfolded, over and over again, senators referred to the data and ewg.org. They even stopped calling it by name—they simply said "look at the web site," as if every other senator knew which web site they were talking about. When the vote came on an amendment to limit subsidies to $275,000 per farm, the Senate voted 66 to 31. More important than impact on agriculture policy were the implications for our legislative processes. A web site had changed a vote in the Senate. No television spots were created, no big newspaper space purchased, no high-powered lobbying firm hired—just a web site.

Eventually, the vote was reversed in the House, primarily pushed by congressional leaders somewhat more immune to this kind of influence, and the subsidy limit was dropped from the final legislation. But, setting aside the policy debate for the moment, the implications of the tactical success are profound. The experiment was proven. A strategy to influence a vote in Congress was centered on an online component, and it worked. As other groups consider the potential for influencing Congress, they should not be constrained by small budgets and huge opposition. They are bound only by their own creativity and the vision of their own leaders to experiment with this new technology that turns Davids into Goliaths.

§6.21 Communicators' and Visitors' Goals

An organization's online goals should mesh seamlessly with its off-line goals. Yet, the web allows public affairs professionals to achieve certain objectives that are difficult or expensive to achieve off-line.

Communicators' Goals

Promote Agenda: Targeted audiences and the general public can be exposed to an organization's or principal's message through web-based communication. Online tools are invaluable for conveying information to reporters, adding to their significance in promoting your agenda and enhancing your strategic image (see § 6.50, Web Site as Journalist Resource). However, promoting your agenda online cannot be the *only* goal, and must not take priority over the audience's goals. Excessive self-promotion (a frequent failing of members of Congress) leads to smaller email lists and fewer page views on a web site.

Increase Membership or Followers (Organizing Tool): Most organizations in public affairs have some connection to a targeted constituency: associations have members, nonprofit organizations have donors, members of Congress have voters. The web is the greatest community organizing tool invented since the soapbox. It allows online communities to be established, messages to spread like a virus, and donations to be collected. Public affairs-oriented organizations should consider online communication as their primary community-building tool.

Enhance Productivity and Efficiency: Depending upon the size of the organization, web resources can be designed to enhance the efficiency of an organization. If your organization provides or sells services or goods (such as publications) in an off-line environment, consider offering them online as well. In addition, a well-organized web site can be a primary source for your staff to retrieve information, answer questions, and coordinate activities. Email is vastly less expensive than direct mail. Moreover, using assessment tools, such as Google Analytics, you can further enhance your productivity and better target your new media strategies, producing greater results and efficiencies.

Enhance Employee Morale: Everyone likes to see her work on display in the marketplace. It may not be possible to get a *New York Times* article on a particular office achievement, but an online link to a section of your organization's web site or a shout-out in an e-newsletter are ways to demonstrate employee achievements and boost morale.

Reputation Management: "Reputation Management" is an essential practice in online communication, springing up from the explosion of sources of influential voices on the web. In the pre-Internet days, a good clipping service could give you a rough assessment of how public opinion was forming on an issue. The web offers a wonderful opportunity for influencing markets, and also the possibility that enemies are populating cyberspace with derisive commentary that could sink a leader's or organization's reputation.

Put simply, reputation management is the ongoing tracking, analysis, and response to any reference to an individual or organization on the web. It requires communicators to: 1) set up tracking systems to monitor news stories, blog posts, and any online comments regarding an individual or organization; 2) establish analytical systems to measure and weigh the impact or influence of those comments; 3) rapidly respond, avoiding the typical slow speed of bureaucratic decision-making, allowing groups and individuals to quickly manage and influence target audiences before a negative message begins setting in the cement of public opinion.

It is impossible to underestimate the speed with which opinions are now formed on the web. Blog entries will occur at 9:00 a.m., commentary will last until 11:00 a.m., and the blogger will be on to two new topics before lunch. If an organization has not responded in that two-hour window, the opportunity to respond and be noticed may be lost. However, two old adages are especially relevant in today's new media environment: "consider the source" and "think before you speak" or post, or tweet. A knee-jerk reaction usually will not help your cause.

There are a variety of tools to track your organization's reputation online, and the list grows almost daily. The easiest and least expensive to set up are Google News Alert and Yahoo News Alert. Your organization may also want to invest in a commercial monitoring tool. Either way, set up redundant teams to monitor your organization's and principal's reputation online, perhaps dividing up monitoring responsibilities. If you work in a small operation, the complexity and breadth of potential commentary on the web can be overwhelming. Have a team in your organization jointly create a virtual "net" to capture keywords, names, topics, etc., that are important to your mission.

Audience Goals

As the web became more sophisticated and interactive, savvy communicators came to appreciate that an audience was not merely a blob of wet clay to be molded. Indeed, "public relations," as envisioned by the profession's pioneer, Edward Bernays, may truly have evolved into something entirely different than a craft to "engineer consent." The idea that we can manipulate public opinion as easily as pulling strings on a puppet was never quite an accurate metaphor, yet the web has taken us to a somewhat different reality.

Whereas in offline communication we consider an audience's values and interests, in online communication we also must consider their immediate needs and goals. People who turn on their computer or smartphone *want* something. And the communicator who does not provide adequate and appropriate content to the audience's satisfaction will quickly become irrelevant.

Access Information: The web has virtually replaced encyclopedias as the repository of all human knowledge. It is a phone book for addresses, a watercooler for gossip, a newspaper for news, a journal for opinion, a cookbook for recipes, a doctor for remedies, and a parent for advice. According to an April 2010 study by the Pew Internet and American Life Project, 40 percent of Internet users go online for data about government spending and activities.

Access Services: The public has become enamored with online services, from buying books to trading stocks to renewing drivers' licenses. Government web sites have made access to the agencies much easier for the online public. As stated earlier, organizations garner efficiency benefits from offering goods and services online. Visitors benefit through conveniently accessing desired services online. The general rule is: anything that does not require a physical presence should be offered online.

Feel Invested in a Cause: While hard to define, people go to many public affairs web sites to get involved. When someone comes to your web site, they've walked in the virtual door of your office and said, "You interest me . . . tell me about your organization." For many nonprofits, associations, members of Congress, even federal agencies, you should enthusiastically respond to that query by offering both information and actions the visitor can take advantage of. While seeking involvement is an important goal of many web users, it is the need least often fulfilled by public affairs web sites. People may have an *interest* in an issue or cause, such as a doctor who will lose money if the government reduces the Medicare reimbursement rate for caring for Medicare patients. Yet research shows the citizens with an *opinion* have more passion and are more likely to take action. (For more on this topic, see *Citizens' Handbook to Influencing Elected Officials*, by Bradford Fitch, TheCapitol.Net, 2010.)

Participate in a Community: Social media tools offer individuals and organizations an opportunity to create like-minded online communities, full of opportunities to exchange ideas and opinions. Some in the public affairs community have been reluctant to create the community, whether through Facebook, Twitter, or their own web site, in part because leaders worried about losing control of "the message." Yet in a hyper-connected world, the organization that doesn't join the conversation loses more than the opportunity to see and hear the conversation, it loses the chance to shape it. The conversation about topics important to you is happening—you can join it, or not.

§6.22 Five Building Blocks of Public Affairs Web Sites

One of the challenging aspects of communicating with new media is the need to differentiate between trends that will affect long-term practices and flash-in-the-pan features. Social media clearly are here to stay, but the all-encompassing online communication tool remains the first innovation the Internet brought us: a web site. Web sites have become the primary communication tool of a public relations professional working in public affairs. For many Americans looking for information on Congress, the first research choice is the web site of their member of Congress, followed by web sites of groups they belong to or support.

When you start to design or redesign a public affairs web site, you must keep in mind that this creation does not follow the same rules as old media public relations campaigns. Unlike a campaign site or commercial site, when a person visits a public affairs web site there is an expectation that they're not going to be "sold" a bill of goods—that they're getting straight information without the spin. To build a successful web site, you want to strive for objectivity in message, relevant and thorough content, and creative and simple ways to present the information. One member of Congress who was learning how to improve his web site said it best: "You need to think like a librarian, not a politician." Intuitive navigation elements and a robust search engine are essential for an effective web site.

For your web site, first consider what you want to accomplish. Like any structure, even a virtual one, you must develop a building plan based on sound principles and goals. A set of principles, or building blocks, for successful public affairs web sites was created by Kathy Goldschmidt of the Congressional Management Foundation. While they were developed with congressional sites in mind, the structure easily fits any other public affairs site.

1. Audience—Any good communication strategy begins with considering your audience. While a web site allows you to reach many audiences, it can't be everything to everyone. One member of Congress mistakenly thought his site should be designated the browser home page of every voter in his state, so he included local news and weather next to his press releases. People come to your web site for a reason, and you should anticipate what those needs are and provide for them. For associations the logical audiences are members of the association, congressional staff, and the media. For non-profits it is probably donors and individuals who may want to volunteer. Start with considering who will be visiting the site and what they want from your organization.

The Department of Housing and Urban Development (<*www.hud.gov*>) thinks about who will be visiting its web site. Its home page offers the following options under the "I Want To" category: Buy a Home; Avoid Foreclosure; Find Rental Assistance; Apply for a Grant; Talk to a Housing Counselor; Get Involved in My Community; and File a Fair Housing Discrimination Complaint.

2. Content—After identifying audiences, ask, "What content will they be seeking?" Tying together audience and content are the most important initial steps to creating a great web site. There should be a clear purpose to the site, with targeted audiences getting their information quickly through no more than two or three clicks. For many public affairs sites, the bulk of the content should deal with issue or policy information. (The exception is federal government sites, which equally emphasize services.) People expect their congressional, national association or nonprofit, and federal agency web sites to have information about what is going on in Washington, so a large share of what's on the site should address that.

Your web site visitors want relevant content, not self-serving brochures translated to an electronic platform. The key is to engage in creative thinking about your target audiences and to anticipate their needs.

3. Interactivity—The key building block that will define the sophistication of a public affairs web site is interactivity. This is the communication characteristic that is unique to the web, allowing for an online relationship to be developed between organization and individual. The simplest form of online interactivity is an e-newsletter, discussed in § 6.41, Tips for E-newsletters. But the best web sites go beyond that basic tool. Nearly every social media tool allows for widget, applet, or some other downloadable tool to be placed on a web site. Many federal government sites have created virtual offices online, offering visitors the capability of doing nearly everything online that can be done over the phone or in a brick-and-mortar office. Congressional offices are offering online polls of pending issues. Nonprofits and associations are creating online grassroots campaigns to rally support for their agendas. Federal agencies offer visitors forums for chats or regular e-newsletters. Associations are integrating social media tools into their web sites. Make getting involved easy and rewarding; make it easy to care and easy to share. Most people visiting your web site want something to do, even if it's just to offer an opinion.

For associations and nonprofits, interactive social media components are inextricably linked to their grassroots organizing efforts. The groups have an opportunity to build a community among their supporters, and to recruit new ones by offering like-minded individuals an opportunity to interact with the sponsoring group, elected officials, and each other. Tactics to create communities include: offering specialized material in password-protected "Member Only" sections; developing bulletin boards for online discussions and information exchanges; and hosting a blog with expert-supporters contributing the content.

Many public affairs organizations, being risk-averse by nature, may resist interactivity. "Someone could say something we don't agree with." "Who has access to the chat tool?" "Facebook is for kids." Any one of these statements could be uttered by a manager who doesn't see the value of interactive web sites. Public relations professionals must recognize that winning this internal power struggle is essential to building a successful web site.

4. Usability—Great strides have been made in recent years regarding the usability of web sites; but many public affairs sites lag behind this trend in the private sector. A 2009 review by a panel of experts put together by *National Journal* showed a pathetic offering by congressional committees, one of the most important sources of legislative information in Congress. "User Interface" is the nexus of information architecture and graphic design in web site design. To get the user interface just right, public relations professionals should consider hiring an outside expert. Put another way, if you had 100,000 people walking through your living room every month, you would probably hire an experienced interior designer.

The key to usability is offering a variety of ways to access and organize information. Web sites also have a non-linear communication quality—people can come to the site from a variety of angles or interests, depending upon where they started. This means that visitors want different things from the organization, as in the Department of Housing and Urban Development site. As a communicator, *you* may have two or three strategic goals; but you must first fulfill the visitors' needs and interests in order to demonstrate your commitment to their immediate objectives.

Usability also includes what designers call the "look and feel" of the site. This covers everything from design layout to graphics and colors. When helping one nonprofit design its new site, the team was asked, "If your web site was a celebrity spokesperson, who would it be?" After a long debate over whether Tom Cruise or Brad Pitt would be the best spokesperson, the nonprofit settled on a more mature image with Paul Newman. They wanted something good-looking, very credible, but with a heart.

One final usability tip: make sure you write for the web. Language must be simple and easy to understand, devoid of jargon, technical terms, and acronyms. And be wary of using slogans to convey information. For example, rather than labeling a section of a web site dealing with taxes "Putting People First," label it "Taxes." Remember, think like a librarian, not a politician.

For information on usability issues for government web sites, see <*www.usability.gov*>. This is a comprehensive web site managed by the U.S. Department of Health and Human Services that offers visitors information on best practices reports, web site analysis tools, and industry guidelines for improving the usability of sites. Also see Jakob Nielsen's usability web site, <*www.useit.com*>.

5. Innovations—Using innovations in a public affairs site means something different than a commercial or news site. If you visit the web site of an upcoming movie, you might expect a quick flash trailer. However, if you visit a congressional web site looking for information on how the member of Congress voted, you're probably going to be annoyed if you first have to take a flash tour of that member's district.

In a public affairs environment, innovation is not about technology alone, it's about applying the technology creatively to meet the needs of the visitor. For a federal agency, innovation may be developing a dynamic interactive questionnaire for someone who wants to calculate retirement benefits in Spanish (see *<www.ssa.gov/espanol/calculador/>*). Stay away from the latest technical gimmick that doesn't offer anything meaningful for your audience. Think creatively about what the visitor wants and consider if there are novel ways to present your information or respond to her needs.

For a lesson in how not to build a web site, visit Vincent Flanders' humorous site: *<www.webpagesthatsuck.com>*. It's only one web designer's opinion, but you might get some laughs and one or two ideas.

§6.30 Tracking and Adjusting Your Site

Unlike old media tools, online media allows public relations specialists to track audience interest. By using web analytics, including tracking logs, available for most web sites, and "heat maps" that track visitor cursor moves and clicks, you can adjust your site design, moving popular page links to the home page for even more usage, and downplaying content of lesser interest. Most web site alanaytic and measurement tools produce specific metrics as to number of visitors, length of stay on a page, and how they found the site.

§6.31 Accessibility and Web Sites

According to the U.S. Census Bureau, 54 million Americans are disabled and many use some kind of assisted technology to gain access to the Internet. The Internet offers a sort of liberation to many of the disabled, offering them an opportunity to gain access to services and information online that are less accessible in the off-line world. For many in public affairs, making a web site accessible to the disabled is not just a good thing to do, it's required by law. Section 508 of the Rehabilitation Act of 1973 (and the 1998 amendments) requires federal agencies and those that do business for the government to make their sites accessible, unless it would cause an "undue burden" on the agency (see *<section508.gov>*). For many organizations in the public eye, making a site accessible is also just good politics.

For simpler sites, making a site accessible may not be hard. But for complex sites, it can be a lot of work. For example, text tags must be written for all graphics and pictures (called "ALT" and "title" tags) so that if a visually impaired person runs her mouse over a photo, software on her computer will transfer the tag text to audio.

§6.32 Cookies

Cookies are pieces of text or software instructions that are downloaded into your computer when you visit a web site, so that when you revisit the same web site, it knows you're you. Cookies are often used to enhance the visitors' experience. For example, when visiting Amazon.com, it knows the books you've bought during previous visits and suggests other new books in that category. Most organizations have a "privacy policy" on their web site and make it clear to the visitor that a cookie is being loaded on your computer. Or, they ask for information on an initial log-on screen, such as *The New York Times* web site, so that you don't have to log on every time you visit the site. Cookies can also be embedded into e-newsletters to inform the sender whether the receiver has opened the message or forwarded it to a friend.

However, any time a public affairs organization puts something in a citizen's computer, the practice can be misconstrued to Orwellian proportions. For example, some would object to the Department of Defense web site putting anything on your computer. However, cookies save the visitor time and enhance the likelihood of developing a regular online relationship. Carefully evaluate your audience and your goals before implementing any cookies or any type of tracking system on your web site.

§6.33 Privacy

One design principle that should be part of every public affairs web site is privacy. People are wary of providing information to politically related web sites, and any site associated with the government must have clear rules on privacy.

Any component or page that collects email addresses must go out of its way to state that the addresses will not be sold or given to any other organization without the expressed permission of the visitor. Privacy concerns are growing in America, especially in light of new laws designed to fight terrorism. Any time a public affairs web site asks for personal information it must be abundantly clear that the information will not be transferred to anyone outside the organization—or the visitor is not likely to be forthcoming, or may not visit the site again.

Your web site privacy policy, internally and posted on your web site, should state clearly what information you collect and what you do with that information. You can find numerous examples on the web.

§6.40 Principles of Public Affairs Email and Viral Marketing

In the world of public affairs, as previously mentioned, the most valuable thing someone can give to you today is her email address. When you run a television or radio ad, you may not have a fully engaged audience—they're fixing dinner, getting the kids ready for bed, yelling at the dog. But when someone is checking their email, they are *focused*. You've got their undivided attention for five to twenty seconds. How will you use that all-important opportunity they are giving you? By telling them about the good deed you've done that puffs you up and makes you look cool and spiffy? Or, by giving them something they want—a piece of information that they can pass on to a friend about an important issue; a way to get engaged in the political process; a method for accessing a service online they normally get off-line, improving their productivity, giving them more time for enjoyable things.

Unlike commercial email, which most people do not like especially when unsolicited, people have a different attitude about public affairs email. If well done, reading it makes them feel like they're fulfilling their civic duty and gives them an insider's perspective because it offers something that was not on the front page of the paper. Organizations that build some connection to the recipient through opt-in procedures or smart email address harvesting, can get a 20 percent to 50 percent open rate.

Email is also a unique tool for "viral marketing." This term is used because a compelling email message can spread like a virus with recipients forwarding it to their personal email lists. The messages have greater credibility because they come from a friend instead of an impersonal organization.

Before an email truly can be considered "viral," it almost always has at least one of the following characteristics. First, it may be funny. Humorous emails are the most forwarded messages on the web. Whether they are David Letterman's Top Ten Lists or the latest joke on a politician caught in a scandal, people like to make their friends laugh and they love taking a thirty-second break from work to check out the latest giggle from a friend.

Second, an email connected to the recipient's values. People rarely forward an email with the cover note, "This is a really stupid idea I wanted you to read." Individuals like to pass on thoughtful ideas to others who share their beliefs. Offering your audience this opportunity not only scores points with the original reader, but allows the forwarder to become a recruiter to your cause by sending it to others who share those values.

Third, the content reflects well on the person who forwards the email.

Think about this when you see a friend post a link to an article on his Facebook page. Yes, the poster is trying to disseminate information he thinks is important, interesting, or humorous. But the poster is also making a statement about himself. He is associating himself with the content and sentiments in the article. Ask yourself, how do I to create email content which not only conveys a message, but which includes a message that someone would be *proud* to be associated with?

§6.41 Tips for E-newsletters

Despite the buzz over social media, email is still the "killer app." E-newsletters share some of the personal connection that social media communicate. "Newsletters feel personal because they arrive in your inbox; you have an ongoing relations with them," said Jakob Nielsen, a leading online communication expert. "In contrast, web sites are things you glance at when you need to get something done or find the answer to a specific question."

A 2010 Nielsen Norman Group study concluded the following:

"Email newsletters are a better way to stay in touch with customers than updates posted on social networks like Facebook or Twitter:

- A newsletter goes into the inbox and sits there, whereas social networks use a stream-based interface, where new postings constantly replace old ones.

- As we found when testing social networks, people turn to these services primarily to keep in touch with friends and family, and corporate content is often mismatched with this mindset.

- Newsletters are under your control design-wise and hold much more information. One user offered the following comparison of newsletters and Facebook updates: *'Facebook to me is more just a general one-liner about something that's going on versus a newsletter that contains content and details on a variety of topics and subjects.'* "

(Source: <*www.nngroup.com/reports/newsletters/summary.html*>)

In the public affairs environment, e-newsletter creators and writers must recognize the high value of their content to the recipient. You are not offering a deal on a mortgage or the opportunity to grow or shrink certain body parts—you're offering the recipient the chance the learn how to improve the world.

Begin with the notion that you are helping someone with the information you convey. Keep that premise, and the following tips in mind, when designing and writing an e-newsletter.

§6.42 Think Before Hitting "Enter"

The web combines two elements that are challenging to a communicator: 1) it's fast; 2) it's permanent. Once you submit a blog entry, send an email, or post something on a web site it lives forever on some archiving site. Be *very* careful before submitting content. For blog comments, it is best to first write it in notepad or a word processor, then have another person review it, and only then cut-and-paste it into the blog comment submission tool. Never offer a comment directly into a web site or blog comments for yourself or your boss. First, the system may not be able to store a copy of what you wrote. Second, you might say something you regret.

1. Keep the Content Subject-Oriented, Not Self-Congratulatory— The worst e-newsletters are those self-serving, "look at what I've done," fawning drivel. While they may work in a direct-mail environment, the online public expects something more and wants it fact-oriented. This doesn't mean that the content shouldn't be persuasive, or even one-sided. Avoid the superficial. Online citizens want steak, not sizzle. Surveys consistently show people are hungry for information that explains how things in Washington affect their lives. The web can be a credible source for that, and organizations can become a trusted reference tool for a targeted audience if you earn their trust with valuable and trustworthy data.

2. The Two Most Important Aspects of Email—The first thing most people look at in an email is the sender's email address. If it is from someone the reader knows, it will likely get read. If you build a relationship with an e-newsletter reader, you can vary the sender's name before the "@" sign to entice him to read on. For example, if your principal is sending out messages from an address that begins "director@" with personal observations on a topic, the next message may be from "research@" for more substantive content.

The second thing most people read is the subject line. It must grab the reader in five to ten words and not sound generic. "New Web Site Launched" will never capture anyone's attention. "Lower Your Taxes—New Web Site" might get people's attention. Make sure there is something unique and timely in your subject line to differentiate it from the scores of other email the receiver is getting. Keep the subject line to five to seven words (about thirty characters).

§6.43 How to Write Great Subject Lines

If a recipient doesn't open your email outreach you've wasted effort. And the best way to get recipients to open email is with a great subject line. In the public affairs arena, the best subject lines fall into two categories: 1) appealing to recipients' better angels, and 2) shock.

In the "better angels" category, a group focused on health care might use the subject line, "Save a Life—Here's How." In the "shock" category, an environmental group focused on pesticides might write, "You're Dying—Here's Why." Some managers will resist bold subject lines, but in the end, the reader will assess your organization based on the *content of the email*, not the subject line. Just make sure the subject line isn't SO over the top that it is inaccurate or misleads the recipients as to what they will find when they open the message.

Another approach is to set up a Question-and-Answer scenario, with the question in the subject line and the answer in the email. Ask a question, then offer a solution. "Fed Up with High Taxes?" "When Will the U.S. Government Get Out of Afghanistan?" "Should People Be Allowed to Marry Their Pets?" Again, the provocative will trump the ordinary.

Try to appeal to their immediate interests. A study of the open rate of mass email messages sent to Capitol Hill staffers revealed that one of the best subject lines to prompt an open included the word, "Invitation." My conclusion is that emails with this word have such a high open rate because the recipients believe there may be a connection to free food through the email. This theory was confirmed by one nonprofit's highly successful open rate of an email sent to congressional staff—182 percent (exceeding 100 percent, which meant it was forwarded to others). The subject line had two words: "Happy Hour." See § 6.43, How to Write Great Subject Lines.

1. Keep E-Newsletters Short, with More Data Available through Links—E-newsletters should be designed just like anything else on the web: scan-able text with more information available through links. Avoid sending out e-newsletters that look like they were designed in the '90s—wordy tomes with no links to more information on a topic. Each e-newsletter idea should have a snappy headline, two to four sentences as a hook, and links to longer articles on the organization's web site.

Also, the top of the e-newsletter is crucial. Many people use Microsoft Outlook at work, and the default configuration sets up a split screen: a summary section at the top listing the email messages in your inbox, and a message below. The lower section usually displays about three to four sentences of the message. This means that you have about two inches at the top of the screen to grab the readers' attention and convince them to hit the "enter" key, bringing up the entire message.

2. Provide Details Not Available in Off-line Media—Create the impression that the receiver is part of a special club that has received information not available to the general public because she has previously signed up for your email communication. This is usually not hard, since you can fill your web site with this content. Reiterate your standard message, but lace it with details not available in the morning papers. *Politico*'s Mike Allen and his "Playbook" daily e-newsletter does this by littering his news of the day with birthdays of celebrity Washingtonians and noting who was the last person to close down the bar at a DC event.

3. Send Emails Frequently—A common question is, "How often should I send an e-newsletter?" Steve O'Keefe, the author of *Complete Guide to Internet Publicity* has the best answer: "Whenever you have something to say." There are no hard-and-fast rules. Some newsletters have relevant and interesting information available every day, like Mike Allen's "Playbook" targeted to a political junkie audience. Others are better in a weekly format. Separating each message by more than a month will probably lead to the reader forgetting you and your organization. So, once you commit to sending the messages, you must feed the beast. When something occurs of importance to your organization's issues, or your principal takes a significant action that affects your audience, by all means break the cycle and send out a special message. Providing the audience with relevant information is much more important than sticking to an arbitrary schedule.

Also, include content to tease readers about new web site content or blog posts. Don't assume they're following your every activity closely. Other than news web sites, people usually only go to public affairs web sites when they need information or when they've been drawn to it through an email or e-newsletter.

It's also a good idea to send an email to new subscribers immediately after they sign up for the regular message. Include the latest e-newsletter to ensure that they become familiar with the offering. This avoids the trap of the recipient who gets so much email he may forget he even signed up for your e-newsletter when it eventually arrives.

Finally, try to pick a time of the day to send your email message when your audience is most likely to read it. For most people in the public affairs community, this is between 10:00 a.m. and 11:30 a.m. This is the equivalent of why telemarketers always call during the dinner hour: because they know you're home.

4. Opt-In Suggestions—First, most public affairs emails are not covered by the CAN-SPAM Act because the law deals with "commercial electronic mail message." A nonprofit organization notifying citizens of a new report on mercury in drinking water doesn't fit this definition. That doesn't mean it's a good idea (or economical) to rent or buy email lists and spam the world.

There are two schools of thought on whether an organization should send an email to someone who did not sign up for it—or, "opt-in" for regular e-newsletters. Technology experts side squarely with the common etiquette rules of the web: you should never send mass emails to anyone who has not opted in. Surveys back up this view, with a large majority of online users clearly stating their preference not to receive unsolicited email. However, direct-mail specialists point out that email is incredibly successful, and there is no ethical difference between sending an unsolicited email and sending a direct-mail piece based on a voter registration file or some other available directory.

However, there is a middle view, which is dependent upon the circumstances and the sender. No federal agency should ever send an unsolicited email except in the most extraordinary circumstances. It conveys a "big brother" mentality and will cause the receiver not to read the email, but to ask, "How the hell did Uncle Sam get my email address?" However, if nonprofits, associations, and members of Congress send unsolicited email on topics they know are relevant to the audience, it's likely to have a positive impact. Moreover, by joining an association or donating to a nonprofit, the audience is communicating, "I want to be a part of your group." The correct balance would be to send them an initial e-newsletter offering, but make the opt-out option more prominent than it appears in your usual e-newsletter. This would meet the ethical standard of not force-feeding a supporter, while still increasing the size of your list.

Another important factor for answering this question is the content of the e-newsletter. For example, if the content from a member of Congress is full of platitudes about his accomplishments, political rants against members of the other party, and conveys the general impression that the sun rises and sets with him, you might get quite a few complaints. If, however, the content is meant to demonstrate transparency and accountability in government, communicating clear explanations for recent key votes, one might be more

§6.44 Spam—The Law, What's Right, What Works

1. The Law—In response to the rapid growth of email in the early years of the Internet, Congress passed a bill to restrict email marketing, the Controlling the Assault of Non-Solicited Pornography and Marketing Act of 2003 (CAN-SPAM Act of 2003). As the name implies, it aims to prohibit unsolicited commercial email—spam—which is difficult, given the technology, diversity, and geography associated with the Internet. Nonetheless, responsible public relations professionals need to be aware of both the legal and public relations implications for violating the law. Luckily, Congress included a key exclusion: the law covers "commercial" email and specifically protects "political" email. You can spam to your heart's content—but that doesn't mean you should.

2. What's Right—The CAN-SPAM Act also points to some good practices, the best of which is to create an opt-in system. For associations and nonprofits, this may not be necessary as the supporter already has opted in by joining the group, although an opt-in check box should appear on the membership form just to be sure. For governmental entities, such as legislators and federal agencies, an opt-in system is mandatory in keeping with best communication practices. CAN-SPAM also requires an opt-out system, allowing individuals to immediately unsubscribe to email messages.

3. What Works—In the early days of the Internet, email list purchasing was very common. People wanted to send messages to the largest lists, thinking this was the best route to success. The wonderful thing about email marketing is the tracking capability: you can know how many people opened your email and which link they clicked on. We've learned that opt-in practices are not only ethical, they're practical. As communicators we collect email addresses of only committed followers who have consciously joined our network. It's not often that efficacy and ethics go hand-in-hand, so celebrate the union.

inclined to send it to those who have not necessarily opted in to receive the e-newsletter.

The ambiguity on this topic is based on a rapidly changing environment and shifting public expectations. So stay connected to your audience and appreciate their needs and desires—that will be the best guide for your approach.

§6.50 Web Site as Journalist Resource

For most public relations specialists working in public affairs, one of the most important web site audiences is journalists. When researching a story, reporters are just as likely to visit an organization's web site as they are to use Google (and most will probably use both). It may sound like common sense to use your web site to provide information to reporters; however, some studies show that many organizations fail to use them effectively. A recent survey of congressional web sites indicated nearly 40 percent of the members of Congress did not provide the name and telephone number of their press secretaries on the site.

In order to maximize your off-line communication, one of the best options is to create a section of the web site targeted to journalist's needs. For those organizations that view the media in a completely adversarial manner, it will be very difficult to get management approval to help reporters in this way. Yet reporters constantly claim that they are generally more inclined to present positive coverage of organizations that are helpful to them in the news gathering process.

The Nielsen Norman Group report, "Designing Web Sites to Maximize Press Relations," outlines the reasons journalists visit a web site. (A summary of the report is available at *<www.useit.com/alertbox/pr.html>*.) Based on these surveys, interviews with reporters, and public affairs specialists, the list below is the *minimum* of what should be available to reporters. Ideally, your web site should have a link on the home page that connects to a media section that provides this information.

1. Public Relations Contact Information—The web has become the new phone book for reporters. Provide a media contact and include phone and email information, so that reporters have a choice of how to contact you. And, if they send you an email, you then have their email address for future use. Many organizations hide the telephone number or email address of their spokesperson. If you want to get covered, you must include basic contact information.

2. Basic Facts of Organization (Names of Key Players, Dates of Actions, etc.)—Reporters know it is quicker and easier to look up a quick fact on the web than to phone a public relations specialist. The PR person may ask too many questions, or for some reason be reluctant to quickly answer a simple question. If this kind of information is not on a media section of the site, make sure there are internal links to other sections of the site where journalists can find it. Organizations should post basic information in the "about us" section of the site.

3. The Organization or Principal Position—A public affairs web site should be the repository of all official actions and statements by any organization or individual. The information should be organized logically, by categories and chronologically. Some organizations tend to organize data by the type of document (press release, speech, letter). However, this system is extremely frustrating to reporters and other visitors; they're usually interested in a specific topic, such as health care, taxes, or agriculture. This section of the site should read like a dictionary—the A–Z on your organization's view of the world. (See most Senate and senator web pages for examples, <senate.gov>.)

This section can also be organized by logical themes that your principal or organization focuses on.

4. Online Media Kits—Many media organizations, especially specialty press and smaller newspapers, want download-able photographs and other easily accessed information that can be used in stories. Offering good artwork can greatly increase the size of a story and the amount of coverage you get. The media often come to your site looking for artwork to accompany a story that's already written and ready to go to press. Media contacts should be offered access to high-resolution artwork that is suitable for use in print publications and television broadcasts. The minimum standard for print and broadcast reproduction is 300 dpi. It's a good idea to use low-resolution (72 dpi) images to show the media what you have to offer, and include a link to high-resolution artwork that indicates the format the artwork is in, the resolution, and the file size (for example, 300 dpi TIFF 1.5MB).

§6.60 To Blog or Not to Blog

When blogging first emerged, some members of Congress began chronicling their daily musings. They and their staffs quickly learned that providing intelligent content on a frequent basis is very hard work. The few members of Congress who do continue to blog often do it as part of a limited event, such as a congressional recess period or a trip overseas.

When assessing whether your organization is a good candidate to blog, consider these three questions.

1. Do we have the resources to maintain a blog? A blog audience expects daily or weekly content. Most public affairs organizations are already strapped for resources, so adding something else to the daily "to-do" list may not be reasonable—especially when you're not sure how many people would read it.

2. Do we have the stomach for a blog? A blog without feedback mechanism for readers is more of an online column than blog. In their early forms, blogs were intended to be running commentaries, with the blogger starting the conversation with interesting ideas and a community of readers chiming in. When newspapers began opening up their sites for reader comments they were appalled at the vitriol they had to endure.

3. Who and what will be our voice? Blogs have the distinctive voice and personality of the author. When Ana Marie Cox first started the political gossip blog "Wonkette," her sarcasm dripped from nearly every entry. You had the feeling you were hearing her thoughts, unedited and unexpurgated. There aren't many association leaders or politicians who would be good candidates for this medium. On the other hand, if you have a principal who is a bit of a character, some wit, and writing ability, blogs are wonderful vehicles that can let personality come through.

4. Who should write our blog? The principal does not necessarily have to be the primary author of a blog. Like all content for the organization, professional communication or policy experts can create the first draft, with the principal reviewing and offering commentary. This takes advantage of the expertise in the organization without putting an unworkable burden on the boss.

Finally, given the manner in which blogs, social media, and mainstream media's online content are merging in form and function, one has to wonder whether the "blog" will remain as an independent, identifiable communication vehicle. An online "post" can now take many forms. In the end, it's either the musings of one individual or a collection of various postings from a variety of sites on a general topic area. Either way, it's pretty much a web site by another name. For more on blogs, see § 5.13, The Internet Medium: Web Sites, Blogs, and Social Media.)

§6.70 What Does a Public Relations Professional *Really* Need To Know about Social Media?

For all the hoopla surrounding social media, in the end Facebook and its related cousins do three basic things: 1) Post content on a web site; 2) Share the content with a selected group of people; 3) Allow those people to comment on the content. There are a lot of bells and whistles beyond the basics, such as using video and mobile technology. Yet for a communication professional and her bosses, it's important to grasp that we're really just talking about basic communication and collaboration principles.

And one of the best things about social media is that most of it is free. Someone else builds the web site, gives you a ton of great communication tools and provides you access to millions of potentially interested parties. Like any online communication vehicle, you need to maintain it. But much of the content is repurposed from other material your organization has already created.

Creating a Facebook page or Twitter account for a public affairs organization also gives followers an opportunity to interact with your group via a platform they're comfortable with. You can communicate directly with interested individuals. And you can provide a degree of background and detail that you couldn't get in a newspaper article. Finally, the magic of social media is the multidimensional communication dialogue that evolves. By allowing people to interact with your content and each other, you can create an engaged community and encourage others to create content that the group will be interested in.

As with any communication effort, one must ask the basic questions: What are our goals? How will this social media site complement our own web site? One might identify two or three issues or time-sensitive campaigns that might logically attract interest on Facebook. Or perhaps there is an upcoming major announcement that lends itself to building a Twitter following. Whatever the message, create extensive links to yours and other related web sites, with the intention of offering a supporter rich content while the communicator collects the supporter's email address and interest area.

§6.80 Everything You Say to Anyone, Anywhere Is Now a Matter of Public Record

An unexpected consequence of the web and social media is the recording of everything we say and do. The generation that has grown up with Twitter seems comfortable with every aspect of their lives being displayed publicly on the web. As college students begin to look for a job, they realize that posting that drunken photo on their Facebook page their sophomore year might not be the best indicator for success a future employer is looking for.

The next time you're giving a talk to a small group of people, and you think that person in the back pecking away at her Blackberry is just exchanging thoughts with her boyfriend . . . think again. In the Networked Age, *everything* is "on the record."

§6.90 The Future

Predictions about the future of the Internet range from the whimsical to science fiction. From a public relations perspective, it's not hard to imagine how a medium can completely transform a society—like television did in the mid-twentieth century. Some, such as Don Middleberg in *Winning PR in the Wired World*, have foretold the end of mass media, where the structure of television networks and dedicated communication channels give way to a completely chaotic environment where messages are quickly disseminated via online vehicles, instead of in clumsy thirty-second TV spots.

Lance Bennett of the University of Washington has examined the sociological implications of this potential transformation, with an eye toward grassroots organizing. He and others predict that as our connected society becomes more individualized, people will cease to gravitate to traditional organizational associations, such as churches, unions, and local clubs. Instead, people will self-select their "image tribes" by merging their varied interests accessed through the online world, instead of by peer and community pressure. Such an environment will require intensely targeted communication and rapidly changing strategies as new image tribes develop.

Already we are seeing the development of a single piece of hardware that merges the computer, television, and telephone into one unit (such as smartphones or tablets), and converges the platforms from which information is delivered. Print, Television, Radio—all presented via the Internet to your hand-held device for your on-demand convenience.

Precursors of this advancement already exist, indicating potential trends in communication. In the 1990s the consumer product and service "Tivo" combined several household devices so that individuals could record any entertainment program on a hard drive, allowing them to watch what they wanted, at any time, commercial-free. Users displayed an almost fanatical loyalty to the Tivo when new. Now many homes have digital video recorders offering the same benefits.

As stated at the beginning of this chapter, we are in the midst of a transition, and by all indications it will be profound.

The public relations profession has used the same basic tools for a hundred years. An earlier pioneer, Ivy Lee, "invented" the photo opportunity in 1914—a tactic still used today. Yet, with communicators able to use the web to communicate directly with constituents, combined with the "crowd sourcing" aspect of social media to communicate and share information, the era of traditional public relations ushered in by Edward Bernays in the early 1900s is giving way to an entirely new communication paradigm based on the oldest form of human communication; talking to each other. To use a phrase from another era: stay tuned.

§6.99 Chapter Summary

- Appreciate the differences between traditional communication and online communication. The web is not a billboard: it requires communicators to present multiple messages, with interactive components, targeting core audiences, while keeping the core values and principles of the organization or effort intact. (§ 6.10)
- The six management principles of online communication are (§ 6.13)
  1. Leadership
  2. Internal leadership
  3. Internal input and cooperation
  4. Catering to external audiences
  5. Connecting to a strategic vision
  6. Connection to the off-line world
- Get your boss to go online by: finding examples or case studies from similar organizations; going slow; building one success on another; lowering expectations; diversifying tactics (but keep it safe); and recruiting allies within the organization. (§ 6.14)
- Public affairs web sites must connect off-line activities with online assets through: directing people to the web site with off-line media, such as direct mail; collecting email addresses of interested people; taking advantage of grassroots organizing practices; and adjusting the web site based on media interviews. (§ 6.17)
- Communicators' goals are to promote an agenda; increase membership or followers; enhance productivity and efficiency; enhance employee morale; and raise money. (§ 6.21)
- Visitors' goals are to access information; access services; feel invested in a cause, and participate in a community. (§ 6.21)
- The five building blocks of a public affairs web site are (§ 6.22):
  1. Audience
  2. Content
  3. Interactivity
  4. Usability
  5. Innovations

- Email should be used to provide valuable data or services to a receiver. Email can use viral marketing to spread a message if it includes one of the following elements: humor; connected to a recipient's values; or would reflect well on the recipient who forwards it. (§ 6.40)
- To get e-newsletters read, a communicator should (§ 6.41)
  - Keep the content subject-oriented, not self-congratulatory
  - Build a relationship with the receiver with an email address and a unique or helpful subject line
  - Keep emails short, no more than three screens
  - Link to the web site
  - Provide details not available in off-line media
  - Send emails frequently, no more than one month apart
  - Strive to provide HTML versions
- Journalists are one of the most important audiences to any public affairs web site. Content should be targeted for their particular needs. (§ 6.50)

Chapter Seven:
Dealing with the Principal

Dealing with the Principal

§7.1 Introduction

Almost every public relations professional has a principal: the primary person who the spokesperson defends, speaks for, advocates on behalf of, articulates achievements of, coordinates interviews for, and sometimes, in rare cases, regrettably—lies for. In nonprofit groups, federal agencies, or companies, the principal is the person who is the face on the organization. If this is an elected official—this is the person who people expect to see on television and the ballot. The visionary, the expert, the passionate advocate, the hero, or the villain (depending upon the circumstances).

Public relations professionals working in large organizations or federal agencies may not have one clear-cut, "go-to" person every time the media calls. They may have a lineup of experts to choose from, and how they match up the right specialist with the right reporter often makes a big difference in the success of a media strategy. These issues are discussed in Chapter Eleven, Communication in a Federal Agency.

Nonetheless, even if you have multiple choices, your responsibility is still going to be the same. You must be the guide who conducts another person through the process of interacting with the media. When you are dealing with a single principal, it is the communication specialist's job to work with him, cater to his needs, train him in the ways of the media, and get him coverage. The goals of the office often flow through the principal. And, your success sometimes depends on your ability to interact with this individual.

This chapter will address how to deal with the most important person in your professional life, the principal.

§7.2 Developing a Relationship

The most successful press secretaries have good personal rapport with their principal. This does not mean you have to be buddy-buddy with your principal, go drinking with him, confide heartbreak stories, and all that other touchy-feely stuff. However, press secretaries are part father confessors. People in the public spotlight rely on their spokespersons to be their confidential public relations advisors. To truly get the confidence of the principal, a press secretary needs to connect with his boss in both professional and personal ways. It might take the form of two people just being comfortable not talking to each other on a long plane trip. Or it might be the ability to talk until 2:00 a.m. about the ten different political permutations of an issue.

There are a few ways you can develop that trust. First, you can convey your support for the organization's mission or the principal's goals. Leaders like to have committed followers, and sincerely believing in your mission is an invaluable asset in public relations. Second, you'll need to perform adequately or better in some tough spots early on. Every public relations professional is confronted with a difficult problem within a few weeks of starting a new job (it's why we think this business is fun, right?). How you handle that first crisis or first tough call will tell your employer a lot about whether you can be trusted with the management of his image and reputation.

However you find a way into the inner circle of your principal's world, it's vital that you make that connection. Part of developing a comfort level with one another requires you to understand your boss' temperament, especially when it comes to dealing with the media. There are some public figures who have a very sophisticated view of the media, appreciating them as a diverse— perhaps difficult—yet important aspect of American democracy. There are others who view them as circling vultures, ready to pounce on any wounded prey, exploit any weakness, and generally attack any potential victim regardless of ethics, costs, or standard of propriety.

Regardless of your view, it's a good idea to quickly learn which way your employer leans. You'll want to understand your principal's perspective, what role you are supposed to play, and under what conditions you can set up communication between the media and your boss. Gaining insight into how the principal views the media, and his level of tolerance for press work, are crucial to developing an effective communication strategy and executing it.

Finally, one of the most difficult tasks of a press secretary is to be the bearer of bad news to the principal. This is not a unique responsibility of a public relations staffer. But, because the bad news that public relations professionals bring into the big office may involve some sort of public humiliation or criticism, the principal's reaction is often strong and, if there are breakable objects in the room, possibly dangerous to anyone else in the room.

Public relations professionals have to tell their bosses everything from, "You just did a live TV interview with spinach between your teeth," to "There's a front-page story coming in tomorrow's paper alleging you committed tax fraud." (The job description of every public relations professional includes, of course, spotting the spinach in the teeth before the principal goes on air and, if necessary, reminding him on a regular basis not to commit tax fraud.)

Regardless of the principal's lack of media skill, arbitrary temper, and inclination to commit misdeeds, communication specialists must accept the fact that some of these errors will be blamed on them.

§7.3 Assessing Strengths and Weaknesses

In getting to know your principal, it's important to honestly assess his strengths and weaknesses. Obviously, you don't want to be overt in this assessment by asking everyone in the office, "What do you think Bill is really lousy at?" Yet, it is vital that you have a correct understanding of what you've got to work with, what makes your boss look good, and what you want to avoid.

President Clinton's communication team seemed to understand this, and through the campaign and early presidency they accentuated his strengths and avoided settings where he didn't excel. The debate settings that his campaign chose to combat President George Bush in 1992 were designed to show off Clinton's "people skills." He roamed around a sunken stage, talking directly with the audience with a hand-held microphone in a town-meeting format—a locale that appeared uncomfortable to President Bush.

Similarly, the Clinton team felt that the new president did not shine in the straight-on, talking to the camera, televised speech as well as some predecessors. Therefore, during his first year, President Clinton did fewer prime-time addresses to the nation than nearly any previous president of the past twenty years.

When a new public relations specialist takes over a communication operation, it's best to conduct a review of the principal's video clips and news articles to provide a clue as to the best forums and vehicles to advance her message. Is this person a ten-second sound bite queen, or does she shine better in live talk radio, where her personality can come out? Does she give good, off-the-cuff quotes, or does she need clear talking points and a printed statement to appear lucid? Knowing the abilities and deficiencies of the principal is fundamental to developing any public relations strategy, and will provide you with a partial road map to the tools you'll use to implement the strategy.

§7.4 "They're Out to Get Me"— Dealing with the Paranoid Principal

It seems that many public figures have adopted the belief that there is a vast media conspiracy out to get them. Elected officials especially see monsters under the bed and in the newsrooms throughout America, and often feel that the job of press secretary includes a responsibility to expose these plots and defend the principal at all costs.

Sometimes this paranoia reaches unhealthy proportions. In the Clinton White House, members of the administration became convinced that *The Washington Post* was bound and determined to spin every minute and irrelevant detail of the Whitewater real estate fiasco into scandal. A report was ordered to document this bias in coverage, with a detailed comparison of headlines and coverage of other major newspapers. The effort came to a crashing halt when Press Secretary Mike McCurry got full wind of the report, and collected every copy to ensure it would never see the light of day (*Spin Cycle*, by Howard Kurtz (Free Press, 1998)). McCurry understood a truism in political communication—even if a bias could be proved, a major newspaper would never admit to prejudices influencing its news judgment.

Officials often look for malevolent motives behind unflattering coverage. Most negative stories are not created out of calculated bias, but out of the industry's cultural tendencies to cover "bad" news instead of "good" news, the drive for competition, or just downright stupidity and sloppiness on the part of a reporter. This is especially true with local news coverage, where reporters have less time for bias and are more prone to errors. A sequence of negative stories that might include a few misquotes or imbalance in reporting facts is more likely to be the result of incompetence than maliciousness. Yet the public official whose name has just been maligned will rarely buy that argument. Two reporters on different ends of the continent can write two negative stories back-to-back for the same publication. They may have developed their ideas independently, found different sources, and never talked to one another—or even have the same editor. And a principal will conclude "Ah HAH! That proves they're out to get me."

The only way to combat this mindset is through education (that's assuming you have the energy to combat it at all). If a media outlet is not biased, then it's best to set the principal straight so that the misperception doesn't interfere with the potential for positive coverage in the future. Sometimes a full summary of the recent coverage will do the trick. Principals will focus on one poor story, or one line in a story that is uncomplimentary. But when faced with the totality of coverage, they themselves may realize that, on the whole, the reporting is generally balanced.

Another method might be to connect the principal with the alleged offending reporter more frequently. This may be a tough sell if the principal thinks that the reporter is biased. But, if the reporter covers the public figure on a regular basis, the principal will know that some kind of relationship is required. One balanced or even non-negative story can begin to persuade your boss that this individual is not on a campaign to destroy his reputation.

If the principal's behavior continues, there may be no way to manage it. It will spiral into a deep distaste for dealing with reporters from any media outlet and severely hamper a public relations professional's ability to do her job. While most of these fits of paranoia are temporary, long-term negative attitudes are dangerous and can only lead to an unhealthy relationship between your organization, the principal, and the media.

§7.5 "It's Not Good Enough"—Dealing with the Media Hog

There's a saying in Washington: "The most dangerous place in this city is standing between Senator (name of current senatorial media hog, e.g., Phil Gramm, Arlen Specter, John McCain, Charles Schumer, etc.) and a television camera." (You may insert almost any U.S. senator's name here, and it will also likely ring true.) Some people just can't get enough media attention. They understand that public policy is largely driven by headlines and sound bites, which motivate the public. While an enthusiastic principal who is a genuine partner in the execution of a public relations strategy is a joy to work with, a boss who is impossible to please can be a frequent nightmare for a public relations professional.

A particularly beat-up congressional press secretary once lamented to me her boss' appetite for attention, and the inability of the press office to ever fulfill his craving. "If I get him a story, he wants to know why it wasn't on page one. If I get it on page one, he wants to know why it wasn't above the fold. If I get it above the fold, he wants to know why his name wasn't in the headline.

And, if it's page one, above the fold, and his name is in the headline, he wants to know why they didn't include a picture."

There's not much a press secretary can do to please a principal who doesn't understand the media and expects that his every utterance is worthy of extensive coverage. A principal with the combination of a large ego and a small amount of public relations knowledge can be lethal to a press officer's daily sanity. But, if you're up to the challenge, you can begin to change the way your principal views the media with the goal that he'll ease up on the public relations team and exhibit more savvy when dealing with reporters.

Before you can effect change, you have to establish your credentials. Some principals respect their public relations advisors implicitly. Others feel the need for constant validation of their staff. A key senior advisor, chief of staff, staff director, or other manager can support public relations efforts at key junctures and help establish trust between the principal and you.

It's also important to document successes. The line between properly evaluating public relations work and looking like a blowhard is a fine one; and it's important not to appear too boastful in your work. Yet, any professional communication specialist should track all press coverage and provide those tracking reports to his employers, not only to justify his paycheck, but to use the data to help plot future public relations strategies.

Finally, you can try to manage the expectations of the principal who seems to have limitless expectations. Make clear and consistent predictions on the amount and quality of the press coverage before an event, release, or inter-view—in writing, if appropriate. A regular and proven record of plotting press coverage will establish your credibility in the eyes of the principal, and make passing on the occasional bad piece of information a little easier to swallow.

Yet, all of this does not completely guarantee your principal will become a reasonable and rational person overnight. A friend who made the transition from journalism to public relations told me the story of one of his clients who had no clue about how the media worked. His client was the president of a large wastewater treatment company that had just developed a new method for cleansing the water that returned to lakes and streams. The president, understandably, was proud of his company's achievement and wanted to shout the success from the highest mountain in the land.

My friend, having just left the world of journalism, had a properly skepti-cal perspective on whether the story was salable. Oh, yes, industry publica-tions would eat up a story on new wastewater treatment. But, this just didn't have the potential to break through in the mainstream press.

The president of the company had a different perspective. "I think I'd like to get on the *Today* show," was the instruction to his public relations agent. "But, don't schedule it on a Monday or Friday, those days don't work for me." Needless to say, no one at the *Today* show did an interview that month on a new way to clean up sludge.

§7.6 "Reporters Aren't Interested in Me"— Dealing with the Media Mouse

It's hard to say which is worse: the principal who gets peeved because she didn't get interviewed this week by a national news anchor, or the one who turns down the interview by a national news anchor because she thinks she's not ready for the big-time. The latter poses challenging questions to communication specialists, as much of their work is not persuading reporters to talk to their boss, but persuading their boss to talk to reporters.

Believe it or not, Washington is full of public figures who are downright terrified of dealing with the media. Or, their sense of public service is so deep and single-minded, they view using news organizations to support their work as only a necessary, but usually avoidable, evil—a diversion from the real task of public policy.

This brand of principal requires extraordinary patience and persistence from the public relations professional. For the scared principal—the one who has a normal fear of public speaking and interaction with reporters—this fear can be overcome with standard media-training techniques. If the principal has a sincere desire to improve her skills, it's simply a matter of working with the staff and perhaps outside consultants to improve her speaking qualities and build confidence in her presentations. For more, see § 8.11, Media Training.

For the leader who thinks she is not ready for prime time, or is just genuinely humble about her work, the task is greater. More than likely, this humble principal is inventing obstacles to avoid interactions with the media. "I don't care if I get media coverage, I just want to get things done." Or, "It doesn't matter what I do, they're going to write what they want anyway." Or, "This really isn't important to the mission of this organization, I've got more important things to do."

These statements are more likely covers for a fear of public speaking than they are true expressions of the principal's opinion. Nonetheless, before you can address the underlying fear, you must provide counterpoints to these misconceptions to encourage the principal to put her toe in the water of media interaction.

You must draw the clear connection between public relations and public policy. Virtually *nothing* of any consequence happens in Washington without a successful communication strategy. Forty years ago a well-researched policy, good relations with key policy-makers, and one good public speech could carry the day. Now, it's impossible to think that the executive branch or Congress could adopt a policy that hasn't been first reviewed in *The Washington Post* or at least on some cable talk shows.

Prove to your principal that if she expects to get anything done she must be a spokesperson for the cause. Provide role models of people she admires and respects who may appear to have similar misgivings about using the media to advance a policy position, and then show how they've used it in ethical and effective ways.

Those resistant to working with the media—the noble nonprofit organization president, the diligent federal agency department head, the rare, shy member of Congress—must appreciate that they've chosen a life that demands they speak out every time their cause gains media interest. They must recognize that there is no way to achieve their policy goals without using the media.

§7.7 How to Defuse the Exploding Principal

Nearly every communication professional has dealt with a boss who has exploded over a news story. There is no one method for dealing with an irate boss, and how you handle the explosion depends on your relationship with him and his personality. But these tips might get you through the storm without completely destroying the relationship between your organization or principal and the offending news organization.

- **Let the principal vent on you.** It's much better if the congressman blows a gasket at his press secretary than at the editor of a local paper. Allow the principal to vent his frustrations. This might be all he needs to get it out of his system.
- **Bring in help.** If the principal has gone completely bonkers over one or two lines in an otherwise decent story, bring in another trusted advisor to provide a reality check. Even if the boss is still raging mad, he'll question whether he should act on that anger if two advisors are counseling against it.
- **Be prepared to act responsibly, but in a limited fashion.** If the offense is real, a response may be warranted—but probably not the nuclear retaliation that the boss is advocating. Usually doing

something has a soothing effect on the enraged public figure
and keeps the media on their toes for errors, no matter how small.

If all else fails, you could try this risky approach: join the rage. I knew a member of Congress who would blow up at small slights in one newspaper. At first, his press secretary argued with the member point by point, defending the news organization and showing how the coverage was actually balanced. This only made the member even madder and led him to question the loyalty of the press secretary.

After many battles, the press secretary tried a different tactic. If the member hit 6.0 on the Richter Scale, the press secretary hit a 7.0. If the member raised his voice, the press secretary shouted and flapped his arms. This led to a reversal of roles, with the member trying to calm down the press secretary, worried that his spokesman was about to do something rash to ruin his reputation with the newspaper.

This strategy will not work with all principals. (Some boss might just respond, "Well, if you're as pissed as I am, let's get that jerk on the phone and tell him what we think of him!") Nonetheless, for those public figures just looking for a good shout, it's not bad to be the cheerleader, encouraging them to get it out. They'll feel better, and then you can begin strategizing some way to rebuild the tattered relationship between the principal and the reporter.

§7.8 "Unofficial" Interactions

One of the best ways to help a principal get comfortable in dealing with the media is to have him interact with reporters in settings that *don't* result in stories. Reporters are intimidating people (although most would have you believe they are benign puppies). Some principals are worried that any errant utterance will result in a supreme embarrassment. Or, that they must be "on" at all times in the presence of a reporter because they don't want to appear as anything less than the model of perfection that the press secretary prints in all those press releases.

The truth is that most reporters yearn to meet newsmakers in settings other than a straight interview. This means more than just coaxing the boss to join reporters at the nearest cocktail party. Non-traditional settings include:

- Coffee or lunch with an "off the record" rule to encourage a frank exchange;
- Regular calls to editorial writers to provide background on important events, knowing that the principal won't be quoted in any way; and

- Chatting with reporters after events where the principal isn't the subject of the event. This is the news equivalent of bumping into someone on the street, with the advantage of a casual exchange and no expectation of benefit.

The idea is to get both parties in the principal-reporter relationship to understand that the other is a real person. Reporters often feel the need to stay detached from those they cover to ensure that their emotions won't interfere with their ability to be a strong critic. Principals are naturally wary of contact with reporters because they are suspicious of their motives. By encouraging "off the record" interactions, you are allowing both to share experiences and opinions, which will make it easier for the press secretary to connect the two when circumstances demand an "on the record" interview.

§7.9 Appreciate that Principals Are Real People

As you get to know your boss, appreciate the strange life he has carved out for himself and the burden it places on him psychologically. The communication specialist is an interloper in the principal's life, acting as a liaison between a person and an impersonal media. It's sometimes hard to appreciate the investment and sacrifice people make when they run for office, agree to serve in the government, or take responsibility of a major company or organization—all positions that put them in the public eye. Press secretaries must never underestimate how difficult it is for individuals to place themselves on the stage of public opinion.

Many public relations professionals view their principals like a product—and why not? We package them like soap, market them like soap, sell them like soap—why wouldn't we depersonalize the "product." But just think about how you would feel if *your* name was maligned in a letter to the editor, even if few people saw it because it was in a puny publication. How would you feel if *your* pet nonprofit project—the one you've championed for years—was just trashed in an editorial? It's hard to transpose yourself into your principal's body and feel his pain—but you must never forget that he sometimes is in pain. The media can inflict a wound on a public figure that press secretaries cannot bandage. Being a good, sympathetic ear is also part of the job description.

§7.99 Chapter Summary

- Developing a trusting relationship with your principal is important to your success. Learn your principal's views of the media and be supportive of his cause. (§ 7.2)

- Assess the strengths and weaknesses of the principal. Find out what he does best when interacting with the media and play to those strengths. (§ 7.3)
- Deal with a paranoid principal by educating him with a summary of news coverage to correct his views. Allowing principals to maintain grudges against reporters can sabotage a long-term media strategy. (§ 7.4)
- Deal with a "media hog" by establishing your credentials, documenting successes, and limiting expectations. (§ 7.5)
- Deal with the "media mouse" by suggesting formal media training. You also must convince the principal that a public relations strategy is essential to achieving public policy goals. (§ 7.6)
- Principals can sometimes explode at negative media coverage. Defuse them by letting them vent on you instead of a reporter. (§ 7.7)
- Set up "unofficial" interactions with reporters and your principal, such as lunches or off-the-record conversations. Every conversation between your principal and a reporter doesn't have to result in a story or quote. (§ 7.8)
- Appreciate that public figures are real people with fragile egos. Being a sympathetic ear is part of the job. (§ 7.9)

Chapter Eight:
Interview Preparation

> ## *"Talk low, talk slow, and don't say too much."*
>
> John Wayne

Interview Preparation

§8.1 Introduction

The operational link in the chain of communication between public figures and the public is the interview. Reporters vie for precious moments with famous officials, while struggling lesser-known agency heads cherish that chance to slip a well-chosen quote on the front page through a brief chat with an influential reporter.

As liaison to both the principal and the reporter, your role is to facilitate access when called for and prepare the principal, or another of your organization's representatives, for the interview. In the public affairs environment, most spokesmen do relatively little spokesmanship. We often become glorified schedulers, trying to play matchmaker between a reporter and our boss. Your job is to ensure that one party, the principal, conveys his or the organization's message and comes off looking good.

This chapter will review the basics of preparing the principal for interviews. Since most of your work is preparing for the interviews, rather than conducting them, this chapter only discusses interview techniques in general terms. (For more detailed texts on the skills of conducting interviews, see § 8.3, Additional Sources on Preparing for and Conducting Media Interviews.) Your primary responsibility is to assess the topic of the interview and prepare the principal for that session. This chapter will offer the basics of those tasks.

§8.2 Assessing the Reporter's Questions

After the reporter says he wants to interview the principal, you should imme-diately shift to information-gathering mode. You want to assess as specifically as possible what the reporter wants to know. In essence, you are the co-writer and director of the play that's about to unfold, where you will "script" both the questions and the answers. The only problem with your play is that your co-writer is a potentially hostile reporter and may not tell you everything he plans for this production.

You'll ask all the standard questions whenever a reporter calls (see § 4.5, Handling Reporter Calls), but you also want to know specifically what the reporter will ask your principal during the interview. Few reporters will pro-vide the exact questions to an interviewee or his representative in advance because they believe to do so shifts the balance of power in the interview too much away from the reporter. Nonetheless, it is the public relations profes-sional's responsibility to probe as much as possible and discern the precise questions.

How much the reporter reveals depends on his particular style, relation-ship with the public relations representative, and the nature of the story. If this is a garden-variety inquiry, such as a reaction to a major news event, there is no need for subterfuge on the reporter's part. However, if the story is likely to be negative to your principal, the reporter will be wary about revealing a clear line of questioning.

If you have some control over whether or not the principal does the inter-view, then you have leverage to find out what the reporter wants to know. Use that power to ensure you get few surprises when the principal gets on the phone or in front of the camera. Find out if the reporter has information being fed to her by another source—perhaps an enemy to your principal or cause. By researching that source, you'll discover other bits of information or possible lines of inquiry that could be pursued. If you work for a federal agency, check and review for any Freedom of Information Act (FOIA) requests the reporter may have filed. (For more, see § 11.6, Freedom of Information Act Requests.)

Most of the time, this dance between reporter and spokesperson is straightforward. Once you get a general subject area, and a few specifics on what the reporter wants to know, you should be able to guess 80 percent to 90 percent of the questions that will be asked in the interview.

Doing your homework will also help discern the reporter's questions and topics of interest. Research what the reporter has been recently writing about—has she been writing on any recent news topics that may be tangential to your principal's position or the agency's point of view? Research recent news reports, especially stories that are not on the front pages, for topics that might prove embarrassing or antagonistic to your principal or agency. A thorough scrub of news aggregators may bring to light issues that slipped through your daily reading. It will also help you review what your principal or agency has already communicated about these issues.

§8.3 Additional Sources on Preparing for and Conducting Media Interviews

Additional resources can be found on the book's web site <*TCNMRH.com*>. TheCapitol.Net offers media training, including public courses and custom, on-site training. See <*TCNMR.com*> for information.

Finally, work out the logistics of the interview. If possible, confine the interview to a setting and time limit that is convenient to your principal and your goals. Make sure the time limit is an appropriate length for the stated topic of the interview, and tell the reporter in advance. While this isn't an adversarial situation per se, it has potential for being one. Make sure you start any potential conflict with some home-field advantages.

§8.4 Pre-Interview Preparation

In preparing for the interview, start with what your principal has already said on the topic. You don't want to put your boss in a situation where he'll say something that contradicts a previous statement, since one of the cardinal public relations rules is to avoid hypocrisy at all costs. Make sure you can answer the question when your principal asks, "What's my position on this?"

Public relations professionals often need help from other staff in preparing a principal for an interview, especially if the topic is new. Be sure to involve them as soon as the interview is set—perhaps even including them in the decisionmaking process on whether to do the interview in the first place. Principals rely on experts for help in forming their opinions; therefore, you need their help in preparing your principal for the interview.

In a federal agency you often have a choice of who does the interview—a high-level administrator with a policy bent or a technical expert with hands-on experience in the field. Government public affairs officers can decide who to offer the reporter, and your choice can greatly affect the story.

For many interviews, communication and policy specialists will work together to create talking points. These should be phrased in short, bulleted

§8.5 Steps for Interview Preparation

With the Reporter

1. Identify the basic topic of the interview.
2. Probe for specific questions.
3. Identify the context of your principal's quotes in the story.
4. Determine the deadline.
5. Settle on logistics.

With Your Office

6. Confirm the interview with the principal and other key staff.
7. Research the topic.
8. Prepare talking points.
9. Conduct a pre-interview conference.

formats, easy for the principal to understand and restate in an interview. Another style is to create the talking points in a question-and-answer format. If you've researched the reporter and the topic carefully, you should be able to craft the most logical questions and propose answers to your principal. This gets the principal comfortable responding to the most likely questions.

Often people new to the profession ask, "Should I create sound bites and quotes for the principal to restate?" The answer is, you should, but not all principals can handle this level of sophisticated communication. To get this right, the principal has to be comfortable with the content, rehearse the quote, and deliver it with skill. Not all public figures have those abilities. In many cases, it's best to let the principal find his own words during preparation sessions and capture them in the talking points. Rather than foisting something clever or quotable on a non-quotable person, let his sincerity shine through.

Still, Washington's largest export is quotes on public affairs. In an article quoting five people, the person with the most clever phrase simply restating conventional wisdom in a pithy way is the one who gets the ink. If time permits, brainstorm the best lines that will garner attention. The key is to sum up the issue in a very short phrase or sound bite—in twenty words or less. It's lamentable that complicated public policy issues often must be distilled down to eight-second sound bites, but those are the realities of modern media.

§8.6 Preparation Sessions

The length and complexity of preparation sessions depend upon the importance of the interview. The executive director of a small nonprofit doing her first *Washington Post* interview on a major policy announcement should spend more time preparing than a senior member of Congress who plans to talk to the local newspaper reporter.

Who participates in this process is equally important. The armchair psychology of preparing a principal for an interview is complex. As the liaison

§8.7 Tips to the Principal for Appearing on Television

- **Rehearse your answers.** Know your talking points and be able to recite them without an "um" in between.

- **Don't rush yourself in advance.** Relax and build in time to get comfortable in the setting. You're talking to tens of thousands of people—if you were doing it in a filled stadium you wouldn't run up to the podium.

- **Keep clothing conservative.** Avoid white shirts, loud outfits, weird ties, big jewelry.

- **Have someone check your appearance in advance.** An un-straightened tie or hair out of place can ruin an otherwise great performance.

- **Wear make-up when available.** Especially in studio interviews, make-up is essential. Guys, get over the phobia—real men wear make-up on television.

- **In taped interviews, avoid hand gestures.** If you talk with your hands, this is tough. But most taped TV interviews are from mid-chest up, and your hand gestures will just appear in the screen from out of nowhere, distracting the viewer.

- **In live interviews, gesture naturally.** It makes you seem enthusiastic and confident.

- **Look at the reporter, not at the camera, unless it's a live interview.** If this much eye contact feels weird, focus on another spot on their head, like an ear or nose.

- **Avoid shifting or blinking eyes.** It makes you look nervous and guilty of something.

- **Keep answers short.** The average television sound bite is about eight seconds.

- **It's not what you say, but how you say it.** This is a basic commandment of television interviews. Research shows the impact of your delivery on an audience is: 7 percent content; 38 percent voice; 55 percent nonverbals.

to the media, you want policy experts present to assist in crafting the message correctly. However, just as communication specialists sometimes cross the line to advise on policy, those responsible for the content of policy sometimes try to become media advisors. I'm often amazed at the hubris of some policy folk who have never been reporters, never been in a newsroom, and rarely watch television news, yet still feel expert advising principals what would sound and look good in a television story. (For a stark example of how this can go terribly wrong, see § 9.6, Potential Message Conflicts with Policy Staff.)

Interviews are part content and part show—especially television interviews. If the principal spews out a lot of extraneous facts or scholarly phrases suggested by an "expert," the chances of getting a quote picked up or communicating effectively are diminished. As discussed in Chapters Three and Four, the message must be short, clear, and precise in order to achieve your goals. Make sure all the participants in the preparation session understand the communication goals before you begin the session.

Preparation sessions also should include some degree of rehearsal. Principals should practice saying out loud the phrases that will be seen or heard by thousands of people before they actually utter them to reporters. Public figures will often spend hours rehearsing in-person remarks to a hundred people, yet spend no time rehearsing remarks that will be read by 100,000. For simple interviews, the rehearsal can be loose, with the boss merely saying out loud, "Well, I'll just tell the reporter . . .". But for more complicated interviews, it's best to engage in role play, with the public relations professional acting as the reporter.

§8.8 Preparing for the Negative Interview

In some cases, a principal must conduct an interview she knows will be used in a negative story. Preparing for these sessions requires much more work. (See § 4.8, Issuing Written Statements versus Doing Interviews for the pro's and con's of doing a full interview versus a printed statement.)

First, make sure the conditions for the interview are as advantageous as possible to your principal. Reporters know that you don't have to grant the interview and that you could provide a printed statement instead. Denying them the give-and-take of an interview prevents them from asking any follow-up questions, or engaging in any grilling (which takes all the fun out of the process for the reporter). Use that advantage to set the parameters of the interview as best as you can. Set a time limit to the interview length to ensure that you get your message through and that you can get out of the session as fast as possible.

You could try to limit the scope of questions as a condition of the interview, but this is usually a fruitless exercise—and even if you get an agreement from the reporter, there's no guarantee he'll abide by it when the cameras are rolling or the recorder is on. And, even worse, he could discuss the question-

§8.9 Tips to the Principal for Various Types of Interviews

Five-minute Phone Interview

This is the verbal equivalent of providing a reporter a printed statement. The principal should relay talking points quickly and efficiently, taking only one or two questions. The key is to get the principal to convey your message early and end the conversation quickly.

Twenty-minute Phone Interview

The principal should be more conversational than during the brief phone interview; make small-talk with the reporter in advance of the substantive questions. The principal should use talking points and have them available. The public relations professional can provide notes to the principal during the conversation only if the principal can process this type of input in this setting.

In-office Interview

Like inviting someone to your home, you and the principal should extend all courtesies you would to a guest. Do not treat the encounter as adversarial, but as a pleasant interaction among professionals. The reporter is there to learn; the principal is there to teach; the public relations professional is there to observe.

ing restrictions in the body of the story, thereby making your principal look scared or defensive.

The research requirements for the public relations professional preparing for a negative interview are also greater.

- Examine all articles on the topic by the reporter to determine all possible lines of questioning.
- Gather a complete internal office document record on the topic, leaving no stone unturned. Ask other staff for assistance, if necessary.
- Schedule more than one preparation or rehearsal session with your principal for the particularly tough interviews. Questions will arise in the first preparation session and you'll need time to clarify those answers and test them in a second session.

Finally, you may need to prepare a principal—to be blunt—to dodge a question. This does not mean you coach a principal to lie, which a public relations professional should never do. But there are situations where public figures should try to shift the focus of the question. In order to do that successfully, you need to be prepared for the question.

Prepare "refocusing phrases" that shift the direction of the question. For example, if the reporter asks your principal a question about your agency's proposal to relax environmental standards on an industry, your principal could reply, "The real question is whether we can balance the environment and economic growth. We can, and here's how . . .". Also, prepare your principal to refute a negative with a positive, rather than merely repeating the negative. Instead of saying, "It's not true—I don't agree that our policy is a failure," the principal should say, "It's not true—our policy has been a success."

In using this tactic, your boss will risk appearing non-responsive. The reporter can always say in his broadcast script or newspaper copy, "The administrator refused to defend the policy," or some other damning phrase. But that is often better than appearing defensive, and you still will have used the medium to get your message out.

The key is to focus on the issue, not the reporter's word choice. The reporter is purposely choosing the most negative phrase in order to goad the principal into saying something rash or emotional. Deny him that victory by rehearsing some refocusing phrases with the principal in advance, and keep him centered on your message and the overall issue the reporter is raising.

§8.10 Preparing for the Ambush Interview

Every public official dreads being ambushed by a reporter. Ambush interviews often occur when public figures have turned down reporters for interviews. Principals sneak out back exits, hide under the noise of helicopter engines, even wear disguises to duck difficult questions from the media. If the reporter has chosen to turn the interview process into a kind of battle, the ambush interview means the principal has lost the strategic high ground. For whatever reason, the reporter has determined that this is the only setting where your boss will answer his questions—maybe because you've refused an interview request, or maybe because the reporter simply wants to catch the principal off guard. Either way, you and your boss are at a disadvantage.

If you think your principal might get ambushed by a reporter, the best thing to do is conduct a preparation session in advance. You'll also want to incorporate this preparation in your crisis communication planning (see Chapter Twelve, Crisis Communication in Public Affairs). In many cases, you may simply prepare the principal to not offer a substantive comment. As stated earlier, "no comment" is not advisable in any public relations context, but it may be the only tool your principal (and his lawyers) are allowing you to use.

If you want to train your principal for handling these encounters as best as possible, offer the following advice:

- **Keep the encounter professional.** Don't let the reporter's tactics rattle you. The reporter is trying to get you to say something because you're not prepared. Don't give in to that tactic.
- **Be pleasant.** When reporters surprise a public figure by jumping around a corner and waving a microphone, they expect an angry reaction. Surprise them with your calm demeanor. Act as if you were just talking to someone who came up to you on the street and asked a legitimate question.
- **Keep the session short.** You only need to say one sentence to avoid a "no comment" line in the paper or on a broadcast story. By using an ambush tactic the reporter has no right to anything more, and probably doesn't expect it.
- **On television, try to avoid the "back of the head" shot.** The television photographer will need to get additional footage of your principal walking away, as if ashamed that he was "caught" by the reporter. Try not to let them get that shot. Walk and talk with the reporter and say the same thing over again in different ways. Walk them to a door of a building they can't enter, or a car, so the only shot they have is the principal walking into a room. This is a very difficult skill to master, especially when someone is firing off negative questions and you're trying to keep the session short. But, by doing so, it keeps you in some degree of control of the visuals of the story, and prevents the public from seeing a starkly negative image. And, if you have to comment for the camera, this is one of those rare cases where calling the reporter's tactics into question works. "This is an ambush. I'd appreciate it if you didn't stalk me outside my home."

The best performance I have ever seen of handling the ambush was not done by an elected official, but by a reporter, Sam Donaldson. In 1993, the reporter who had become famous ambushing presidents found the tables turned on him over a personal investment. Donaldson owned a sheep ranch in New Mexico and, as a ranch owner, was entitled to the same federal "wool and mohair" subsidies as other ranchers. However, this reporter who frequently impugned the reputation of public figures for wasteful spending now got a taste of his own medicine. Anti-government spending groups used the ABC reporter as a poster child for excess because of the $97,000 he received for the subsidy. (The point was even juicier because

Donaldson had previously done a segment on *Prime Time Live* attacking farm subsidies.)

A news crew for one of those quasi-news programs, "Inside Edition," wanted to nail the celebrity reporter, and staked out his apartment-house garage. As he walked from the elevator to the car, the reporter peppered Donaldson with questions. Years of being on the other side of the microphone was perfect training for Donaldson. His voice was calm, but firm. If the reporter asked an accusatory question, Donaldson interrupted, "You've made a mistake," and refocused the question. If the reporter pushed an exaggerated fact, Donaldson replied, "You've got your facts wrong . . . you need to do better research," as a master would teach an apprentice. All the while, he never broke a steady pace toward his car. As he put the key in the door, he flatly said, "And that's all there is to it," and drove off. It was a masterpiece performance that left the viewer confused as to who was in the right.

Similarly, in 2004 then-CBS News anchor Dan Rather was in the midst of a controversy over a *60 Minutes* story ("Rathergate") that used bogus materials related to President George W. Bush's Air National Guard service during the Vietnam War. (See § 5.14, What Blogs Do Well: Get People Fired.) He was in Texas to interview a source after the controversy had erupted, and was greeted at the airport by a news crew, hoping to get a juicy soundbite from a rattled national anchorman. They were disappointed. "So nice that you came to greet us," Rather said pleasantly. "Are you here to give us a ride?" He also greeted the cameraman—an unusual gesture that made it even more difficult for the reporter to get rough with Rather.

It's no surprise that the best people at playing "defense" in an ambush are experts at "offense."

§8.11 Media Training

Every public figure who does interviews—especially television interviews—on a regular basis needs media training. (TheCapitol.Net offers non-partisan media training, see *<www.WorkWithTheMedia.com>* for information.) It's as basic as requiring kids to get swimming lessons before they jump into the deep end of the pool. Many people feel they don't need any training because they have watched countless television interviews. This is the equivalent of thinking you can be a major league baseball player or play basketball in the NBA because you watched the World Series or the NBA Playoffs on television. Watching and doing are two entirely different things.

Ideally, your organization can afford a professional consultant to coach your principal. The best time to suggest such training is soon after you've been hired, or when your boss has taken on new responsibilities and will be required to do multiple television interviews.

There are significant advantages to bringing in an outside consultant. First, they likely have more experience than you in the specialty of training executives who have to do interviews. While you may have general skills in the area, consultants usually have a greater body of knowledge and more examples to draw upon. Second, principals respect outside consultants. For some reason, outsiders often have more credibility than insiders, even though they may be dispensing the exact same advice. Finally, outside consultants can say things to a principal that his personal public relations advisor may be unable or unwilling to say. Appearing before the media is a very personal thing, and your principal may have some fundamental flaws, like a bad toupee or horrendous choice in clothes. It's often much better to have someone else impart this kind of advice privately, and then leave the circle of advisors.

If you cannot afford such training, you'll have to play the role of media consultant yourself. Conduct a couple of sessions in front of a camera. Try to re-create an interview setting as best as possible. Review the video with the principal to highlight strengths and weaknesses. Again, this is much less advisable than hiring a professional consultant. However, some training is better than nothing. Your principal might actually enjoy the experience and it may convince her to put up the fee for some professional advice.

Finally, be wary of who you allow into these training sessions. A lot of people think they'd make great media consultants, but they end up merely confusing the principal with goofy suggestions, such as encouraging the boss to be more aggressive, when a more subdued, confident approach would be better. If your principal is going to be in front of tens of thousands of people, make sure the person advising her isn't an amateur.

§8.12 Things to Monitor during the Interview

While the interview is being conducted, there are a few things you need to monitor. The obvious point is that you *must* monitor all interviews with the media. This is important for a few reasons: 1) to be a check on any reporter errors or slants; 2) to get a better understanding of the points the principal wishes to stress on the topic; 3) to be able to follow-up with the reporter, in case the principal makes a mistake.

Other points you'll need to keep in mind.

- **First, pay close attention to ensure the boss makes no factual errors.** If the principal gets a date or number wrong, both he and the reporter will want you to fix it. If he gets it wrong in a broadcast interview, you'll need to encourage the reporter to not use that sound bite.

- **Second, identify points you may need to nuance.** Public relations spokesmen sometimes have to "play down" or "play up" points their principals make. This is hard, since reporters view this as blatant spin. But you may have additional facts that the principal didn't mention that add strength to a point and will be relevant to the reporter. One subtle way of doing this is under the premise of a follow-up. Sending a backgrounder or additional points via email is a good way to reinforce points you'd like to see in the story.

- **Third, consider whether to record the interview.** There are no hard-and-fast rules on this topic, but here are the points for and against.

    Some feel the costs of using a recorder far outweigh the benefits. Unless this is a one-time interview with a reporter who you expect to write a biased story, then there is little value in having a second recording (assuming the reporter is recording it either with a pocket recorder, or for broadcast purposes). Putting a recorder on the table before an interview is like putting a big, fat sign in front of the reporter's face, "I DON'T TRUST YOU." If you intend to have a long-term relationship with the reporter, there must be a degree of trust.

    On the other hand, if you have an established policy of recording all interviews, it could remove any potential offense to the reporter. You will have a useful tool that can be used to check any error in fact the reporter might convey. If the reporter *knows* you have a recording, it can impose a greater degree of diligence on the reporter to accurately record the facts. Also, the recording can be helpful if the principal gets upset by the coverage and claims to never have uttered a quote. Your recording can clear up that misunderstanding immediately. Finally, transcripts of interviews can be used to inform staff of policy positions (sometimes determined on the spur of the moment during interviews) or on the organization's web site.

Finally, what do you do when the reporter asks a completely unanticipated question? Obviously, this is where the principal earns her pay. If it's a print interview, hopefully she'll brush off the question with something like: "I didn't know you would be asking about that topic. I'd like the chance to consider your question in detail. Maybe we could talk about it another time." This response can also be used in some ambush interviews. If it's a broadcast interview, that's a tougher issue.

During the 2000 presidential campaign, then-Governor George W. Bush sat down for a TV interview with a Boston reporter on domestic issues. Instead, the reporter gave the future president a pop foreign policy quiz, asking such questions as, "Who is the new president of Pakistan?" Bush flubbed the answers and looked unprepared (which was the reporter's goal). The reporter was later criticized by some of his colleagues in the media for misrepresenting the purpose of the interview and playing "gotcha" journalism.

It is unethical for a reporter to lie in order to get an interview, and if you catch a reporter in such a lie, one approach is to end the interview immediately. However, this is difficult when the cameras are rolling. As the public relations specialist standing by, you can do very little other than force an ending off-camera—which will look terrible on the screen. You have to judge whether a disembodied voice off-screen saying, "Okay, the interview is over," is going to look worse than your principal's unprepared answer.

The only way to effectively handle a reporter who has misrepresented the purpose of the interview is to make *that* the answer. "Wait a minute, you said this was going to be an interview on health care, and now you're asking about foreign policy. I know that foreign policy is important, but I don't think you need to lie to get me in front of a camera to talk about it." Making journalistic ethics an issue is always difficult and often ineffective, but it might be better than having your boss answer an off-the-wall question and look stupid in the process.

§8.99 Chapter Summary

- Before setting up an interview between a reporter and your principal, assess the reporter's questions. Find out what the reporter knows, and confine the time limit of the interview in a way that benefits your principal or organization. (§ 8.2)
- Prior to an interview, coordinate with other staff and create talking points. If appropriate, create exact sound bites and quotes for the principal to memorize. (§ 8.4)
- Conduct preparation sessions with the principal before interviews. Only include in these sessions personnel who understand the media and message goals. (§ 8.6)

- When preparing for an interview that could result in a negative story, engage in additional research; conduct additional preparation sessions; and prepare the principal to refocus hostile questions. (§ 8.8)
- When handling ambush interviews, principals should try to keep the encounter professional, pleasant, and short. (§ 8.10)
- Use professional media trainers if the budget allows. They are often viewed more credibly by the principal, and can say things to him you can't. (§ 8.11)
- Monitor all interviews. Pay attention for factual errors made by the principal and correct them immediately after the interview is completed. (§ 8.12)

Chapter Nine:
Internal Issues:
Experts, Policy, Numbers,
Leaks, Lawyers, and Language

Internal Issues: Experts, Policy, Numbers, Leaks, Lawyers, and Language

§9.1 Introduction

One of the harsh realities of being a press secretary is that you can't create the policy product *and* sell it. Public relations specialists, campaign consultants, and political advisors often lament that they don't control all phases of the public policy process. On the eve of a key vote that a Senate press secretary *knows* will earn someone's wrath on the front page, she might be heard saying, "It would be so much easier if we just didn't have to vote that way."

But members of Congress have a nasty habit of following their conscience, federal agencies sometimes do noble things that are hard to explain to the media, and meager, do-gooder nonprofit organizations usually stick to their guns in the face of awesome, well-financed opposition. It is often the responsibility of communication specialists to take whatever public position the policy specialists have created, put the best face on it, and sell it to the media and the public.

At the same time, public relations specialists are beholden to policy experts within their organization to do their job—responding to reporter inquiries and translating the organization's initiatives into press coverage. Questions posed by reporters often require diverse resources of an organization to answer. Moreover, proactive public policy and communication campaigns must be coordinated perfectly if they are to be successful. This means that "working and playing well with others," as you learned in elementary school, is as important to successful public relations as knowing how to write a good press release.

This chapter will address the typical internal issues that communication specialists face in a public affairs environment and how to deal with them.

§9.2 Gathering Information from Experts

Within every public policy-oriented organization there is a brain trust, a group of people responsible for generating the ideas that will drive the work. In a Senate office, legislative assistants are largely responsible for conceiving, writing, and negotiating the bills that the senators get credit for. In nonprofit organizations, researchers write reports to influence government policy and to change the way people think about the world. In federal government agencies, bureaucrats draft the regulations that dictate how the agency accomplishes its mission.

Identifying sources *within* the organization to help shape the message is as important as identifying the sources *outside* the organization that will convey the message. You must learn who the reliable producers of newsworthy information are, the projects they are working on that could result in media exposure, and assess whether they understand the connection between their policy initiatives and the public relations process.

The best way to ensure that you are kept in the loop for valuable data is to set up your own internal research system. For a Senate press secretary, this may be as simple as strolling into the legislative director's office on a regular basis. But the press officer of a federal agency or the director of communication for a large nonprofit association must set up a more formal process for ensuring that information comes across their desks. Attending the correct meetings, making sure the relevant documents on upcoming initiatives are provided, and getting phone calls returned by the right people within an organization, are all instrumental in keeping abreast of potential public relations opportunities and threats. For more information on how to accomplish this goal in a federal agency, see § 11.5, Information Flow: How to Stay Informed.

In addition to setting up an information flow system, it is important to build personal and professional relationships with the experts within the organization. Policy experts seem to have a natural suspicion of public relations types. They often view the profession with skepticism, fearing that some flack will rip apart and dumb down their carefully woven policy just to grab a one-day headline (which, to be fair, we sometimes do). Policy experts sometimes even view their own press departments *as* the media, fearing they might immediately release valuable information before the policy experts deem it appropriate. This lack of trust, for example, could lead a federal agency official to conceal a major policy announcement from his press department until the day of its publication in the *Federal Register*, preventing any coordination with a public relations expert. It's important for the policy experts you work with to understand the value of public relations, the role you play, and the importance of your mission to the organization or principal. They need to view you as an asset to their cause, not a threat. These goals can also be incorporated into your media training.

Ideally, public relations specialists want a team of press-savvy policy experts aiding in the communication process, developing ideas that are great policy *and* can be easily translated to media. When the policy and communication teams are in sync on developing initiatives and public relations strategies, there is no public affairs achievement too great to accomplish. Abraham Lincoln put it this way: "Public sentiment is everything. With public sentiment, nothing can fail. Without it, nothing can succeed."

§9.3 Interpreting and Translating Information

One of the greatest challenges when working with policy information is translating it into language that the average person understands. Depending on which study you look at, the average American reads at a sixth- to eighth-grade reading level. (*The New York Times* will likely be written at a twelfth-grade reading level—*USA Today* will be closer to the fifth grade.) Reporters know this, and have trained their eyes and ears to filter out technical jargon, confusing terminology, and any errant fact sent by public relations professionals that could cause an editor to ask, "What the hell is this mumbo-jumbo?"

In order to translate complicated policy into ordinary language, public relations experts first must understand it themselves. This can be one of the most interesting and frustrating aspects of the job. Every day you must learn a new field and become a quasi-expert. When examining new topics, look for the diamond in the rough—the fact that will jump out to reporters because it might interest their audiences. Probe for facts that will connect with your target audience and force the policy expert to explain the effect of the policy.

When sifting through a sea of statistics, find one or two salable facts. Experts will often create large charts with mammoth amounts of numbers and

§9.4 Translating Technical Information into Plain English

Translating technical jargon into simple language is one of the most important roles of public relations specialists in Washington. The city thrives on the use of techno-babble and acronyms—especially lawyers, scientists, and the military. Deciphering the terminology is imperative if your message is going to get through.

Here are a few ways to unravel the language puzzle that policy experts create.

- **Organize the information in a simple list.** If a report has a good executive summary, use that as your guide. Reports should be condensed to simple salient points. Proposals should be reduced to a series of ideas, rather than complex concepts. It will be much easier to understand an idea that is put into a manageable form.

- **Identify the two or three points that are most relevant to your audience.** Even if there are ten ideas that a policy specialist may be pushing, reporters are only interested in the first two or three. They may touch on all ten in their story, but to get the process going, you have to make choices and pick winners.

- **If you're not satisfied with the data and consider it not worthy of a news story, ask for more data.** Experts sometimes don't know the gold in their own reports. Do some additional data mining to see if they've overlooked a nugget of great information that could make it to the front page of the local paper.

- **Analyze the information with the policy expert; explore conclusions they may not have considered.** Push their thinking and force them to speculate on the potential impact of the information. Policy specialists will often be reticent to engage in speculation, but you must encourage them to overcome this resistance. Reporters will ask you, "What does this mean?" Answer that question first in the privacy of your office with the expert, not on the phone with a reporter.

hundreds of data points. Reporters want no more than two or three key statistics to convince them to cover a story. You need to search through that puzzle of data to find the sexiest pieces to attract media coverage.

It is equally important for the principal of the organization to speak in clear, understandable language, devoid of technical double-speak. Brainy

§9.5 How to Use Numbers

Numbers are one of the most powerful persuasive tools available to public relations specialists. As much as I adore Mark Twain, he missed the point when he said, "There are three types of lies: lies, damn lies, and statistics." While numbers can certainly be misleading, the fact remains that they are believed. Use them to bolster an argument or to support an initiative.

When using numbers related to policy, here are a few things to keep in mind.

- **When using numbers in text, be careful not to overload the reader.** Make certain to use only two numbers in a sentence; no more than four to a paragraph. When possible, round up to use "half" or "two-thirds," or other non-numerical fractions. Lead with your most powerful numbers, and include comments on those statistics before you include other numbers in the press release or other public relations document. Let the impact of your primary findings sink in before you overwhelm the reader with more data.

- **Always translate the meaning of the numbers into human terms.** The quotes for a release can often do this effectively. For example, if you're putting out a report that states that a high percentage of seniors in nursing homes are subject to physical abuse, include a quote from your principal stating the impact this has on people's lives. Or, better yet, include a quote from someone who is actually affected by the numbers, like a victim or a victim's family member. Disembodied statistics are useless unless you can demonstrate their significance to your audience.

- **Purposely using false or misleading statistics is wrong, and honest mainstream news organizations will catch your ploy and expose it.** Supportable, well-researched data can be an effective instrument in any public relations strategy.

leaders are often the curse of public relations specialists. Erudite principals who speak in *magna cum laude* terminology wreak havoc on reporters seeking a simple quote or digestible sound bite. Help these poor, overly educated souls by interpreting the information *before* they do the interview. Test them with tough questions and determine if they use long sentences with multi-syllable words when simple phrases will suffice. Your message can be the most valuable information in the world, but if you can't translate it into terms the average person in Peoria can understand quickly, then it's virtually worthless.

§9.6 Potential Message Conflicts with Policy Staff

The conflict between policy staff and public relations staff is almost unavoidable, in part because of each group's differing goals. Policy staffs are supposed to create a perfect world, often in spite of messy political realities. Their societal prescriptions are often complicated, and sometimes come at a high price to powerful groups and interests. In contrast, public relations staffs' mission is to promote the policy through the widest coverage possible, forcing them to latch on to simple themes that reporters and the public can understand. While controversial and politically unpalatable messages might make good policy, they also invite criticism and negative coverage. The result of these competing goals often leads to debates within organizations as to whether policy initiatives should be altered to improve the likelihood of positive press coverage.

Of course, there is no set formula for how and when, or even if, policies and principles should be "compromised" in the interest of politics or press coverage. Individuals or groups that take firm stands based on committed ideology can be viewed as ethical stalwarts, unwilling to bend to the pressure of "special interests." They also can be viewed as extremists, out of touch with the people who will be affected by their work. Finding the right mix in developing and managing the public relations campaign behind an initiative is an important element in its success or failure.

Public relations and policy staffs also often disagree over priorities, especially when the organization has multiple objectives. Every policy person thinks his issue should be paramount and pitched to *The New York Times*. However, press staff must prioritize; if they go running to leading reporters with every little new idea, they will lose credibility with their media contacts—becoming the proverbial person who cries, "Have I got a story for you!"

The best way to resolve these conflicts begins and ends with the organization's or principal's goals and how well they are articulated and followed by staff. The organization's strategic plan should include both policy and communication components. Employees should understand their roles and responsibilities so priorities and resources can be properly allocated. If the strategic plan is not clear (or does not exist), then public relations personnel should look for avenues to resolve these conflicts, rather than ignoring them.

Often a change in a few words can solve the problem (for example, instead of calling it a "cut" to a program, terming it a "reduction in growth"). Sometimes a change that a policy person may think is minor can make a huge difference to a public relations expert, like postponing the "reduction in growth" for a year until after an election. If all else fails and the conflict between public relations and policy staff persists, it may be necessary to have a staff member who is senior to both combatants resolve the conflict. This should be avoided at all costs because no organization can succeed if inter-departmental feuds continue.

The best of all situations is to resolve the conflict by collaborating on the policy initiative as it is created. A policy or program has a much better chance of success if a public relations strategy is developed in concert with the policy planning. This is often difficult, as "experts" are territorial about their work and don't value the input of individuals not versed in policy. However, it's important for press staff to demonstrate their value to the process; convince the policy expert that by working together you can create a great policy *and* get it adopted. This doesn't mean that public relations specialists and policy experts need to be joined at the hip. But, as soon as the organization begins considering committing significant resources to an initiative, the public relations staff should be called in to offer an opinion as to whether it's worth the effort, and how best to sell the idea. There's a saying, "Politics is too important to be left to politicians." The same is true with the policy-crafting process: public relations specialists are instrumental to programs and initiatives being successfully enacted and accepted by the public. To turn the phrase, public policy is too important to leave to policy experts.

§9.7 Lawyers

First, a disclaimer before I comment on lawyers. I am not a lawyer, but some of my best friends are lawyers. Lawyers perform a great service in society, defending the poor, righting great wrongs, and helping to maintain the Rule of Law. A plurality of Congress is lawyers (and I mean that as a compliment), as has been the case since the Continental Congress, which helped found this great nation.

They are also, as a group, some of the worst public relations "experts" and are, by nature and training, ill-equipped to work with the media. Some lawyers, often the ones groomed in media relations through handling high-profile cases, have overcome the lessons of law school to become good spokespersons. But one must never forget that a lawyer's top priority is to *win in court*, not on the evening news.

Lawyers are taught to withhold information, avoiding disclosure at all costs because it could hurt their client in court. Unfortunately, this strategy breeds suspicion among reporters and invites further investigation. Many pundits and former Clinton administration insiders believe that some of President Clinton's problems might have been avoided if he had released documents related to his Whitewater business investment in early 1997. By withholding mostly innocuous information from the press, reporters felt there was something to hide and went on a feeding frenzy. Reporters are absolutely relentless when they think a public official has something to hide. It is an irresistible mystery that may land them a promotion or a Pulitzer Prize, and they will hunt down any cloaked detail with a gusto that is unmatched in the professional world.

Lawyers also are extremely defensive of their clients and unwilling to accept blame—which, if you're on trial, is a very good thing. However, the world of crisis communication often demands a different strategy. When the Exxon Valdez ran aground in Alaska in 1989, Exxon's legal team urged extreme caution for fear of liability (even though a drunken captain was allegedly responsible for the crash). By failing to properly accept even a small amount of responsibility for the incident, Exxon looked defensive and destroyed its reputation with customers.

In contrast, when Johnson & Johnson faced a crisis in 1982 involving a maniac who tampered with their Tylenol bottles and killed seven people with cyanide, its president stepped in and ordered the product immediately taken from the shelf. New packaging was created, and the entire industry was forced to follow Johnson & Johnson's example. No reasonable person was blaming Johnson & Johnson for the deaths, but by taking responsibility for the crisis and by solving the problem, the company saved the brand. Prior to the crisis, Tylenol controlled 37 percent of the market for headache medicine. When the panic hit the airwaves, the share dropped to 7 percent. Just six months later, after a successful effort by the company and its president, market share was back at 30 percent. (For a more detailed analysis of these cases, see § 12.7, Contrasting Case Studies: Systemic Crisis—Exxon and Tylenol.)

One of the best examples of the dangers of legal advice being transplanted to the public relations realm occurred in the 1996 presidential campaign. Vice President Gore was accused of misusing his office by placing fund-raising calls from his government telephone and not using campaign resources for the calls. In a press conference in the White House Press Room on January 7, 1996, Gore defended himself, claiming he was innocent of the charge because there was "no controlling legal authority" on the matter. He was so confident of this legal defense he said the phrase seven times.

Not only was the public completely mystified by what he was talking about, most reporters needed a Black's Law Dictionary to interpret what "no controlling legal authority" meant. Translated to layman's terms, it loosely means, "no one has ever been tried for the crime that I have been accused of committing." (Not exactly bumper sticker material for the campaign.) The "no controlling legal authority" press conference was considered a disaster for the campaign. The criticism of his legalistic defense of a questionable practice remained etched in many voters' minds and reinforced the belief that Vice President Gore was inflexible and unwilling to take responsibility for his actions.

The key to balancing a public relations strategy and legal strategy is knowing *when* to follow a lawyer's advice. Public relations specialists wrestle with many issues that have legal implications, and it pays to develop legal sources within your agency or organization to help keep you out of trouble. Often, consulting legal experts before developing strategies and talking to reporters can help you avoid serious long-term damage. Moreover, if you work in a federal agency, certain agency policies or federal law govern the release of some information (such as national security or confidential commercial information), and you must follow an attorney's guidance when handling this data.

When it comes down to the difference between legal mandates and public relations savvy, public relations specialists David Shea and John Gulick said it best: "Lawyers tell their clients what they must do. Public relations specialists tell their clients what they should do." Use the right expert for the right battleground. If you're standing before a judge in a courtroom, would you want a press secretary defending you? Similarly, if you're standing before the court of public opinion, get someone versed in the rules of that court, its nomenclature, and how to best present your case; more often than not, that's not a lawyer.

§9.8 Leaks

Leaks to the media have plagued Washington policy-makers since the inception of our government. President Richard Nixon was so obsessed with leaks that he created an illegal group, known as "the plumbers," to ferret out and "plug" the leaks. Policy-makers will work months on initiatives and engage in countless hours planning the perfect announcement—all to have it spoiled by some sub-cabinet level underling who gets a thrill over being the first kid on the block to spill a secret.

Despite the ample lesson President Nixon demonstrated about the futility of trying to plug policy leaks, and the countless examples before and after him, there is no workable way to investigate leaks after the fact. "Witch-hunts" for the malcontent or office irritant who used the media to advance his own policy view or to kill someone else's are usually futile, and always devastating to an organization's morale. The water analogy that gives us the term "leaks" also points to the only way to stop them—build a big wall to stop leaks before they happen. Leaks are not just the result of individuals craving attention; they are symptomatic of organizations that do not have disciplined internal communication policies.

The Clinton administration had a reputation for fighting its policy debates on the front pages of *The Washington Post* and *The New York Times*. Dissent was aired in public and initiatives were killed by well-meaning people who chose to use external means to achieve what they could not achieve internally within the administration. This does not mean the Clinton team was not expert at controlling and manipulating the media—they were. They just had trouble controlling their own staff.

In contrast, President George W. Bush's team is seen as the most disciplined press operation that ever worked in the White House. As the senior staff member in charge of communication, Karen Hughes was known as the "enforcer." The key to the success was instilling a mentality (and fear) in the administration that information would flow only through approved channels. From the campaign and into their installation in power, the Bush White House established a regimented communication policy—they built a wall that no leak could seep through.

Reporters decry these closed-mouth operations, as they often result in only the sanitized, organizationally endorsed message being released to the public. And sometimes this penchant for secrecy can lead to dangerous misjudgments and abuses of power. But public policy groups and public figures have a right to determine their own fate and to articulate their own messages. Reporters often highlight lone dissenters as relevant policy-makers, when they may only be lowly staffers with an ax to grind. Wikileaks has added data dumps consisting of thousands of documents to the concept of a "leak." Creating policies that result in fewer surprises may make for duller newspaper reading, but it sometimes can lead to a more efficient and successful organization.

§9.9 Trial Balloons

Some have used the high degree of interest in the policymaking process to test proposals before they may actually be proposals. The launching of a trial balloon is used by some in Washington to initiate a debate over an idea without having to claim credit for the idea. This is usually done by the White House or federal agencies, which can more easily float proposals in an anonymous fashion than any other entity because of their size. For example, a story may appear in *The Washington Post* stating that the administration is considering changing rules on who is eligible for food stamps. Officials can gauge the level of support or opposition to the idea based on the reaction, without the official baggage that accompanies actually proposing the initiative. And, if it blows up, anonymity protects the author from direct attack.

Public relations specialists should be wary of using trial balloons. First, there are ethical problems in advancing ideas anonymously. If it's such a good idea, why not own up to it? The answer is the proponent may not think it's such a good idea or that he may be criticized for it, which is why he's looking for a public reaction (hopefully, a positive one). Second, trial balloons may not be fair tests of the merit of the proposal or its ability to survive the public policy process. It's like sending one lone soldier up against an army. Without the full weight and support of an administration, how can you know whether the idea will be given the consideration it deserves?

Finally, trial balloons are often used because proponents cannot achieve their goals through the standard policymaking process. A person senior to the proponent has killed it, so its creator wants to try to do an end-run. Perhaps a sub-department head has a proposal that was rejected by the White House, but clings to the notion it can survive. By ignoring the decision of a high authority, the proponent is thwarting the regular policy process and the appropriate chain of command.

If, after these considerations, a public relations specialist still wishes to float a trial balloon in the media, she must choose a very friendly reporter to do the story. The proposal must be conveyed in a very favorable light, with almost no dissent present. Lastly, the evaluation process of the proposal's first flight into the public world must be fair. Often people will latch onto one or two criticisms and say, "See, I told you it was a dumb idea." Collect all the public commentary and put it in a clear memo, assessing the weight and strength in support of or opposition to the concept.

§9.10 Rogue Press Secretaries

Washington is full of people who love to see their name in the paper—or, if not their name, at least their handiwork. This penchant for publicity leads many people who are not deputized by their organization to deal with the press to interact with reporters. The media fosters this habit out of its own interests to get sexy quotes from undisciplined staff (or sources closer to the real action and the truth) instead of the professional, and sometimes duller, mouths of the designated spokesperson.

This type of rogue press work should not be confused with whistle-blowers—dedicated employees trying to expose wrongdoing that often can only be corrected by using the media. I'm talking about the headline hunter disguised as a policy expert. People who secretly want to create the policy *and* sell it to the papers—often because it's *their* policy idea.

Usually, having a press-savvy colleague is a great asset for a public relations professional. He knows that if he gets a policy specialist on the phone with a reporter, the expert can skillfully help the organization's goals by explaining dense material, or offering an inside view of a breaking story— often better than the communication specialist can. However, it must be made clear to all staff that they should deal with the media *only* when authorized by the public relations team. Loss of control over communication can be a disaster for an organization, leading to public controversy and loss of credibility. If the communication director is saying one thing to a reporter, and another staff member is saying something different, the reporter will highlight that conflict for all it's worth.

Most organizations have policies against staff talking to reporters, but this is hard to enforce in large organizations. If this occurs, and the person responsible makes himself known, it's best to clamp down as quickly as possible. Usually, senior management takes a very dim view of unauthorized contact with the press and will aid in this effort. This isn't a witch hunt, which, as stated earlier, is usually a failure. This is merely an organization making clear to its staff that there are policies that guide its communication strategies. If it's a good organization, most staff should have the opportunity for input into those strategies. The time to articulate what should be presented to the media is at staff meetings, not after the meeting in a secret call to *The Washington Post*.

One Capitol Hill chief of staff puts his office policy very succinctly to his non-press staff: "If I ever read your name in the paper, it better be in the obituaries . . . or it will be."

§9.11 Motivating Staff with Press Coverage

The policy-creation process is often a thankless one. Most federal government, nonprofit organization, and think-tank work yields much less pay than the private sector and often results in little praise. Principals often appropriate the great ideas as their own, which is often in the best interest of the organization. This leaves the bookish expert only getting credit for her work through the kudos from fellow staffers and knowing she served the organization and principal well.

Yet nothing can be so rewarding to a policy person as seeing her work appear in the news. The release of important policy initiatives is often accompanied by commentary from other experts, and this may be the only public feedback that a staff member gets for her work. It may also be the only tangible result. Most policy initiatives are not enacted into law, adopted as regulations, nor have any major effect on the world. But the *public discussion* of those ideas may have a profound impact on encouraging constructive dialogue and may lead to change.

While press personnel are used to seeing their efforts translated on the evening news on a daily basis, most Washington residents involved in any policy-creation process rarely see their work bandied about in the headlines. This is heady stuff for the policy staffer who may have labored on an idea for months or years before it sees the light of day.

Use these occurrences to motivate staff and to demonstrate the importance of public relations to the policy-creation process. Make sure a clip system is established that distributes press coverage to the entire staff, and credit the creator of the policy as the reason behind the coverage. Also, be certain that the principal of the organization sees all coverage generated about policy staff work, and push the principal to make note of that coverage as a way to encourage other staff to emulate the example of working with the press officer.

It's at times like these when shy, reserved experts get their fifteen minutes of fame—even if it only lasts thirty seconds on the evening news or is one line in a paper. They may say that it's no big deal and that they really just care about creating good policy. But I'll bet that clip will be secretly mailed off to their mom and dad before the end of the day.

§9.99 Chapter Summary

- Identify sources within your organization who will provide you with the information essential to doing your job. Set up information flow systems to ensure you are kept apprised of important developments within your organization. (§ 9.2)
- Always translate complicated jargon into plain English. Be wary of too many numbers. (§ 9.4)
- Conflicts between policy staff and public relations staff are inevitable. Work with the policy staff to convince them of the value of working with the media to achieve common goals. (§ 9.6)
- Lawyers are often poor public relations advisors, but can be valuable in avoiding major errors. Consult legal experts before developing strategies or releasing sensitive information. However, sometimes in a crisis, following a legal strategy instead of a public relations strategy can be disastrous. (§ 9.7)
- Investigating leaks after they occur is often fruitless and demoralizing to an organization. The best way to stop leaks is to prevent them before they happen—establish a clear and disciplined internal communication policy that no leak can pass through. (§ 9.8)
- Motivate staff by circulating press clippings and media reports. Media successes are sometimes the best achievements for an organization. (§ 9.11)

Chapter Ten:
How to Interact
with Congressional
Campaign Operations

How to Interact with Congressional Campaign Operations

§ 10.1 Introduction

For congressional press secretaries, interacting with the member of Congress' campaign can be one of the most challenging, exciting, and difficult experiences of a career. Our political system demands that incumbent members of Congress maintain two operations during election season—one official and one political. Most of the functions of these operations are distinct and have little overlap.

The official staff administers the member's legislative duties, coordinates with other congressional offices, answers correspondence from constituents, and handles people's problems with the federal government through "casework." The campaign staff organizes volunteers, coordinates with political parties in the state or congressional district, and creates television, radio, direct-mail, and online media strategies to help the member get re-elected. One function—the communication departments—have nearly identical missions: promote the member of Congress and his agenda through the media.

The intertwined nature of the missions forces congressional press secretaries to walk a difficult tightrope during election season. They must act as a primary liaison to the campaign, work closely with the campaign consultants and staff, and respond to reporter questions—often generated by the member's opponent. And, during this chaotic time, congressional press secretaries must make certain they cross no ethical or legal line merging official funds, resources, and time with the campaign's, lest they open their bosses to charges of misusing taxpayer funds for political purposes. They should expect to spend a lot of personal time (nights and weekends) helping the campaign, whose success will determine whether the press secretary has a job after election day.

This chapter will address the unusual task of balancing these interests, helping the member of Congress get re-elected, and keeping one's sanity in the process. Note: this is not a how-to section on being a campaign press secretary. The Democratic and Republican parties put out very good publications and conduct training programs on that topic. This chapter is about carefully and legally using the tools of a government office to advance the governmental and political goals of a member of Congress during an election campaign.

§10.2 Getting to Know Your New Partners: The Campaign Team

The modern, well-financed congressional or state office campaign has become a multi-headed hydra, with hired consultants, ad hoc advisors, campaign staff, and other sources of input from well-meaning, and well-financed, interest groups. The average congressional press secretary who thought his legislative director was tough to handle will be in for a shock when he has to deal with a media consultant who has twenty years' experience, countless campaigns under his belt, and, most important, the member's ear. A campaign consultant holds a special place in a member's inner circle; their relationship was forged in the heat of political battles, making that bond very powerful. Developing a relationship with this new team is the congressional press secretary's first job.

After months (in a House office) or years (in a Senate office) of running the communication operation, press secretaries must join forces, and sometimes relinquish control of the message during campaign season, to a team of part-time campaign consultants and full-time campaign staff. While consultants usually are resistant to suggestions from congressional staff on how to run the campaign, they frequently offer advice on how the congressional office should function, either through the press secretary, chief of staff, or the member directly. This advice will flow whether you like it or not, so it's best to stay on good terms with the consultants and campaign manager if you want to continue to have a significant influence on communication issues.

The best way to develop trust with campaign consultants is to demonstrate your value to the team and your understanding of common goals. New consultants will want to educate themselves on the member's background and public profile, and they'll rely on press secretaries to supply them and their staffs with reams of newspaper clippings, television news stories, and web page archives and links. A properly designed web page can be a wealth of information. Include a well-designed archive and you can capture the member's public record. Become the consultant's information source; it's their responsibility to become experts on the member of Congress. Organize background and accomplishments related to the member of Congress in a logical way that follows the anticipated themes of the campaign, and put it in an easy-to-read format, such as a briefing book or database. Be sure to include and highlight all the negative coverage that could be used by an opponent. For more information on preparing this material, see § 10.6, Self-Research.

§10.3 Role of Consultants

In a campaign, most consultants work as a team, advising the campaign staff as a group. But, they also have independent responsibilities. Listed below is the cast of characters.

- **General Consultant:** Oversees the general strategy of a campaign; coordinates the other consultants' work; often the senior advisor to the candidate or member of Congress.

- **Media Consultant:** Creates and produces radio and television spots; advises on most earned media questions.

- **Pollster:** Creates, administers, and analyzes campaign polls; advises on many earned media questions; coordinates message with other consultants.

- **Direct-Mail Consultant:** Creates and produces direct-mail material, advises on some earned media questions.

Most relationships between campaign consultants and congressional press secretaries are positive. Campaign consultants have a great deal of political experience, and you can learn a lot about politics and communication strategies by working closely with them. Congressional press staff often have campaign backgrounds and understand the goals of the consultants. But never forget who's in charge; during a campaign, a candidate is much more likely to listen to a consultant being paid a million dollars in fees and commissions than to a government employee making $60,000.

§ 10.4 Merging Policy Message with Campaign Message

Ideally, the message of the congressional office and the message of the campaign is a perfect chain of communication, seamlessly linked in the public's mind from the first campaign, throughout the term in office, and onto the re-election campaign. The advent of elections should always be on congressional press secretaries' radar screens, and as Chapter Three outlined, message discipline is vital to any successful public relations effort.

The two or three primary themes the member has chosen for his message must be consistent, whether coming from a congressional office press release or a campaign commercial. After all, the re-election of an incumbent is about what he or she achieved in office. If you have done your job, the voters should already have a solid idea of what the member stands for and has accomplished. The campaign's responsibility is to translate that reputation into digestible thirty-second commercials. In the best operations, the only difference between the congressional office message and campaign message is a choice of words and communication vehicles. Campaign commercials articulate the lawmaker's values, promote legislative accomplishments, and find symbols (usually people) to provide testimonials to the value of the member's work.

Disputes sometimes erupt on matters of language between congressional policy staff and campaign staff, with the press secretary acting as arbitrator. For example, the media consultant will want to say in a campaign commercial, "the legislation put a thousand new cops on the streets." But the policy staff will argue that statement is untrue because, "some of those police officers work in offices, not on the streets." The consultants usually win these debates in order to use the strongest language possible to sell the candidate. But these victories come at a cost.

Campaigns and candidates sometimes can go overboard, exaggerating accomplishments and threatening their own credibility. This is most frustrating when the accomplishment alone, without embellishment, is impressive enough. Vice President Al Gore is still ridiculed for an off-hand claim that he "created" the Internet—which, of course, is not true. What *is* true is that Al Gore was one of a small handful of forward-thinking members of Congress who in the 1980s recognized the extraordinary potential of something the Pentagon had developed, called ARPANET, and promoted its conversion to a non-military environment—quite an amazing feat by itself!

Catching members of Congress and candidates in exaggerations during a campaign is the full-time job of many reporters and congressional opponents' staffs. The media has created a cottage industry of debunking the campaign ads of every candidate. Each sentence is parsed to skewer any overstatement or unprovable fact. Opponents use examples of exaggerated language as evidence of the congressman's lack of credibility and untrustworthiness.

As the communication professional working for the member's government office, you must sometimes be the balancing force between the policy staff, who want to keep language safe and ordinary, and the campaign staff, who want to hype every minor accomplishment. Even if the topic in question is used in a campaign commercial, if it relates to the work of the congressional office, *you* may be called on to defend its accuracy. It's important that the congressional office staff and the campaign staff are of one mind on the language used in campaign material, and it is often the responsibility of the congressional press secretary to ensure that such information is accurate and defendable.

§10.5 Polls and Policy Positions

In the 1996 presidential campaign, President Clinton's operation was criticized for having his agenda driven by polls. The administration's early advocacy of gay rights and health care for all was replaced by Rose Garden ceremonies on v-chips for television sets and photo ops on the value of school uniforms to combat juvenile violence.

As polls have become more sophisticated and used by politicians, their use has become more controversial. As a presidential candidate, George W. Bush claimed he would not be guided by polls to set his policy positions. In 2002, when Al Gore was asked how he would conduct any future run for the presidency, he said, "To hell with the polls, tactics, and all the rest."

Each candidate gauges for himself the degree to which he allows his policy positions to be influenced by polling. In some respects, honest scientific polling is the most "democratic" guidance a candidate can follow—certainly more representative of the public interest than the influence of campaign contributions. Political scientists and philosophers have argued for centuries how our leaders must balance their responsibility to lead by principle and their obligation to follow the will of the people. For example, if our leaders in the mid-1960s followed the feelings of the masses, blacks in the South may have been denied civil rights for decades longer.

Where polling may play its most crucial role is not in determining a policy position, but in articulating it. Politicians and their aides use polls and focus groups to test language—which phrases capture the public's attention and resonate with an audience, and which phrases fall flat.

The GOP made extensive use of this tactic in a 1995 debate over Medicare reform. The Republican Revolution was in full swing after the GOP took over the Congress in the 1994 elections. House Speaker Newt Gingrich and company were in the midst of their hundred-day campaign to enact the Contract with America, a platform of ten initiatives that House Republicans were seeking to turn into law. Most of the Contract polled well and could claim a good degree of popular support. But as part of the Republican promise to balance the budget in five years, Congress needed to reduce the rate of growth of the country's health-care system, namely, the popular Medicare program. The GOP Congress needed $270 billion in savings over five years, and that made for a tough sales job on Capitol Hill and in the media.

GOP strategists struggled with language and forced unusual discipline on their members' word choice. House Budget Committee Chairman John Kasich even forced his GOP committee members to put a dollar in a hat every time they used the term "cut Medicare." Weeks of polling, focus groups, and strategy meetings finally resulted in the "trinity" of words that would lead them to the promised land: Congress was going to "preserve, protect, and improve" Medicare through reforms. However, pollster Frank Luntz found out in focus groups that the word "improve" led seniors to think of lower deductibles, more benefits, and better services—something the GOP Congress would have difficulty delivering on. So, he recommended a replacement word—the Congress would "strengthen" Medicare.

The new trinity was echoed by every GOP spokesperson. The strategy had the desired effect—the Republican leadership won the key Medicare vote in the House with 231 votes, with all but six in the party supporting it.

The lesson here is that words are the paint applied to the canvas of the message in a public relations campaign. And polls can guide public relations professionals to the best words to articulate that message. The candidate usually will decide *what* to say—polling can help you decide *how* to say it. (For a good review of public policy polling, see Public Agenda Online at <*www.publicagenda.org*>, or the Pew Center for The People and The Press at <*www.people-press.org*>.)

§10.6 Self-Research

One of the most valuable jobs a congressional press secretary can legally do to help the member's campaign is to conduct "self-research" on the member. The term "self-research" is similar to what campaigns do when probing into an opponent's background, known as "opposition research." This is one area, if done correctly, that the congressional ethics committees, outside watchdog groups, and even the media will never criticize—you're supposed to know your boss' record in Congress. Press secretaries can compile lists of the member's voting record and rationales behind positions and votes; organize speeches, statements, or letters; and itemize accomplishments for the congressional district or state—any type of research that reviews the member's official activities.

One important ethical and legal note: How that data is used, and the degree of coordination between the campaign and the congressional office, *may* violate ethics rules, and congressional press secretaries should consult experts if they think they're getting close to the line. For example, it's perfectly legitimate to provide a constituent, the campaign staff, or a reporter with the list of the key environmental votes that the member of Congress has cast in the last two years. However, if the press secretary spends a Monday afternoon in the congressional office writing a three-page summary of the member's environmental record, and that summary is delivered word-for-word as a campaign direct-mail piece less than a week later, that might be interpreted as a misuse of official resources.

For more information on the rules and regulations governing the use of office staff during campaigns, consult the House Ethics Committee (<*ethics. house.gov*>; see the "House Ethics Manual" and the "FEC Campaign Booklet") and the Senate Select Committee on Ethics (<*ethics.senate.gov*>; see the "Senate Code of Conduct" and "Campaign Guidance").

Campaigns are another reason why it's important for the press secretary to concentrate on the basics—create an ongoing research system that anyone can use and that can be accessed in a variety of ways. The system can be used for a variety of purposes to assist in the official functioning of the office, in addition to aiding the campaign, and, therefore, cannot be viewed as solely created to assist in the re-election effort.

The key components of congressional self-research are:

Voting Record. A complete, searchable record of every vote cast by the member, with descriptions of the votes in layman's terms. The *CQ (Congressional Quarterly) Weekly* has good terminology for explaining what the votes mean. Short rationales or accompanying statements should be prepared for any controversial or important vote.

Bills Introduced and Cosponsored. Tracking bills sponsored by the member is easy, since most offices thrive on this activity and keep *Congressional Record* statements, press releases, and other related matter. Tracking *cosponsored* legislation is sometimes a more difficult challenge. Some bills have hundreds of cosponsors, since members can easily add their support to any bill introduced and sometimes do it verbally without notifying staff. While databases exist (such as <*thomas.gov*>) that easily track cosponsorships of legislation, identifying the *reason* behind a member's decision to cosponsor legislation is another matter. Occasionally, when fielding a question from the campaign, a congressional legislative director will shout to the rest of her staff in a crowded office the question, "Does anyone have the faintest idea why the congressman cosponsored a bill declaring November the National Save the Curled-Toe Hippo Month?" The lesson here is: build and track the legislative record before you get the obscure calls.

Key Positions and Public Statements (Especially News Articles). Often members of Congress will articulate new positions in ad hoc public meetings or in conferences with newspaper editorial boards. These statements often result in small-town newspaper articles, and may be the only time the member has stated his position on this particular issue. Collecting and cataloguing these statements may be crucial to defending the member, especially if the opposition gets hold of these potentially incriminating statements.

Public Schedule. The member's past schedule should be prepared if anyone questions his activities—especially on days when he might have missed votes. Ideally, this is kept in a searchable database and can be catalogued by location, subject category, staff member present, and participants.

Accomplishments. Press secretaries and legislative staff should create comprehensive documents that catalogue the accomplishments of their member of Congress. Rather than rushing to complete these before each election, the compilation should be an ongoing collaborative task of the congressional legislative and press operations. Each accomplishment should include a brief paragraph describing the accomplishment, with longer documents created for more important achievements. Each item should include or refer to supporting documentation, such as the actual legislation, official correspondence, or other paper trail that proves the member actually was responsible for this achievement. Ideally, a hard copy of the supporting documents should be kept in a single file and the details should be logged into a searchable database that can be sorted by subject category, area of the state or community in the congressional district that benefits from the accomplishment, and priority to constituents or the member.

"Accomplishments" is probably the most important area of self-research and the most valuable to the campaign. It is also the one that comes closest to violating ethics rules and the law. According to congressional institutional rules and federal law, congressional offices can use official resources to document the activities of a member of Congress. However, staff cannot work for the member's campaign on the taxpayer's dime. Accomplishment memos can be provided to constituents, the media—even the campaign manager. But, if they are taken verbatim and turned into campaign literature, the congressional office and the campaign have crossed the line and opened themselves up to various investigations and penalties. If congressional press secretaries create the material that is going to be used verbatim by the campaign, they must do so on their own time and using their own resources or the campaign's resources.

There are other research areas related to the member's activities that campaigns often conduct. Some candidates will hire opposition research firms to do thorough self-research on themselves—background checks done just to make sure there's nothing in their records that may unknowingly spell disaster for their career. Past business dealings, unusual complaints from disgruntled employees, messy divorce proceedings, all can be dug up, for a price. And, in tight campaigns, no price is too high for a hungry opponent looking for a silver bullet to win a congressional seat. There is a vast amount of information avail-

§10.7 Use of Congressional Press Clippings in a Campaign

Congressional office media coverage often plays an important role in the connection between congressional and campaign messages. Consultants will often use the headlines from newspaper stories to establish a congressman's credibility in campaign television commercials (or destroy it, depending on the headline). News articles and those headlines have an image of unchallenged, independent veracity to them that, when used briefly in campaign commercials, can be extraordinarily persuasive. Tracking, documenting, and being able to retrieve these articles on a moment's notice is often an indispensable talent for a congressional press secretary. Create a database of articles that include topic, source, and, most important, text of the headline. For more on developing a clip system, see § 2.23, Tracking and Filing Systems.

§10.8 Fact-Checking Organizations

The media has always seen itself as vigilant watchdog against campaign and candidate exaggerations and falsehoods. Often, the story can be one or two exaggerations rather than the speech or debate performance itself. Today, instead of some enterprising reporters taking up the challenge of combing through every statement, there are organizations (many of them associated with newspapers, such as Politifact.com) and web sites dedicated to fact checking. Below are some of the more prominent sites.

- **Factcheck.org**—Run through the University of Pennsylvania's Annenberg School for Communication, this nonpartisan web site is a self-described consumer advocate for voters. The web site monitors the accuracy of claims by "politicians, political ads, and chain e-mails."

- **OpenSecrets.org**—A nonpartisan guide to campaign contributions.

- **"The Fact Checker" from *The Washington Post***—Glenn Kessler runs this page on *<Washingtonpost.com>*, which hands out "Pinocchios" based on misleading information.

able in the public record, and some campaigns will hire private investigators to dig it up. But those headaches are usually for the campaign press secretary, not the congressional press secretary.

The key to self-research in a congressional office is for the press secretary to spot potential problem areas in the official record—positions that are most likely to be attacked by an opponent, special-interest group, or the media. Being prepared to answer the tough questions isn't a misuse of taxpayer dollars, even if it helps your member's political career—it's part of your official responsibility to be the expert on every possible aspect of your member's official activities.

§10.9 Campaign Attacks on the Member's Official Activities

In campaigns, incumbents are frequently attacked for their record and actions. If a campaign organization is fully staffed, then a campaign manager or press secretary usually responds to the attack. But in many campaigns, there is no full-time spokesperson to respond, either because the campaign can't afford one or it's too soon in the election cycle. Moreover, with the advent of the permanent campaign, the growth of special-interest groups, and the media's willingness to cover any charge or attack, congressional office press secretaries can find themselves defending their boss in near campaign-like environments—sometimes before they're even sworn into office.

Congressional rules and federal law permit the member's press secretary to respond to reporter inquiries, even if they are campaign-related. (House and Senate rules differ slightly on the degree of campaign involvement, and congressional press secretaries should acquaint themselves with the subtleties.)

If the attack relates to a member's vote or position, it's often best to let the record speak for itself. A written statement that's already been submitted in *The Congressional Record*, or a statement from a spokesperson may be appropriate. Sometimes the response should come from an aide, not the member. If the give-and-take in the newspaper is an opponent versus a congressional flunky, it appears as if the opponent is on the level with the aide and not the member of Congress. The member should maintain the role of statesman as long as possible before he assumes the role of candidate. Strong incumbents should view weak opponents like minor annoyances—acknowledging them only encourages them to attack more, and often results in more headlines.

The closer you get to the election, the more the rules tend to shift—attacks cannot be allowed to settle into the mind of the electorate. Chris Matthews, in his book *Hardball* (Free Press, 1999), argues that campaigns should "leave no shot unanswered." Certainly in a presidential campaign or in a heated congressional contest, this is now an absolute. But crafting these retorts should not be the responsibility of the congressional press secretary. In tight races members of Congress usually can afford a team of media advisors to craft responses to attacks. In those cases, you play a supporting role—be ready to respond to requests from the campaign to do quick research on the record, to help develop potential responses to attacks, and perhaps to make yourself available after hours to help coordinate strategy.

Ethics rules and laws prohibit *official* press secretaries from conducting campaign work on government time and utilizing government resources. But congressional staff can do whatever they want with their own hours, and most are prepared to put in the extra time to ensure their member is re-elected (and their jobs are protected).

§ 10.99 Chapter Summary

- Get to know the campaign consultant team. Provide them with background on the member of Congress in a notebook or database form that includes accomplishments, position statements, and legislation supported. Be certain to include anything potentially negative that can be turned into a campaign attack. (§ 10.2)

- The congressional message should flow seamlessly to the campaign message. Press secretaries should be intermediaries between congressional policy staff who are wary of hyping accomplishments and campaign staff eager to exaggerate achievements. (§ 10.4)

- Polls are best used to set priorities and clarify language rather than to establish policy positions. (§ 10.5)

- Congressional press secretaries should conduct self-research on their members of Congress. This research should include: voting record and rationales; bills introduced and cosponsored; key positions and public statements, especially press clippings; the member's past public schedule; and list of accomplishments, sorted by category, area of the state or district affected, and priority to constituents. (§ 10.6)

- Congressional press secretaries are permitted to respond to attacks generated by campaign opponents, but should coordinate all responses with the campaign team. (§ 10.9)

Chapter Eleven: Communication in a Federal Agency

Chapter Eleven:
Communication
in a Federal Agency

> *"It has reached the point where the CIA has to reveal its sources and* The New York Times *doesn't."*
>
> I. Mee

Communication in a Federal Agency

§11.1 Introduction

"We're from the government; we're here to help." Those words, presented seriously in the 1950s, are now a common joke both inside and outside of Washington. Many things associated with the gargantuan federal government are considered suspect by the public. And any public relations campaign with a U.S. government stamp is often criticized as being unsophisticated, politically motivated, and sometimes untruthful.

Yet consider the extraordinary importance of federal agency public affairs information specialists in our society. How would disaster victims get access to immediate and sometimes life-saving information without clear and professional instructions from a Federal Emergency Management Agency spokesperson? How much better prepared are we for terrorist attacks because of warning and emergency preparedness campaigns? And how many lives have been saved by the federal government campaign against drunk driving with the slogan created and run by some bureaucrat: "Friends don't let friends drive drunk."

Those who choose careers to communicate the programs and goals of a federal agency, and to respond to the myriad of requests for information from reporters and the public, play a vital, yet often unheralded, role. As our government has grown in size and complexity, explaining how it works, promoting the programs available to the public, and executing public service campaigns to improve our society are profoundly important to our democracy.

This chapter addresses some of the unique tasks of government public affairs information specialists. Much of the advice offered throughout this book applies to this group. However, working for federal agencies offers some clear advantages, disadvantages, and quirks that one is wise to learn prior to signing on for a tour with Uncle Sam.

§11.2 What's Different about Federal Agencies

For those making the transition from the private sector to the public sector of public communication, after a few weeks on the job a person might be seen mumbling to himself, "I don't think we're in Kansas anymore, Toto." A key difference between working in the federal government and working in a non-profit, association, or Congress is the *bureaucracy*. Unless you've worked in a large corporation, you've never seen anything like the internecine intricacies of a federal agency. This is discussed in more detail in § 11.4, The Bureaucracy.

Federal agency communication work also differs from other forms of public affairs public relations work in that it is often nonpolitical. The outside observer might think that all federal government work is political. But the mission of thousands of public information specialists who work for the federal government is often straight, nonpartisan, garden-variety communication. As a longtime veteran of federal government put it: "Our job is to tell the U.S. taxpayer how their tax dollars are being spent."

Because the communication product has the authority of the United States government behind it, the federal agency public relations specialist has an added responsibility to double-check facts, authenticate statistics, and engage in reviews that other communication professionals can treat more casually. Any statement, press release, or web site entry is an official record of a federal agency. While you may consider a government report such as "Mating Disruption of Grape Moths with Pheromone as a Pest Control Strategy in Vineyards" a dry subject for a press release, it is extremely important to vineyard owners (as well as to grape moths).

Another key difference between federal agency and other public relations work is the use of web sites. While the web plays an important role in any public relations effort, government web sites are much more prominent information dissemination tools for federal public information specialists. First, the government has *much* more information to distribute than most organizations. This wealth of data has a perfect home on a well-designed web site. Second, people like dealing with the government online. A web site is the first choice of both the public and reporters who are seeking government information. (See the "A–Z Index of U.S. Government Departments and Agencies" on USA.gov, <*www.usa. gov*>.) And through various e-government initiatives, the government is mandated to make information increasingly accessible online. While all public relations professionals should make maximum use of their web sites, federal communicators should consider it an even greater priority, and commit significant time and resources

§11.3 *Communicators Guide* by the Federal Communicators Network

While a bit outdated (published in 2000), the *Communicators Guide for Federal, State, Regional, and Local Communicators* is a compilation of advice, guidance, and tips, written by veteran federal government public relations specialists. It includes many Items specifically tailored to the federal communicator. It is available online for free by searching on the title.

to ensuring its success. More information is available on what people want in federal government web sites in Chapter Six, Online Communication.

Finally, the government has unique legal and ethical responsibilities to provide information to the public and the press regarding its deliberations. The same cannot be said of an association or nonprofit group. As the liaison to the public and the press, federal public information specialists are partly responsible for maintaining the public trust between government and the governed. You often must play the role of advocate for disseminating information inside organizations that may have tendencies for secrecy.

U.S. Supreme Court Justice Louis D. Brandeis said that sunlight is the greatest disinfectant. It is partly the responsibility of public relations specialists to ensure the light shines through to all corners of the federal government. For more on the legal responsibilities, see § 11.6, Freedom of Information Act Requests (FOIAs).

§11.4 The Bureaucracy

The federal bureaucracy is a different beast than a standard organization or corporation, with enough nooks, crannies, quirks, and obstacles to frustrate most public relations professionals. Over time, each agency develops a character of its own—whether it be the Pentagon or the Federal Motor Carrier Safety Administration. But federal agencies often have a common characteristic of being restrictive with information. This makes the public relations job more challenging.

Probably the most predominant characteristic that affects federal agency public relations work is the time it takes to get publicly releasable documents approved and the number of reviews they must go through. This is partly because the federal government has such broad influence over people's lives and our economy that everything with the official stamp on it must be absolutely correct. However, it also is caused by a variety of factors that generally plague the federal government, including many layers of slow-moving reviews and the occasional unmotivated employee. This requires public relations professionals to build long lead times into the release of materials and to develop extraordinary patience.

Public information specialists also can become frustrated with the cautious nature of their coworkers in federal agencies who don't deal with the media. People who deal with the media are usually looking for some degree of excitement. They want to make things happen, even if it means taking some risks. This is contrary to the modus operandi of those federal bureaucrats who prize job security above all else. Change and innovation do not happen quickly in the federal government. Be prepared for some brick walls being erected by people who have been building those walls since the Taft administration.

This should not be construed as a criticism of federal workers. Most are dedicated employees who have answered the noble calling of public service. But the structure of the federal workforce is not conducive to the quirky, the unusual, nor will it turn on a dime for your brilliant idea. The deliberative processes within the government are not designed to be speedy—they are structured to be thorough, fair, inclusive, and correct. Fashioning a quick response to an ongoing news story will likely be difficult. But if you foster relationships and trust with key people in your agency and department, your chances of success are much greater.

§11.5 Information Flow: How to Stay Informed

Being a public relations specialist in a large bureaucracy means acting like a reporter, and your organization is the subject of your investigation. It seems odd to think that you have to dig for information in *your own* agency, but a lot of the best stuff will not flow freely to you. You'll need to develop systems and protocols to ensure that you are kept informed of what's going on in your own agency so you can translate it to the outside world.

It all starts with support from the top. If your principal is supportive of the public relations mission, then others in the agency will cooperate more freely and coordinate their efforts. Before accepting a position in a federal agency, get a good understanding of the principal of your prospective particular unit or department. Does she understand the importance of communicating successfully with the media? What resources is she willing to commit? Will she intervene with other counterparts or others outside the agency to assist in your mission? If the principal has no taste for the public spotlight and does not want to advance the goals of the organization through public relations, then your job will quickly devolve into writing boring press releases and saying "no" to interview requests.

Another key factor to staying informed is having access to the right data and personnel. This often means getting access to the right meetings. If information is being exchanged and decisions are being made, and you're not in the room, it's pretty likely that a public relations component will not be considered or developed. Find out early where the action happens and get in on it.

Set up information networks to get the news inside the agency. Which regular reports are best to review to get a broad understanding of upcoming projects or releases? Which key department heads should you network with on a regular basis to find out what's being considered? Are there alternative pathways, such as informal listservs or email lists, that you should develop to stay in touch? Individuals not trained in public relations often will not recognize the press value in the agency work. It's your responsibility to spot the agency's diamonds in the rough and display them to the public and reporters.

Another frequently frustrating aspect of public relations within the government is agency colleagues who will tell you great news—too late to plan a release. Getting a phone call from an excited source: "Two weeks ago, we gave $100,000 in grants to tribal nations to help with homeland security efforts" can push you over the top. Had you been involved in the story earlier, you could have worked with tribal officials and congressional offices to plan a pitch strategy to garner inches of ink. Instead, you have a cold story that is truly yesterday's news. It's not uncommon to hear colleagues indicate that stories weren't "ready" to be released, and thus you were not informed.

You must work patiently with your colleagues to help educate them—although you are a link to the media, you are not a direct, always-on, tell-all link. You must demonstrate the value of working together to plan strategies—as well as the appropriate timing—to publicize important events. Media relations training for technical experts in your agency can offer an opportunity to educate colleagues about your work, the value of working together, and help better prepare them to deal with the press.

Likewise, some individuals will contact you daily with "great" story ideas that simply won't sell to reporters. Nonetheless, cultivate these sources and educate them about the nature of what you need. Try to pitch a few favorite small stories to specialty media—it'll go a long way to developing a relationship with both your agency source and a trade reporter. And, if you get frustrated gently explaining (again) why the latest research study on widgets is not news, remember—it's easier to temper enthusiasm than to foster it.

§11.6   Freedom of Information Act Requests (FOIAs)

The Freedom of Information Act (5 U.S.C. § 552), or FOIA, is supposed to create a porous flow of information from the government to the people. Passed in 1966, the law was given real teeth in the post-Watergate era in 1974, and updated for the Internet in 1996. In 2007, President George W. Bush signed the OPEN Government Act (P.L. 110-81, 121 Stat. 735), which made administrative updates to FOIA, including clarifying the definition of "news media" and establishing a new Office of Government Information Services (<*www.ogis. archives.gov*>) to review agency compliance with FOIA. In concept, the law states that the people have a right to access whatever government information they want, so long as it doesn't violate certain standards involving national security, personal privacy, trade secrets, or other logical exemptions. In practice, FOIA opened a new window into government deliberations by providing activists, scholars, reporters, and civil libertarians with extraordinary access to information. Simultaneously, it added an enormous burden on federal agencies to process more than half a million requests each year, and subjected federal officials to numerous lawsuits when they refused to divulge requested information.

Within each agency are "FOIA officers," who process and respond to the FOIA requests from companies, reporters, and citizens. This may or may not be a public relations specialist, depending upon how that particular unit is organized. For a list of FOIA contacts at different federal agencies, see the Department of Justice web site, <*foia.gov*>.

When a FOIA request is received, the agency has twenty business days to respond to the requester. According to the U.S. Government Accountability Office, more than 80 percent of FOIA requesters receive some kind of response within the twenty-day period, if not the actual information requested. Some fees may apply for copying and extended searches.

While there are a series of appeals that can occur using administrative avenues, the only real enforcement of a FOIA request is to take the government to court. News organizations and public advocate organizations have the resources to use this course of action, but most citizens have to hope that the government gets back to them with the information requested in a timely manner.

There are nine exemptions to the act that allows agencies to withhold information.

1. **National Security:** military plans, scientific data, or CIA records;
2. **Internal Agency Rules:** internal personnel rules and agency practices;
3. **Information Governed by Other Statutes:** information that other legislation has deemed not public, such as individual income tax data;
4. **Business Information:** trade secrets, manufacturing processes or formulas;
5. **Internal Government Memos:** information prepared for a trial or other material regarding officials' recommendations;
6. **Private Matters:** medical records or other material that would compromise an individual's personal privacy;
7. **Law Enforcement Investigations:** information that would interfere with law enforcement proceedings, deprive a person of the right to a fair trial, or endanger the safety of an individual;
8. **Regulation of Financial Institutions:** records related to financial institutions such as banks, the Federal Reserve System, and the Office of the Comptroller of the Currency; and
9. **Oil Wells:** geological and other information related to the location of oil wells.

There can also be penalties for releasing information that is considered to be "commercial/confidential," that is, information that will harm a business if its competitors have access to it. The government often has access to such data that should not be made public—and the FOIA officer can be your friend to help keep you from releasing this kind of information inappropriately. Predecisional information (if a decision is expected) may also be withheld—but do not think that a document is "protected" by merely stamping "DRAFT" across the top. And, once a document is released or made public to one audience, it automatically becomes public for all audiences.

Over the years, Congress and the courts have clarified federal officials' responsibility under FOIA. But the reality is that the government retains some discretion on whether or how to respond to a request—especially if the

§ 11.7 FOIA References

For more information on FOIA, access the information available from the American Civil Liberties Union's FOIA site <*www.whatisfoia.org*>, the Paul Galvin Library at the Illinois Institute of Technology <*www.gl.iit.edu/govdocs/foia. html*>, and the Department of Justice's FOIA web site at <*foia.gov*>.

request requires an extensive search for the information. Each individual department and division will have its own FOIA procedures, and public information specialists should get to know those procedures and the FOIA officers.

While policies for each agency vary, many agencies will distribute requested documents without a FOIA unless: they contain information that must be withheld due to privacy or commercial concerns; there is a FOIA statute that the agency wishes to apply; or, gathering the documents involves a huge effort. It pays to work with reporters to make the process as easy and productive as possible for both the agency and the media. This often means explaining the process to a reporter as to why FOIA requests must be filed for some information and help them define what they want to ask for.

Be prepared to engage in a balancing act of protecting the interests of the agency with your responsibility to the reporter, and to know the laws and agency policies about information release. Ask yourself: "Has this information already been released in another forum? Is it legitimately covered by FOIA? Are aspects of this document legitimately withheld under FOIA? Even if the information is legally withheld, should (or must) it be withheld? What are the consequences to our relationship with the reporter if we do not respond within a short period of time?"

Also, keep FOIA in mind when you create documents. As a federal employee, documents you write are considered official government documents—even your email may one day receive public scrutiny. When writing memos or emails, remember that your personal views should be kept in check. One public relations specialist referred to a local reporter as a "nefarious little weasel" in an email that he subsequently received under FOIA. Needless to say, that lapse in judgment affected her future working relationship with the reporter. Your actions may eventually be subject to an administrative or legal review, so make sure they are defensible and ethical.

One aspect of the FOIA process that can be very helpful to the public relations officer is that when reporters initiate a FOIA request, you now have a record of what reporters are looking for. Work with your agency's FOIA officer to routinely review the list of incoming FOIAs. Many agencies keep a running list of FOIAs received by subject and source to track timing and responses—that same list is useful to you for other purposes. If a media outlet is focusing on a particular issue (and you haven't already worked with the reporter), call him and offer assistance. Begin a relationship and perhaps the story can grow beyond the document.

If an aggressive investigative reporter is requesting numerous documents, begin to prepare for the story. You can often get a sense of the angle of the story by the documents that have been requested. Work with the FOIA officer to review the documents before they are released and plan your strategy. Do you offer an interview now or later? What story do these documents tell? How do you plan to respond? Are there mitigating actions you can take? And be sure to notify agency officials of the pending FOIA request. You don't want the administrator to be surprised with a CBS News *60 Minutes* expose when their pursuit of the story was a matter of public record within your own agency.

§11.8 Civil Service Professionals, Political Appointees, and Political Events

There are two types of public relations specialists in federal agencies—civil service (or career) employees and political appointees. Civil service professionals usually have extensive experience in the federal government—often including years of service with a particular agency, may have little background in political work or election campaigns, and are most interested in advancing a public relations agenda focusing on the long-term goals of the agency. Political appointees are temporary employees (in the sense they are likely to be in their positions less than four years), usually come from campaign backgrounds, and are interested in advancing a public relations agenda focusing on the person who heads the agency or their benefactor.

The friction between agendas is a crucial and strategic difference that can cause problems between public relations professionals. A career public information specialist may be interested in promoting *all* parts of a particular agency from a to z, from the animal husbandry research to the zoological expeditions. Political appointees will shun this alphabet soup public relations approach, and usually seek to promote a few select programs championed by the department head or other political appointees within the department or agency.

If a conflict breaks out among the competing agendas, the political appointees usually win, since their patron usually outranks any career employees. (This is another reason why a web site should successfully marry the two agendas. Web sites can be all things to all people, yet still use prominent space to promote two or three key messages.)

Both types of agency public relations professionals must take a backseat to planning and execution any time they are working on an event where the president, a cabinet member, or a member of Congress is involved. Agency public relations personnel sometimes complain that the politicians "steal" all the good victories that their department worked months, maybe years, to develop. This is just a fact of life in Washington that you must accept—the politicians get to one-up nearly everyone on the public relations stage.

If you're planning an event at your agency where a president, cabinet official, or member of Congress is involved, you also have to be prepared for a LOT of extra security precautions and a gaggle of reporters who might not normally cover your agency. Those loyal reporters from the small newsletters and blogs who faithfully publish every little utterance from your agency, no matter how mundane, will sometimes feel upstaged by the big boys from the networks who swoop in like loud, unwanted party guests. During these events, agency public relations professionals must make sure that they pay proper attention to the needs of their regular reporters, who will still be around after Elvis has left the building, and who you'll need to cover the daily goings-on of the agency when things go back to normal.

Dealing with Congress is a whole 'nother story. Unlike the president, Congress *will* be here in four years. You may be called on to coordinate events with members of Congress and their staffs. For example, at a press conference, the pecking order is a bit more complicated. The department secretary trumps the freshman member of Congress from the minority party, but doesn't outrank the chairman of the appropriations subcommittee that funds the agency. In coordinating any event with members of Congress, it's best to be courteous and deferential—that freshman member may be in the majority next year, and she may be the subcommittee chair a few years after that.

Public relations professionals also may find themselves coordinating the testimony of agency officials before congressional committees. You may want to acquaint yourself in advance with the reporters who cover the committee, identifying key targets to talk to before and after the hearing. However, be cautious about releasing testimony in advance. Committee press secretaries consider the hearing their show, and they can get upset when agency staff disrupt their choreographed events.

However, if your agency official is being called to testify before a hostile committee, these rules do not apply. You'll want to do all you can to promote your message with key reporters. Contact them in advance, possibly even providing them testimony on an embargoed basis—anything to improve the conditions of the confrontation. (See § 4.14, Using Embargoes.) Members of Congress are playing on their home field when you go before them in a committee setting. Usually only a skillful performance, like the kind that Oliver North executed during the Iran-Contra hearings, can save the day.

The key to successful public relations tied to congressional testimony is preparation. (TheCapitol.Net offers custom one- and two-day training courses, "Preparing and Delivering Congressional Testimony," <CLTBC.com>, and a book, *Testifying Before Congress*, by William N. LaForge (TheCapitol.Net, 2010).) The testimony should be edited by a public relations professional or speechwriter. This makes it more palatable to the media audience and to the congressional audience as well. Most hearings are incredibly boring, partly due to the formats, and partly due to the dry and poorly written material of the witnesses. Exercise the same rules for public testimony as you would for a press release or interview. Remove all unknown acronyms or technical terms; ensure that the most important information is up front and presented in an interesting fashion; and prepare sample answers to questions that are likely to be posed by members.

In addition, many Capitol Hill hearing rooms are now equipped with video and PowerPoint presentation capabilities. If these are available, make sure the official uses them. While you don't want to over-produce the testimony, a well-done multimedia presentation can be a persuasive tool.

Finally, public relations professionals in federal agencies cannot escape the reality of the political calendar that offers the public the opportunity to throw the rascals out in two-year and four-year cycles. The democratic process intrudes on the orderly dissemination of information in many ways. First, political types will get much more active around elections. They need to demonstrate to voters their value and accomplishments, so the sheer amount of press work can double or triple in the months leading up to an election. Second, senior agency officials will be traveling more, either campaigning for the administration or helping members of Congress. This may put an added burden on those staying back in Washington to keep information flowing with fewer personnel. And third, if you are a career person, the song sheet from which you sing may change drastically before and after the elections. Regulations published and promoted or defended by you before an administration change may be thrown out or drastically altered—and again defended by you. Remember, your name and reputation will follow you no matter who is in charge.

§11.9 Summary of the Hatch Act

The Hatch Act (5 U.S.C. §§ 7321–7326) restricts the level of partisan, election activity of federal employees and some state and local government employees who are paid with federal funds. The act, originally passed in 1939 and significantly amended in 1993, is designed to protect government employees from being forced to support candidates who may have influence over their jobs and to protect the integrity of the electoral system, which could be corrupted by improper influence by federal employees. Political appointees are not covered by the Hatch Act.

The 1993 amendments replaced the draconian prohibition on employees from engaging in "any active part" of an election with a series of somewhat complicated regulations, open to various interpretations. If you think you are going to engage in any kind of partisan activity, it's best to consult your office counsel on your agency's restrictions. Also, the U.S. Office of Special Counsel, which enforces the act, has a series of publications and some helpful information on its web site, *<www.osc.gov/hatchact.htm>*.

Below is a short summary of the major do's and don'ts.

Permitted and Prohibited Activities

Permitted	Prohibited
• May be candidates for public office in nonpartisan elections	• May not use their official authority or influence to interfere with an election
• May assist in voter registration drives	• May not solicit, accept, or receive political contributions (some exceptions apply for labor union members)
• May attend political fund-raisers	
• May campaign for or against candidates and referendums in partisan elections	• May not engage in political activity while on duty
• May distribute campaign literature	• May not be a candidate for public office in a partisan election
	• May not wear political buttons on duty

There are strict rules and laws separating governmental and campaign activities. Civil service personnel are covered by the Hatch Act (5 U.S.C. §§ 7321-7326), which was amended in 1993 to allow some political activity, but still prohibits federal employees from getting too involved in federal campaigns. Political appointees do not have the same restrictions. Hatch Act guidelines are somewhat confusing, and each agency has its own interpretation, so it's important to get a briefing on your agency's guidelines when you begin work.

§ 11.10 Public Information Campaigns to Change Behavior

More than other public relations professionals in the public affairs arena, federal agency communication specialists sometimes are tasked with the colossal challenge of changing public behavior—using communication tools to solve some societal ill, such as getting the public to use seat belts in cars or encouraging people to exercise more and eat fewer fatty foods. These campaigns may be tied to regulatory or legislative initiatives, or they may be intended to stand on their own as the sole federal effort to enact change in our country.

These types of campaigns pose some of the greatest opportunities and challenges for public relations specialists. In these cases our skills are not just aimed to puff up someone's ego or deflect some errant criticism; our efforts are intended to have a tangible impact on citizens. However, unlike similar public service campaigns supported by the private sector, public sector efforts usually have small budgets, and television networks are leery of getting in bed with Uncle Sam lest they jeopardize their perceived independence.

Federal communicators are also hampered by the government's resistance to engage in bold marketing strategies. The government must walk a politically sensitive path and carefully target audiences who could be at risk of the malady or are engaging in behavior the government wishes to affect. For example, young men living in inner cities are more susceptible than suburban males to falling into a life of crime. But if federal officials engaged in a public relations campaign to change their behavior, they might be charged with reinforcing stereotypes. For example, a campaign originating from Washington targeting youths in Detroit would probably be ineffective.

This means that federal public relations experts must use a strategy that empowers intermediaries, or "esteemed others." The public is often biased against national programs; it is usually more effective to work through local programs to empower trusted individuals and groups in the community to spread a message.

So, in order to reduce drunk driving, federal campaigns are aimed at restaurant and bar owners to encourage them to act more responsibly, and provide information to police departments to encourage them to add a public education component to their law enforcement activities. One of the most famous public education campaigns wasn't targeted to at-risk groups. The federal government has spent $160 million over twenty-five years to reduce drunk-driving accidents not by targeting the drunk drivers, but by targeting their companions: "Friends don't let friends drive drunk."

For those joining the ranks of federal communicators, this concept of empowering intermediaries is fundamental to the success of public service campaigns. With limited resources, public relations specialists must develop strategies that leverage the power of other groups and individuals. And campaigns must be designed to incorporate a middleman who will be the actual deliverer of the message to the intended audience.

§ 11.11 The Greatest Public Relations Challenge: When Government Works

Years ago I was on a trip to New York with a group of Senate press secretaries and had a meeting with then-NBC News anchor Tom Brokaw. The legendary anchor cheerfully answered our questions and engaged in a good give-and-take about the media and offered excellent advice on how to get our bosses more airtime on his network. I played the proverbial skunk at the party by indelicately asking a question about his network's coverage of Congress.

I pointed out that both ABC and NBC seemed to have an anti-government bias with two segments on their nightly newscasts, ABC's "Your Money, Your Choice" and NBC's "The Fleecing of America." Both regular segments on the newscasts focus on government waste, fraud, and abuse, usually exposing some member of Congress or administration official as having squandered millions of dollars based on some nefarious motive, usually political.

It seemed to me that these segments constituted a "quota system for negative government news." The producers and reporters had to dig up something bad about the government on a weekly basis or lose their coveted jobs. What about good government news? Don't the networks have a responsibility for balanced reporting by investigating when the government does something right?

Brokaw did not flinch at the question and seemed eager to defend his industry. He pointed out that a big part of journalists' responsibility is to expose what is wrong in society so that it can be corrected. He conceded that this may play to the more negative impulses in the industry and may be a form of "gotcha" journalism, but the motive was sound. Finally, he finished me off by quoting an icon of broadcast journalists, Walter Cronkite, who once said, "We only cover the story when the cat runs up the tree."

Right or wrong, the media does not like to cover good stories about the government. Unless it is a whistle-blower exposing some wrongdoing, federal bureaucrats also are largely an ignored group. This places an added burden on the federal communicator to aggressively challenge reporters' assumptions about government and to highlight the numerous good stories available.

In a post-9/11 world, the public is slightly more open to appreciating the role of government in protecting their well-being and advancing the public good. From ensuring our airplanes are safe to fly to ensuring our water is safe to drink, the federal government is intertwined in our daily lives, and there are many positive stories to tell. It is the responsibility of a federal government public relations specialist to ferret out those positive stories, develop strategies to communicate them in interesting ways, and persistently hound reporters into recognizing that our nation's government sometimes has a positive influence on the public. It's a tough sell—but a worthy one, and one that has benefits both to the communicator and our society as well.

§11.99 Chapter Summary

- Recognize that federal agencies are different from other organizations and pose different challenges to public relations specialists. Agencies are comprised of difficult bureaucracies, require public affairs officers to be meticulous about all released information, make greater use of web sites, and have special legal and ethical obligations to make certain information public. (§§ 11.2, 11.4)
- Set up information flow systems to stay informed of important developments. Do not wait for information to come to you—cultivate sources within your agency to provide it. (§ 11.5)
- The Freedom of Information Act (FOIA) requires agencies to release information to the public, except under certain conditions. Work with your FOIA officer to learn what information cannot be released, what information can be released without a FOIA, help reporters understand how best to use the law to ease the data collection burden on them and your agency, and regularly review FOIA requests to see what reporters are requesting. (§ 11.6)
- Understand the different objectives of civil service employees and political employees. Be prepared to bow to political pressures and demands when dealing with the White House, Congress, and during election season. (§ 11.8)
- Federal government public information campaigns to change public behavior can be the most important and tangible work of a public relations specialist. Empower intermediaries to aid in the campaign. (§ 11.10)

Chapter Twelve:
Crisis Communication
in Public Affairs

Crisis Communication in Public Affairs

§ 12.1 Introduction

Some consider the ultimate measurement of any public relations professional to be how he handles a crisis. For some in public affairs, that test can be given five days a week—and on weekends during a particularly bad week. Crises are regular occurrences in many public relations jobs. Whether they are caused by natural disasters, harrying critics, enterprising reporters, or by the actions of an organization or principal—responding to crises is a central part of the job description.

This chapter outlines the types of crises you might encounter and how to handle them. In any crisis often the greatest challenge is not dealing with those things outside the organization beyond your control, but managing those elements within your organization that are supposedly within your control. Identifying the crucial issues, marshaling your resources, and coordinating your message are usually the greatest tasks in handling unforeseen events.

This chapter provides guidance on how to deal with the multiday story—the one that can spiral out of control without effective public relations management. While public relations must often take a backseat to other priorities within an organization, effectively handling a crisis is of paramount importance in the world of public affairs, because mishandling a crisis can lead to the demise of an entire organization or a public figure's career, loss of life, or threaten the public welfare. For information on dealing with the one-day story, see § 4.7, Handling Negative Stories. Some of the concepts in this chapter are derived from *Communicators Guide for Federal, State, Regional, and Local Communicators*, written by the Federal Communicators Network, discussed in § 11.3.

§12.2 Preparing for the Crisis— Crisis Communication Plan

In Washington politics, it can be argued that most public relations profession-als work in full-time crisis mode. But, there's a difference between the run-of-the-mill attack on an agency policy position and a six-month-long front-page investigation into its financial mismanagement or the agency's responsibili-ties in response to a disaster. How one prepares for a crisis often determines whether an organization and principal will survive with reputations intact. Crisis experts for years have started all crisis management lectures with one rule: *Once you hear the thunder, it's too late to build the ark.*

Here are some general principles to follow to prepare a crisis communica-tion plan.

Sell the Idea to the Organization and Principal. Many principals may want to take a Pollyanna approach to the possibility of a crisis—ignoring various scenarios that could threaten the organization simply because facing negative consequences is unpleasant. One of your responsibilities is to help your organization or principal plan for the worst.

There are two categories of crises, extraneous and intrinsic. An extrane-ous crisis happens outside the control of the organization, such as Hurricane Katrina and the attacks of 9/11. An intrinsic crisis is one that concerns the policies or procedures of the agency or principal. It is perceived to be under the control of the organization. In an extraneous crisis the communication focuses on public safety and response management, responding to the crisis, mitigating the effect, rescue, and recovery. In an intrinsic crisis the communi-cation focuses on reputation management and public trust.

Begin by conducting a risk assessment and consider the worst possible disaster scenario. Events like these cannot be ignored by any leader and immediately get their attention and usually their cooperation.

- Understand your agency's responsibilities to disaster response
  and public safety.
- Identify and engage with the communication specialists in agencies

that share responsibilities in disaster response and begin coordination on crisis communication response plans.

- Identify the needed public response that will ensure public safety.
- Develop messages to communicate the risk, cultivate the response, and manage expectations.

Beginning here gets the crisis communication plan started and in this process then you can consider the more intrinsic risks and:

- Brainstorm scenarios that could lead to consistently negative or catastrophic news coverage.
- Call on all key members of the team to develop possible situations that could hurl the organization into a crisis.
- Get agreement in advance on what assets and personnel can be utilized by the public relations staff in the event of a crisis.

Often, when a crisis is in its infancy, debates between the press staff and policy staff will go like this: "We need more research to answer these questions from the press." "But this doesn't justify me taking time away from our other priorities—it's just not a big enough deal." The problem is, crises that could be diffused in their initial stages are sometimes ignored by all but the public relations staff, resulting in small problems growing into large crises. Get everyone on board with the idea that a crisis communication plan is essential, and involve key organization members in the planning process.

Establish an Internal Crisis Communication System. The larger the organization, the greater the need for establishing clear communication systems for employees. "I had no idea what was going on," is a common refrain from employees after a crisis when no system has been established. Collect all phone numbers (especially mobile phone numbers), establish email protocols and conference call procedures that will kick in during the crisis—and make sure that all the information is distributed to staff in advance.

Similarly, establish a crisis communication team. This will include the principal, the key policy or administrative staff member (such as a chief of staff), and a public relations staff member. Other members of the team will vary depending upon how the organization is set up and each person's expertise. Let key staff know prior to a crisis that when a fire starts, they'll be called on to grab a hose and pitch in to put out the flames.

Consider Who Should Talk with the Media. In a crisis, reporters will want to talk to more than a spokesperson. Filtering all information through a public relations source implies a degree of anxiety and, indeed, paranoia about the crisis. Preventing the media from talking to key organizational players can heighten reporters' suspicions and cause them to speculate as to why certain personnel are not speaking publicly. At the onset of the Chandra Levy-Gary Condit scandal in 2001, the only quotable statements were emanating from staff, leading the media and the public to infer, "Well, if he's not talking, he must have done something wrong." It is especially important to make experts available in any crisis when the public safety or health is at stake. People just don't believe flacks in such situations—they want to hear from engineers, doctors, Ph.D.'s (someone with a smock, badge, or hard-hat)—anybody with a title other than "spokesman."

Also, consider the optics of who is doing the talking. During the initial days of the BP oil spill in 2010, the chief spokesman for the company was its CEO, British-born Tony Hayward. He had a disastrous performance before a congressional committee, showed his priorities during an interview when he said he "wanted his life back," and at one point went to back home to England to watch yacht racing (not a sport that connected with many Gulf residents). Hayward was replaced as chief spokesman by BP executive Bob Dudley, who was from Mississippi, and Hayward was later forced to resign as CEO. The contrast of the British accent for the neighborly Southern accent could not have been more tangible.

Prior to the crisis, identify the people on your team who might have to deal with the media during a crisis. Provide them with basic media training, offer them assurances they'll have help in talking with reporters (their greatest fear), and walk them through the possible types of questions they might get. When a crisis occurs, you'll be much better off with a policy expert or principal who has been briefed in advance on his potential role.

Preparation is key and can make the difference in surviving a crisis. When one considers the public appearances of former FEMA Director Michael Brown (in the aftermath of Hurricane Katrina), former Attorney General Alberto Gonzales (facing controversies over the dismissals of U.S. attorneys), and former BP Chief Executive Tony Hayward, it's fair to ask how they prepared for their moments in the spotlight. They may have not been able to survive their PR crises, but their damaging public appearances hurt their causes, hurt their organizations and patrons, and largely contributed to their losing their jobs.

Create a Crisis Communication Plan. Create a document that covers all the details of your advance planning:

- How to reach people in an emergency; home phone numbers and email addresses;
- Conference call information; and

- Key reporter information (back-up files of press lists, in case you have to leave the building).

It is also wise to keep a copy of this document at home, in case a crisis hits when you're not at the office. The plan and associated files should be updated a few times a year.

Integrate Social Media into the Plan. The web and social media can be a useful tool—or a dangerous element—in a crisis. Good planning can help ensure that the new media works to your advantage. As with any plan, identify your assets, including your web site, Facebook, and Twitter. Then determine how you will use these tools. How will you update your web site? What is the approval process for posting on Facebook and Twitter? Do you have one staffer who can monitor Facebook and Twitter during a crisis so you can respond quickly to falsehoods and answer questions? Are there sympathetic bloggers whom you can turn to?

Keep in mind that even more than traditional media, new media interactions require constant monitoring and activity. You can't let anything slip through, lest it go viral and travel around the world while the organization leader is napping.

Tips for PAOs and PIOs in a Crisis. An essential piece of the crisis communication plan is the risk communication plan.

For extraneous disasters, the risk communication is on what the crisis communication is predicated and should be focused on expectation management by:

- Defining the threat
- Defining the response
- Defining the expected public behavior
- Creating the channels of communication to be used in the crisis response

Basically:

- Here's what we think
- Here's what we're going to do in the event
- Here's why we're going to do it
- Here's what we will expect for you to do in order to ensure public safety
- Here's where we will be and what you can expect from us

That way during the event your communication can stay focused on:

- Here's what we know
- Here's what we're doing
- Here's what we need you to do

§12.3 Recognizing the Crisis and Adapting the Organization

While many public relations and political experts are good at recognizing a crisis when they see one, many leaders and policy experts are not. They are often fixed on a pre-set "business-as-usual" plan and are reluctant to allow unexpected events—especially those generated by the media—to interfere with their schedule.

When a crisis strikes an organization—communication or otherwise—the organization must respond in its entirety. This doesn't mean that everyone has to stop what they're doing and watch the press secretary craft a reply to a negative news article. However, all the resources of the organization must be at the press secretary's disposal in order to respond effectively.

Some managers have difficulty accepting this temporary shift in priorities and assets. But consider the consequences of not shifting personnel to a crisis. A public relations crisis can cost an organization immeasurable losses due to destroyed credibility and demoralized supporters. For example, the United Way has been repairing its public image for years as a result of a financial scandal in 1992 resulting from fraud committed by its then-president, William Aramony. How much damage could have been averted if the United Way leaders had transferred all available resources to investigating the malfeasance and demonstrating a sincere and thorough effort to expose any errors, no matter how embarrassing in the short term?

When faced with a single day's negative story, most leaders fail to recognize how it can mushroom into a crisis that can encompass the entire organization until it's too late. Agencies, nonprofits, and congressmen rarely, if ever, "over-respond" to a crisis by devoting too many resources to deal with it. But "under-responding" may lead to serious damage to the reputation of an individual or organization.

§12.4 Getting the Boss to Admit the Crisis Exists

Usually the largest obstacle to admitting an intrinsic crisis exists is the principal. A leader's common reaction to an intrinsic crisis is denial. They want no story at all—much less the multiple stories that comprise most communication crises.

It is ironic that many principals want an entire army of public relations writers to respond to one letter to the editor in a small paper, yet will scoff

at the idea of devoting necessary resources to defusing a genuine communication time bomb. They view any negative coverage as a reflection on their
leadership, and want not even a hint of public condemnation. Getting a principal to admit that a crisis exists is most difficult when no law or institutional
rule has been broken, and when the media is challenging an action or decision
based on their own values or their perception of public values.

Leaders achieve success in part due to their self-confidence. However,
that trait can often lead to a downfall in a crisis. In 2010, then-House Ways
and Means Committee Chairman Charlie Rangel faced a series of allegations
that he had received sweetheart rental rates on his New York City office, used
official resources to raise money for a center at the City College of New York
named after him, and not paid the appropriate amount of taxes and failed to
report income on a property in the Dominican Republic (a big deal if you're
the guy who writes U.S. tax law). He refused to admit any wrongdoing, despite
a rather impressive array of evidence in the public domain lined against him.
In March 2010, under criticism from his own Democratic colleagues in the
House, Rangel stepped down as chairman of the House Ways and Means Committee. Here was a long-term senior career politician, a decorated Korean War
veteran, clouding all those accomplishments and losing one of the most powerful posts in Congress, all because he wouldn't admit he made mistakes.

In situations where the principal does not understand the magnitude of
the communication crisis, it's your job to convince him. Usually, a solo effort
using reasonable arguments and logical precedents is not enough. It's helpful
if you find a close advisor to the principal, possibly even someone outside the
organization, who shares your view. People inside organizations often want
to tell leaders what they want to hear, thinking this is a fast track to success.
Friends of the principal outside the organization usually have no such career-
enhancement agenda, and the principal knows that. While a principal will
shun a friend's opinion about topics central to the organization's professional
mission, he will often turn to a confidant in a time of crisis. If you have built a
relationship with your principal's outside advisors, communication crises are
the time to activate that network and get them to whisper the truth in the
king's ear.

You can also help the principal to visualize what's to come by playing out
the future—outlining the potential coverage that will result if the crisis is not
dealt with forthrightly. Having an arsenal of case studies of previous crises is
always a sobering presentation for the accused. These books paint vivid pictures of leaders who failed to see that it was raining and it was time to load up

the ark: *Shadow: Five Presidents and the Legacy of Watergate*, by Bob Woodward (Simon & Schuster, 1999) is a primer on presidential scandals; and *Torture and Truth: America, Abu Ghraib, and the War on Terror*, by Mark Danner (New York Review Books, 2004) includes an account of how U.S. political leaders failed to recognize how the story would damage America's reputation. For additonal resources, see *<TCNMRA.com>*.

§ 12.5 Types of Communication Crises in Public Affairs

As mentioned before, there are two categories of crises, the extraneous crisis and the intrinsic crisis. The extraneous crisis is very straightforward: know your role, speak to your role, protect the public. It is the intrinsic crisis that is the most complex and is the subject of this section.

People who are not versed in crisis communication have a tendency to respond to all crises the same way. It's the equivalent of seeing smoke and pulling the fire alarm. While this is an exceptionally wise precaution in dealing with fires, all communication crises are not alike. And, many press secretaries would argue that there should be a law against yelling "Crisis!" in a crowded office.

In Washington, the public affairs community is faced with three types of crises: *systemic, adversarial,* and *image*. Systemic crises involve something dealing with the people, processes, or operations of the organization—an accident, a layoff of employees, a problem with a product or service, or misuse or waste of resources (see § 12.6). Systemic crises are caused by circumstances that are under the organization's control but in extraordinary conditions and, as a result, systemic crises are difficult to anticipate. Adversarial crises are contests, initiated by an opponent, usually attacking a view, position, or policy held by the organization (see § 12.9). Finally, image crises are those that call into question the ethics of an organization's leader or leaders, such as allegations of illegal activity, unethical conduct, or questionable judgment (see § 12.10).

A systemic or adversarial crisis can sometimes lead to an image crisis if it is not handled correctly. The most famous example was the Exxon Valdez, which began as a simple but colossal accident, where leading company officials bore little or no blame, and ballooned into a public relations disaster costing the company millions. (See § 12.7, Contrasting Case Studies: Systemic Crisis—Exxon and Tylenol.) Each category of crisis and how to deal with each is discussed below.

§ 12.6 Systemic Crises

There are three subsets to systemic crises: facilities crises, employee crises, and consumer crises.

A **facilities crisis** is most often a physical disaster that damages the organization's infrastructure or operations where the organization is now putting people's lives at risk or endangering public safety. Examples include the damage done to Japan's Fukushima nuclear power plant by an earthquake in 2011, the 2010 Deepwater Horizon oil spill, the 1984 Union Carbide plant gas leak in Bhopal, India, and the NASA Space Shuttle Challenger disaster in 1986.

An **employee crisis** is the kind faced when the workforce is affected in some way, either through loss of life, layoffs, or changes to job routine. In these crises, often the primary audience of communication isn't the general public but the workforce, and management finds itself speaking to its employees through the local television news.

A **consumer crisis** occurs when public confidence in the organization is lost through an unexpected error in operations, such as a defective product or an inability to provide service. These crises can quickly lead to image crises if they are not dealt with rapidly and effectively.

Methods for Handling a Systemic Crisis

So, it's just been discovered that the agency's building was lined with asbestos, or the large nonprofit needs to lay off a hundred people just before Christmas, or the association's professional accreditation system is under fire because the chief auditor fudged his credentials on his resume. How do you respond to a systemic crisis?

From the onset, understand that your problem is not necessarily an image problem, but one based on the operations of your organization. Do not compound the crisis by misreading the meaning in the events. The primary goal in handling a systemic crisis is to quickly, accurately, and broadly disseminate information—the *exact same information* over and over again through as many outlets as technically possible. Here are some general principles to keep in mind.

Communicate Freely. An organization's natural fear of the media combined with some kind of unexpected event often lead people to curl up into a fetal position and hide under a desk. Resist the urge to recoil. Hopefully, you merely have to pull your crisis communication plan off the shelf, modify it based on the developing circumstances, and go to town. In a web-driven 24/7 news environment this might mean a constant updating with information.

§12.7   Contrasting Case Studies: Systemic Crisis—Exxon and Tylenol

In college public relations classes around the U.S., every student is taught the two classic case studies in how to handle a crisis. These twin stories form the opposite ends of the positive and negative lessons to be learned and are slowly growing to legendary status in public relations education. Wearing the white hat, and forever ensconced in the eyes of practitioners as the model for handling a communication crisis, is Johnson & Johnson, and its public relations management revolving around customers' deaths resulting from taking Tylenol capsules laced with cyanide in 1982. At the other end of the spectrum, wearing the black hat and forever labeled as the buffoons of crisis public relations management, is the Exxon Corporation for its handling of the oil tanker Valdez's crash in Alaska's Prince William Sound in 1989. In both cases, a systemic crisis led to a threat to the image of the corporation, rocking it to its foundation. In one case, corporate leaders stepped forward and rose to the occasion, in the other, they hid behind spokespersons and lawyers.

Tylenol Killings

The Tylenol killings of 1982 shocked the entire nation, and made all Americans question every pill container in their medicine cabinet. In September 1982, seven people died after taking Tylenol capsules that authorities reported had been injected with cyanide. National news covered every detail of the story, showing how easily the bottles of over-the-counter medicine could be tampered with. Early in the crisis, it was unclear where the tampering occurred, but Johnson & Johnson knew it had to act and act fast.

Before federal authorities could make a decision on what to do, Johnson & Johnson, on its own, recalled *31 million* bottles of Tylenol. The company's president, James Burke, led the public relations effort to restore faith in the company and product. Instead of playing the role as corporate leader or legal defender, he played the role of public-health protector. He offered advice to consumers on programs such as *60 Minutes*. He opened up the Tylenol manufacturing process to cameras. He created an 800-number for concerned consumers to call. And, he established (and heavily promoted in the media) new packaging procedures designed to protect against tampering—forcing every drug manufacturer to follow his lead.

The campaign worked to an astonishing degree. At the beginning of the crisis, Tylenol products accounted for 37 percent of the over-the-counter analgesics market. After the poisonings, the market share dropped to 7 percent. Six months

(Continued on page 243)

§12.7 Contrasting Case Studies: Systemic Crisis—Exxon and Tylenol (continued)

later, after the reintroduction of the drug and accompanying public information campaign, the company's share was up to 30 percent. President Ronald Reagan praised Burke, saying, "In recent days you have lived up to the very highest ideals of corporate responsibility." Philip Seib and Kathy Fitzpatrick, in *Public Relations Ethics*, call it "the greatest comeback since Lazarus."

Exxon Valdez

In sharp contrast to Johnson & Johnson is the case of the Exxon Valdez. Late at night on March 24, 1989, the oil tanker Valdez hit a reef in Alaska's Prince William Sound. More than 10 million gallons of oil spilled—the largest oil spill in American history. The company CEO, Lawrence Rawl, reportedly was awakened with the news of the accident at his home. He assigned a deputy to handle the public relations end of things, and went back to sleep.

In the ensuing weeks, Rawl was rarely seen on the evening news. Instead, people saw pictures of Alaskan birds, covered in deadly crude oil; vast helicopter shots of spoiled shores; and angry local residents complaining of the company's insensitivity to their destroyed lives. The company's public responses to the crisis were equivocal and sounded like they were drafted by lawyers, which they probably were. The company became the object of public attacks and to many the epitome of what was wrong with corporate America.

One anecdote crystallized the depth of public mistrust for the company. In Washington, an apartment dweller used his perfectly positioned property, nestled on a hill directly opposite Washington's Key Bridge at the edge of Georgetown, and above an Exxon Station on M Street, to make a point. For years after the incident, the environmentally minded resident hung a bed sheet with big red letters saying, "Remember the Valdez." Each day thousands of Virginia-to-DC commuters, many of them involved in the policy formation process, got a homegrown public relations message damning the company. For public relations professionals in corporate America, it doesn't get worse than the Exxon Valdez crisis.

The general rules of dealing with a crisis are addressed throughout this chapter, but the specific lessons the Tylenol and Exxon Valdez case studies show:

- **Fast communication is imperative**. When the house is burning down, get out of bed and grab a fire extinguisher. I'm sure Exxon CEO Lawrence Rawl got a good night's sleep on March 24, 1989—probably the last good night's sleep he got for months after that.

(Continued on page 244)

§12.7 Contrasting Case Studies: Systemic Crisis—Exxon and Tylenol (continued)

- **There is no replacement for a CEO, principal officer, or other leader of an organization.** In Johnson & Johnson's situation, James Burke was the only person who commanded the necessary credibility to calm public nerves and to demonstrate the company's commitment to the public.

- **Lawyers are not the best public relations agents.** I'm sure Exxon got the best legal advice immediately after the crisis and followed the correct legal course. But if you choose to fight a public relations problem with a team of lawyers, remember that it could be a long fight, and what you may win in a courtroom may be lost in the court of public opinion during the months or years spent fighting the battle.

For additional resources, including links to more analysis and related publications, see <TCNMRA.com>.

Even if you have nothing new to report, offering interviews feeds the media beast and calms the public, employees, and other stakeholders in the midst of a crisis.

Focus on the Victims. In many crises, people are hurt, possibly even killed. Focusing on anything other than the victims makes your organization look cold-hearted. No matter how many times major companies get caught in industrial accidents that result in the loss of life, they still kick into cover-your-ass mode when the TV cameras turn on. Offering sympathy, practical assistance, even just a shoulder to cry on, is what the public wants to see in a crisis. No major organization ever lost in court simply by saying, "I'm sorry for your loss. How can I help?"

Be Available at All Times. In times of crisis, the media want answers on their timetable, not yours. But despite the major change in circumstances, principals sometimes become very pig-headed, and refuse to change their schedules. In a facilities crisis, the leader will say to the public relations team, "We don't have anything new to report." In an employee or consumer crisis, the leader will say, "We haven't made up our minds yet." When an organization is under siege, silence is tantamount to an admission of guilt. When the reporter writes, "The spokesman was unavailable for comment," the reader sees, "The spokesman was scared to look like an idiot because his organization

§12.8 How to Use Online Communication and Social Media in a Crisis

Your best tools in any crisis, but especially a systemic crisis, can be found online. In addition to being available to the public 24/7, your web site, Facebook, Twitter, and other online tools offer the added advantage of allowing you to disseminate information completely unedited by the media. It is also a great way to get information to reporters. There are six simple ways you can take advantage of your web site and social media as soon as a crisis breaks:

- On your web site, create a special section on the crisis for the public. Make it the most prominent item on your web site. Regardless of whatever message or mission your organization has, during a crisis nearly 100 percent of your web site's visitors will be coming for crisis information—don't make it hard for them to find it.
- On your web site, create a special section on the crisis for the media. Reporters have different needs than the public, and good web sites tailor different sections of the site to the differnet needs of different types of visitors. Include detailed information, such as background on your organization's efforts, reports related to the crisis, the latest statements from the organization's officials, and media contact information.
- Engage your contacts on Facebook and Twitter. In a crisis, you will see a significant increase in the number of "fans" and "followers" you have. Post and link to your most recent statement. Correct falsehoods. Provide new information when appropriate. This can be a full-time job by itself, so as part of your planning identify a staffer who can update your feeds and, when appropriate, respond to comments or questions. Remember, social media is a two-way street. Be proactive so that false information is corrected in real time and doesn't become accepted as fact.
- For all your online and social media tools, post updates at regular intervals. During a crisis, a web site, Facebook page, and Twitter feed must be current. And, in a crisis, "current" means they've been updated within the last two hours. Even if it's simply to say there is no new information, demonstrate that the principal and organization are on top of the situation.
- Promote links with related web sites. Make contact with other web sites and Twitter feeds, such as news organizations, and provide them easy links to your web site. You share the same goals in a crisis—getting the information to the public quickly. Take advantage of the shared mission to advance your message.
- Work with bloggers. As part of the new media, bloggers can be your allies—or adversaries. Identify potentially sympathetic bloggers who can post your statements and push back against falsehoods. For adversarial bloggers, don't ignore them. Be open and accessible and respond to any inaccurate postings—in real time.

screwed up massively, so he didn't answer the phone." In some adversarial crises, it is wise to pick your response times and not be completely available. But in systemic crises, being available conveys a sense that you have nothing to hide and increases the likelihood your message will get out.

Coordinate All Messengers behind the Same Message. If your organization's leader is not the only person authorized to speak in a crisis, make sure everyone is singing from the same hymnal. Divergence in message reveals a lack of coordination in your organization and saps public confidence. During the 2002 sniper attacks in Washington, various law enforcement personnel spoke to the media, sometimes offering views or theories conflicting with those in charge of the investigation. The result was additional panic and reduced confidence in the ability of the police to catch the killers.

Use All Available Means to Disseminate Information. Many public relations strategies call for a targeting of certain messages using certain vehicles to manipulate and enhance impact. In a systemic crisis, use the print and broadcast media, email, web sites, social media, the town crier, smoke signals, tom-tom drums—anything that spreads the word. Your goal is to get out as much information as quickly as possible to the public. Don't be choosy about the messenger.

Tips for PAOs and PIOs

Preparation is paramount in crisis communication. Risk assessment and risk communication plans lay the groundwork for communicating in a crisis. But when the ship hits the fan-tail:

- **Go ugly early:** "Here's what we know . . ." If the event is yours, you must be the bearer of bad news and own the event.
- **Be available:** "Here's what we're doing . . ." Even if you don't have anything to report, listen to the questions, reiterate what you've said previously with coordinating input from your leadership.
- **Provide leadership:** "Here's what we need you to do . . ." Protect the public at all costs.

§ 12.9 Adversarial Crises

Much of Washington spends most of its time in some kind of adversarial crisis. Our constitutional form of government was established to create an adversarial system through checks and balances to ensure a degree of healthy and nonviolent conflict. Since the mid-1980s, the vestiges of nonpartisan cooperation have been ripped away, leaving the Congress in a virtual permanent campaign.

And policy debates—gun control, abortion, environmental protection—have created legions of advocates on both sides, constantly locked in a struggle to win public opinion.

For these reasons, the tactics for dealing with a crisis created by an adversary's attack may best be studied in campaign texts provided by political parties, or manuals on special interest group lobbying techniques. Nonetheless, there are some general rules to follow when attacks come in any public relations environment. These rules can be especially helpful if your organization is not accustomed to mixing it up in the mud with an opponent. For more on responding to congressional campaign attacks, see § 10.9, Campaign Attacks on the Member's Official Activities.

Methods for Handling an Adversarial Crisis

Put Your Best Argument Forward and Don't Pad It. It may seem like a simple rule—use the best argument to win the debate. But many in the public policy field muddle their message with extraneous arguments or by going overboard. Think about what convinces you to vote for a candidate, to support a particular policy view, or to develop respect for an organization or agency. It's usually two or three key points, not fifteen or twenty. And when advocates go overboard, exaggerating their claims, they reduce their credibility in the eyes of the audience and give their opponents something easy to attack. Al Gore did a great deal to promote the Internet and to get government agencies to support the burgeoning communication environment in the 1980s and '90s. But by claiming he "created" the Internet, his credibility was lost, his opponents pounced, and his genuine good work was ignored.

Define Your Motive/Define Your Opponent's Motive. As discussed in § 12.16, Transparency of Motive, motive is a key persuasion element in a crisis. *Why* you are doing something tells an audience as much about you as *what* you are doing. In an adversarial crisis, define your motive in the best possible terms. When environmentalists fought to protect the Arctic National Wildlife Refuge, it was hard to argue that their effort was intended to line their pockets. Conversely, they could argue that their opponent in the battle, the oil industry, was merely seeking profits at the potential cost of significant environmental damage, and could use the ghost of the Exxon Valdez to help with their claim.

To reporters and the public, explaining your motive and your opponents' motive helps to define the story and puts the debate in context. For more on contrasting your message with your opponent, see § 3.6, The Message Box.

§12.11 Travel Advisory— How to Avoid Travel Scandals

Travel scandals are some of the most common ethical attacks in Washington because there is a gap between what is permitted by law and government rules, and what the media will choose to highlight and attack. Members of Congress, agency officials, even nonprofit heads can find themselves in perfect compliance with the law and regulations, yet still wind up on the front page of *Politico*, *The Hill*, *Roll Call*, or *The Washington Post*.

In order to avoid any potential trouble, follow these rules:

- **Don't go anywhere sunny or fun.** If the taxpayer or association member is paying the tab, you're not supposed to be having fun, you're supposed to be working. If you go on a fact-finding trip to Hawaii in December, bring home some macadamia nuts for the reporters who will be on your case for taking a government- or association-sponsored vacation.

- **Don't go anywhere outside the U.S. with indoor plumbing.** For some inexplicable reason, the media has decided that no one should travel outside the United States. Any public figure taking a foreign trip will have his itinerary scrutinized, meal menu examined, and expense account audited by any reporter who sees the potential for a story here. The exception to this rule is travel to any place where reporters would not want to go themselves. Congressman Tony Hall (D-OH, 1985-2002) made fighting hunger a central part of his mission in Congress and traveled to more unpleasant locales than any other recent member of Congress. Getting pictures taken next to starving kids will never get you in trouble with the media, but going to a NATO conference in Brussels, no matter how important, could end up in the "In The Loop" column in *The Washington Post*.

- **Don't go anywhere with spouses.** This rule only applies to members of Congress, since no other government or non-government entity usually covers the costs of spouses' travel. Surprisingly, members of Congress often do not understand why they shouldn't be allowed to take their significant other on junkets. The media, in this case quite understandably, questions why it is necessary for a congressional wife to engage in shopping expeditions as the price for having the husband attend official meetings.

- **Don't use government planes or helicopters for personal use.** Despite the ethics briefings that administration officials attend at the start of their tenure, some senior officials seem to think their time is so valuable

(Continued on page 249)

that the use of a government aircraft is justified. Former President George H. W. Bush's Chief of Staff John Sununu ended up losing his job in part because he used a government plane to visit his dentist in Boston. Clinton White House aide David Watkins took a government helicopter to go golfing. And President George W. Bush administration Army Secretary Thomas White had questions raised about a trip he took on a military jet to meet with a real estate agent in Aspen (he said it was on the way to a meeting in Seattle).

- **Don't go on any trip without a full itinerary.** A few years ago former Senator Arlen Specter was criticized for asking the State Department to help him find a squash partner overseas so he could continue to exercise during an upcoming trip to Africa. While the trip had a lot of important meetings scheduled, the squash scandal was enough to raise questions about the whole trip, and the mission was aborted. When you're traveling on someone else's dime, you're expected to work, do only work, and nothing but work.

§12.10 Image Crises

The history of government and politics is rife with public figures who have faced image crises—and failed miserably at handling them. Presidents and politicos, senators and staffers, consultants and courtesans have all found themselves in the eye of a political storm, seeking a safe port to harbor their leaky ship. In some cases, they may have been able to save their weak vessel if they had handled the initial onslaught more effectively and honestly.

An image crisis is an attack on a public figure's character and usually involves allegations of his doing something wrong. The catchall words of "misdeed" or "wrongdoing" are nets that encompass a litany of errors including violations of law, institutional rule transgressions, sexual misconduct, financial mismanagement, and downright stupidity. At the heart of it, an image crisis raises questions of honesty and public trust, and can be professionally deadly to any public person.

Methods for Handling the Image Crisis

The public figure or organization in a scandal has a menu of tactics that have been tried and tested over the years. Remarkably, with this rich history of case studies, many public officials continue to rely on their own instincts, family member's advice, or, worse, their lawyer when handling an image crisis. Specific tactics for dealing with an image crisis when you're wrong are provided in § 12.12 and when you're right in §12.14. Regardless of whether you think your principal has done nothing worthy of the scandal, or recognize that he has done something wrong and is deserving of scrutiny, there are some general principles and tactics for handling an image crisis.

Full Disclosure. There was a short time in the last decade when the political community once again thought "clamming up" was a good media relations strategy. In 2005, *The Washington Post* ran a Page One article, "In Recent Scandals, a Rethinking of Capital's Conventional Wisdom." The article quoted some prominent officials suggesting that, in part, because then-embattled House Majority Leader Tom DeLay was "riding out" his controversies by not "coming clean," perhaps the traditional thinking of "getting ahead of the story" was not the best strategy. However, DeLay was later forced to resign from office and was later sentenced to three years in prison on a money-laundering conviction. This proved not to be a successful media relations-legal strategy.

The cardinal rule of any image crisis is full disclosure. No public figure ever got out of a scandal by hiding from the media. And for many, reticence to talk or additional lying led to their doom. The Clinton administration might have avoided years of public scrutiny if it had handed over to the media documents related to their Whitewater land deal. Instead, they stonewalled, leading to further investigations, scandal, and impeachment.

Marathon News Conference. The embodiment of the full-disclosure commandment is the marathon news conference. The sheer stamina of standing up before cameras and unceasing questioning for hours is supposed to demonstrate you have nothing to hide from the media. While this tactic makes sense on paper, and *should* exhaust reporters' interest, it has had mixed results. Democratic Vice Presidential candidate Geraldine Ferraro was one of the first pioneers of this tactic in 1984 when the media raised questions regarding her husband's investments, including a possible link to organized crime, renting warehouse space to a pornographer, and failing to pay taxes. Ferraro got kudos from the media for endurance under enemy fire, lasting nearly two hours, and the press conference largely knocked the story off the front page, but some questions remained unanswered—in part because her husband was the subject of inquiry, and he *didn't* have a marathon press conference.

Then-First Lady Hillary Clinton sustained more than one hour of questioning from reporters in 1994 to answer inquiries regarding some commodity trading that resulted in quick profits for her family. The press conference quelled the immediate controversy, but the Clintons' many critics continued to raise the issue as an example of the couple's questionable ethics.

Advancing Facts to a Friendly/Fair Reporter. If you're in a media maelstrom, you probably have a good idea which reporters will treat you fairly, and which ones are going to toast your demise. When you've got information to advance the story or put your principal in a better light, use the media source most likely to present it favorably. Follow up any positive newspaper article with renewed pitches to television reporters and assignment desks. Television reporters, who get most of their information from newspapers, are more likely to follow a lead story with new information.

End-run Around Adversaries by Getting Ahead of the Story. When a public figure finds himself in an image crisis, the vultures usually begin circling. Opponents try to collect damaging information and release it on a timetable most unfavorable to the principal. If you know the information is going to be leaked, it's best to release it yourself, rather than have enemies divulge it in a manner designed to do the most damage.

During the investigation of the 1996 Clinton campaign's fund-raising irregularities, the White House short-circuited much of a Senate committee's investigation efforts by releasing information publicly *before* giving it to the Republican-led committee. They chose the best sources, the best time to release information, and created an apparent full-disclosure campaign instead of letting their opponents parcel out the damaging information on their timetable. The Clinton White House engaged in huge document dumps, leaving Chairman Al D'Amato off balance and looking for scraps in the mounds of information.

Contrast the Clinton strategy with how former U.S. Attorney General Alberto Gonzales handled the growing controversy over the firing of nine United States attorneys in 2007. Instead of getting ahead of the story as Clinton did, Gonzales repeatedly stonewalled requests from Congress and the media to produce information—including emails—about the firings. Each day Gonzales failed to put out information and each time he said he "did not recall" something, the scandal received more coverage and calls for his resignation grew stronger. Also compare how Representative Charlie Rangel handled his ethics problems and the charges in 2010, ending up censured by the House and forced to step down as chairman of the House Ways and Means Committee.

§12.12 Image Crises— Rules When You're Wrong

In most image crises, somebody screwed up. The congressman has had an affair with an intern, the agency head used a government plane to check out some vacation real estate, or the association president mixed personal and organizational funds to a degree that confused even the best accountants.

There will always be people within the organization, especially the principal, who will want to endlessly debate the degree of guilt, the severity of the offense, and the potential damage to the organization's reputation. This is a worthy debate *after* you've begun implementing your crisis communication plan. As stated earlier in § 12.4, getting the organization or principal to admit that a crisis exists is the first hurdle.

As the public relations professional responsible for keeping this mess from destroying the organization or principal, you've got to take charge of the situation and follow a clear plan for addressing the crisis. Here's a three-step procedure for managing an image crisis when your organization has done something wrong.

Step 1—Gather All the Facts. The rules for dealing with a potential communication crisis are similar to any news story—first find out what the story is about. Public relations professionals usually find out about impending crises in one of two ways—either from reporters, which is not very pleasant, or from their own organization that has discovered the wrongdoing or error. In either case, your first responsibility is information-gathering, either from the reporter or fellow employee. Ask every question you can properly ask.

With a reporter, you can ask anything without concern of bumping into any legal issues. However, if your organization has uncovered some malfeasance on its own, you may want to stop and consider the legal ramifications of your inquiry. Public relations professionals enjoy nothing like attorney-client privilege, and many a flack has been hauled into court or a deposition, incurring steep legal fees along the way. While you have a need to gather information to fulfill your public relations responsibilities, be wary that other *legal* responsibilities also exist. For more information on balancing these concerns and dealing with lawyers, see § 9.7, Lawyers.

Step 2—Assess Liability. In a public relations image crisis, your assessment of potential damage is instrumental in developing a communication strategy. What is the extent of the organization's wrongdoing or error? Is this a one-day story, or does it have "legs" that will carry it through many days? Are there other facts yet to be uncovered that could lead to additional coverage? Will there be an additional external investigation, either through law enforcement authorities, congressional committees, or some other body vested with regulatory powers, which will lead to additional coverage? Map out a worst-case scenario for your principal and key advisors. In an image crisis, the worst-case scenario is often the one most likely to occur.

Step 3—Create a Plan. An organization in a communication crisis without a plan is like a blind man trying to feel his way out of a burning building while getting punched in the stomach around every hallway turn (see § 12.2, Preparing for the Crisis—Crisis Communication Plan). Someone has done something wrong and atonement will be demanded by the proper authorities, the media, and the public. At the initial stages of a crisis, most people feel they have four options: 1) kill the story; 2) stonewall the reporter and refuse to answer questions; 3) deny the allegations; 4) fully disclose all information.

If there are any legal implications, lawyers will oppose option 4, full disclosure. As discussed in § 9.7, lawyers are trained to withhold all information until forced to divulge it. However, in an image crisis those in an organization must weigh the loss of reputation versus the potential legal ramifications. In 2001, Firestone faced a huge legal and public relations disaster when reports surfaced that their tires used on Ford Explorers allegedly ripped apart on very hot days, resulting in as many as 200 deaths from accidents. Firestone followed a strict legal strategy publicly and before congressional committees, denying responsibility and blaming the auto maker Ford for the malfunctions. While Firestone may eventually win its day in court and protect itself from millions in lawsuits, how many millions will it cost the company in lost customers?

In an image crisis, full disclosure is the quickest way to a resolution. Killing the story is usually not an option when wrongdoing has been uncovered. Refusing to answer reporters' questions simply confirms guilt, causing people to think, "Well, if they aren't talking, they must have done something wrong." And, denying the allegations simply puts off the inevitable. In any image crisis, the truth will eventually come out. You can either divulge it willingly, or have it pried from you by the media or some other investigator. Follow the sage wisdom of Mark Twain in this instance: "Always acknowledge a fault frankly. This will throw those in authority off their guard and give you an opportunity to commit more."

For the best contrast of the differences between dealing with an image crisis through full disclosure, or denial and stonewalling, see § 12.13, Contrasting Case Studies: Congressional Sex Scandals—Barney Frank and Gary Condit.

§12.13 Contrasting Case Studies: Congressional Sex Scandals— Barney Frank and Gary Condit

Sex scandals have been a part of Washington since the founding of the republic. In the presidential election of 1804, President Thomas Jefferson was accused of maintaining a "Congo harem" at his Monticello plantation, and of fornicating with slave Sally Hemmings. In 200 years, the script for how to handle a public relations crisis stemming from a bedroom liaison has changed. Prior to the 1980s, the media would largely refuse to publish such content, determining it to be immaterial to the public official's responsibilities of office.

However, in the last twenty years the media have now collectively determined that any personal relationship remotely raising the specter of moral variance is worthy of coverage. The Bill Clinton-Monica Lewinsky scandal broke all sorts of new journalistic ground and effectively rewrote the rule book for sex scandals in Washington. (Although public figures such as John Edwards, Mark Foley, John Ensign, Christopher Lee, Mark Souder, David Wu, Anthony Weiner, et al., continue to add new chapters to that rule book.) Within two years of the Clinton impeachment, another sex scandal captivated Washington's and the nation's attention: the Gary Condit-Chandra Levy scandal.

Gary Condit eventually lost re-election in the 2002 Democratic primary as a result of his mishandling of the public relations crisis. He failed, perhaps in part, because he was following President Clinton's lead, who was evasive throughout much of the Monica Lewinsky affair, only fully disclosing the nature of the relationship in a nationally televised speech eight months after the story broke. But, Condit had a much better role model to follow—a member of Congress who, like Condit, was engaged in a sexual liaison that most of his constituents and House colleagues found morally questionable, and where a similar allegation of illegal activity on the part of the member was raised. Gary Condit's role model shouldn't have been Bill Clinton, but his colleague from Massachusetts, Congressman Barney Frank.

The Facts of Both Cases

The facts of the Gary Condit scandal dominated the news in 2001. In May 2001, a young woman working on a paid internship with the Bureau of Prisons, Chandra Levy, was reported missing by her parents, a few days after she was to return home to California. Soon after, media reports indicated she had some kind of relationship with her local congressman, Gary Condit. Condit merely called Chandra "a great person and a good friend." But reports leaked of the two meeting regularly, having dinner together, and of his counseling her on

(Continued on page 255)

§12.13 Contrasting Case Studies: Congressional Sex Scandals— Barney Frank and Gary Condit (continued)

career matters—a pattern of unusual behavior for a married congressman and a twenty-four-year-old woman.

The police reportedly talked to Condit on two occasions, and he revealed nothing about their intimate relationship. More details emerged from family members and friends indicating that the two were having an affair. Finally, the police leaked to the media that Condit had 'fessed-up to them, but he still refused to talk to reporters about the relationship, continuing to have his staff speak on the record.

The 24-hour cable networks went bonkers, covering the story like it was a matter of national importance. Old Condit flames were dug up, every detail repeatedly examined, and commentators began to openly speculate about whether Condit was involved in the disappearance. Finally, after months of evasions and denial, in August Condit began a public relations effort—first with a letter to constituents, followed by a nationally televised interview with Connie Chung on ABC. The interview was a disaster: Condit refused to be fully honest about his relationship with Chandra Levy, and the near-universal reaction was negative.

Within twenty-four hours of the interview, Condit's last line of supporters, his House Democratic colleagues, began to jump ship. House Minority Leader Dick Gephardt said Condit's answers "fell way short" and implied that he might be removed from his position on the select House Intelligence Committee. The rest was left up to the Democratic voters in his California district, who ousted Condit in the September primary election. The tragic story of Chandra Levy's murder ended with the conviction of Ingmar Guandique in 2010 for her murder. Guandique was sentenced to sixty years in prison in 2011.

The episode was remarkably similar to a sex scandal that shocked Washington thirteen years earlier involving Congressman Barney Frank. However, Frank's handling of the controversy was a model in crisis communication and ethics, and he continues to serve in the Congress.

In 1989, news emerged that Congressman Frank was engaged in a homosexual relationship with convicted felon Steve Gobie. As the coverage continued, it was discovered that Gobie was running a prostitution service out of Frank's Capitol Hill apartment. Moreover, it was alleged that Frank used his influence to fix some of Gobie's parking tickets, and had written a misleading memo on congressional stationery to Gobie's probation officer.

Frank went before the House Committee on Standards and Official

(Continued on page 256)

§12.13 Contrasting Case Studies: Congressional Sex Scandals— Barney Frank and Gary Condit (continued)

Conduct, which recommended a reprimand. On the House floor, Republicans pushed for a stiffer sanction, a censure, which would have forced Frank to give up his subcommittee chairmanship. However, Democrats held to the committee's recommendation, and the reprimand stood.

How did the two members handle the public relations and ethics crises differently? Why did Frank survive and Condit fall? While both engaged in various actions and issued statements dealing with the crises through the months-long ordeals, the best comparison of the two's attitudes and strategies can be found in the letters that they sent their constituents explaining their actions. Both felt the need to tell their stories to their constituents, but the two took vastly different approaches.

The Issue of Apology: Barney Frank minced no words in his letter of September 1989 to his constituents. "What I did was wrong. . . . I owe my friends an apology and an explanation." Later he repeated, "I hope you will accept my apology." In contrast, Condit refused to take responsibility for his actions, blaming circumstances on some unnamed force. "I'm sorry that the pain the Levy family and Chandra's friends are feeling has grown worse with each passing day," Condit said. The implication was that Condit was not in any way responsible for the "pain" the Levy family was feeling.

Accepting Responsibility: Barney Frank made it clear that he was responsible for the troubles he was experiencing. "I made some serious mistakes in judgment." Condit at one point in the letter said that he was "not perfect" and had made his share of "mistakes," but this was not a clear reference to his handling of the Chandra Levy matter, and his tone throughout the letter was defensive. He went on to blame the media for not being fully open. "When tabloids turned the tragedy of Chandra's disappearance into a spectacle and rumors were reported as facts, I decided that I would not discuss my private life in the media."

Working with Investigators: In Frank's letter he said, "I need hardly tell you that this committee [the House Committee on Standards and Official Conduct] will have my full cooperation." In fact, Frank himself formally requested the committee investigation. Condit, on the other hand, remained equivocal to the end. "I will be interviewed on television and hopefully I will be able to answer questions that help people understand." "Hopefully" he will be able to answer questions? By this point in the crisis, he had reportedly misled police, refused to talk to any reporters, and had not cooperated with

(Continued on page 257)

§12.13 Contrasting Case Studies:
Congressional Sex Scandals—
Barney Frank and Gary Condit (continued)

the private investigators hired by the Levy family, and the best he could tell his constituents was "hopefully" he would answer questions.

Dealing with the Media: Throughout the crisis, Frank dealt with local media regularly, holding long news conferences and explaining his version of events. At the time, his former paramour, Steve Gobie, was doing his best to discredit the congressman. Condit refused to talk to local reporters. And when he finally gave an interview, it wasn't to a local reporter, but to a national one, enhancing the spectacular nature of the event.

How Condit Could Have Saved His Job

If Condit had followed Frank's model performance, he might still be in Congress. Instead, he broke some basic crisis public relations rules.

Full Disclosure Early: Frank disregarded the advice from lawyers and counselors and completely disclosed everything regarding his relationship with Steve Gobie very early in the crisis. If Condit had been honest from the beginning, the only sin people would have tagged him with was adultery. By withholding information, even if it did not relate to Levy's disappearance, it led the media and the public to speculate he had more to hide, possibly even facts related to her safety.

Be Motivated by Public Interest, Not Private Interest: At one point in the scandal, Barney Frank openly discussed resigning his seat. Frank appeared genuinely torn by the controversy and upset that others might be harmed as a result of his errors. Condit, on the other hand, appeared motivated by self-interest and political survival. He needed to ally himself with Chandra Levy's parents, in essence playing the "worried boyfriend." This sounds odd for a married man, but the media was ready to cast him in a role in this morality play, and he could either play a concerned beau or sleazy old man trying to cover his butt. Condit chose the latter and sealed his fate.

There's no guarantee that his constituents would have tolerated Condit's infidelity and re-elected him. But it's a sure bet that his handling of the crisis only amplified the public's mistrust of his judgment and honesty. Moreover, by becoming a national spectacle, Gary Condit further eroded the public confidence in all elected officials and cemented an unfair and largely inaccurate public perception of the ethics of members of Congress.

For additional resources, including links to more analysis and related publications, see <TCNMRA.com>.

§ 12.14 Image Crises—
Rules When You're Right

Like the defense lawyer who, after years of defending the guilty finally has an innocent man walk into his office, public relations professionals will occasionally find themselves enmeshed in a scandal where their principal or organization is wrongly accused. Getting out of this trap is a little like Houdini getting out of the straitjacket while immersed in a tank of water. Yet there are some methods for trying to save a reputation about to be savaged in a media feeding frenzy.

Third Party Defenders. The accused in an image crisis has already lost some credibility due to the accusations against him. Having a third party vouch for his innocence is one method for restoring public confidence. A member of Congress once found himself on the front pages for allegedly influencing a federal agency on behalf of a friend and business partner. The member immediately called on the House Committee on Standards and Official Practices (commonly called the Ethics Committee) to investigate the matter. The committee gave him a clean bill of health after a few weeks, and the local papers dropped the line of inquiry.

Media Defenders. The accused can also try to find allies in the media, especially among editorial writers and columnists. This is a risky strategy, because columnists are just as easily swept up in the coverage and, being former reporters, could likely conclude something like, "While his guilt remains in doubt, serious questions have been raised." Play this card *only* when you have confidence that the writer is on your side and will write a favorable column or editorial.

Full Disclosure. As discussed in § 12.10, full disclosure, such as a marathon news conference, is a possible tactic in a situation where your principal's or organization's reputation is at stake. However, when using this tactic you accept that the story will be continued for another day and the allegation will be repeated: "Smith held a news conference today to deny allegations he stole candy from babies." Your goal in this case is to get the media to put the story to bed once and for all after answering *all* of their questions, giving them nowhere else to go.

Online Media. As described in § 12.8, the online and social media can be helpful or harmful to your crisis communication efforts. Since it moves in real time, you can use your web site, other web sites (including blogs), Facebook, and Twitter to correct falsehoods and to set the record straight. Don't wait to do this—when it comes to online media, be aggressive and fast. The Internet can be self-correcting, but don't assume that bad information and false charges will be addressed on their own.

§12.15 Eight Mistakes to Avoid in a Crisis

If truth is the first casualty in a war, common sense is the first casualty in a communication crisis. People who normally plan out their bathroom breaks suddenly become panicked when a reporter calls. Or, worse, they try to avoid the crisis altogether. Here are eight common mistakes you want to avoid.

1. Ignoring the Problem—Not Changing Priorities: It's hard to implement a good crisis communication plan (§ 12.2) if the boss decides to keep his golf tee-time. Many organizations fail to recognize they have a communication crisis and don't shift priorities and resources accordingly.

2. Not Changing Decisionmaking Apparatus and Team: The most common way organizations mistakenly deal with crises, communication or otherwise, is to simply work harder. A communication crisis adds considerable burden and work on a probably already-overworked team. New decisionmaking protocols must be established to deal with the crisis—maybe even establishing a separate communication team to address the crisis. In the Clinton White House, all impeachment inquiries were directed to a newly installed spokesman in the office of White House Counsel, freeing up the White House press office to continue to push the president's agenda.

3. Letting Lawyers Direct the Public Relations Policy: If I'm headed to a courtroom, I want the best lawyer defending me. But, if I'm headed to a press conference, I want an expert advising me how to win in the court of public opinion. Firestone and Exxon let the lawyers craft the public relations strategy when their companies faced communication crises, while Johnson & Johnson, during an incident involving Tylenol-tampering, pursued a public relations course. Pick the right advocate for the right battleground.

4. Allowing Systemic Crises to Become Image Crises: Exxon Valdez, Firestone and tire treads, United Way, even the Deepwater Horizon oil spill, all started as systemic accidents that may or may not have reflected on the judgment and decisionmaking abilities of these organizations' leaders. However, *how* those leaders handled the crises led to questions being raised about their ethics, judgment, and concern for public welfare. If it's an accident or mistake, treat it like an accident or mistake.

5. Withholding Information: People underestimate the power of Washington investigations to ferret out *every* detail in a crisis. Information that is not disclosed will eventually come out, adding stories to the crisis and making the holder of that information look as if he had something to hide. Former political advisor Chris Matthews, in his book *Hardball*, suggests that politicians who discover their own problems should "hang a lantern on their problems."

6. Not Correcting Errors Immediately: The general public, even reporters, understand that people make mistakes. However, mistakes made during a communication crisis are amplified. If you say something erroneous, correct it immediately or reporters will think you purposely misled them— and then tell a few million of their readers, listeners, and Twitter followers that you're a liar.

7. Using the Wrong Spokesperson: When the media first reported that Gary Condit had an affair with Chandra Levy, Condit's chief of staff said that it wasn't true and characterized the two as just friends. Gee, that convinced me. In a crisis, usually the leader of an organization must face the public. In the case of Johnson & Johnson and the Tylenol killings, company President James Burke showed confidence, caring, and genuine concern for the public in a way that only a company leader could.

8. Not Being Honest: It's almost embarrassing that this must be said, but public figures break this rule in a crisis so often, it must be stated plainly: DON'T LIE. If you don't believe that this is an instant ticket to public relations hell, there is an ample supply of former CEOs, agency heads, congressmen, and even a president or two, who will tell you that they wished they'd told the truth at the onset of a crisis.

§12.16 Transparency of Motive

When Gary Condit was twisting in the wind during the media feeding frenzy of the summer of 2001, what bothered people more: that he had committed adultery with a young woman, or that he was not forthcoming about the affair and helpful to investigators trying to find her? Most people consider politicians' sexual shenanigans rather blasé, or at least a matter best left to those directly involved. But *lying* to or misleading investigators and the public as to the true nature of their relationship struck many people as a greater misdeed than the adultery. Why?

The simple answer is that a public official was lying and possibly obstructing the investigation into a young woman's disappearance. But, *why* was he lying? The deeper answer is this: the congressman was placing his political image ahead of the safety of a young woman. His *motive* was selfish, not altruistic. In the Networked Age of "always on" media coverage of every public figure's actions, *motive is transparent.* In every communication crisis, the media will find a motive for any misdeed or questionable action. In Washington, if a motive is not put forth by the individual or organization in question, one will be provided in the court of public opinion. That motive will always be negative—based on political contribution, personal benefit, or to provide assistance to a friend or family member.

One of the most common errors public figures make in an image crisis is to invent an implausible motive for their actions. During his nationally televised interview with Connie Chung, Gary Condit said he would not divulge the true nature of his and Chandra Levy's relationship out of respect for the Levy family. The national television audience response was a collective "Gimme a break." Condit had displayed very little interest in the family's situation prior to the broadcast; it was implausible that his motive now was to protect their privacy. Within minutes after the statement was aired, the Levy family called on Condit again to be honest with investigators and the public. Condit's motive remained crystal-clear—he was trying to save himself the embarrassment of admitting to an affair.

The lesson for all public figures is to honestly examine the motive behind any action or statement. The source of your motivation will have a profound effect on how you are judged in the media. A judge will usually announce a different sentence to a man who robs to feed his family than one who robs to feed his drug habit. The original questionable act will still bear scrutiny and will sometimes overshadow even the noblest of motives. But motive will always cloud an ethical breach. To this day, millions of Americans consider White House aide Ollie North a hero for ignoring the Congress, and allegedly violating federal law to funnel money to the Nicaraguan Contras who were fighting a communist government. While he might have broken the law, his *motive* was to fight communism, and was, therefore, a mitigating and, for some, an exonerating circumstance.

While "the ends justify the means" is worthless in a structured debate or in court, the media and the public still weigh motive in judging guilt. For this reason, you must accept the reality In crisis communication: motive is transparent and underpins the public's opinion in any public relations situation.

§12.99 Chapter Summary

- Prepare for a crisis by: establishing an internal crisis communication system; considering who should talk to the media; and creating a crisis communication plan. (§ 12.2)

- Know the signs of a crisis and adapt your organization to the changing environment. Use all means available, including outside advisors, to get the boss to admit that you're in the midst of a crisis. (§§ 12.3, 12.4)
- There are two categories of crisis: extraneous and intrinsic. (§ 12.5)
- There are three types of intrinsic crises: systemic, adversarial, and image.
  - **Systemic Crisis:** Dealing with the operations of the organization—an accident, layoff of employees, or problem or defect in the product or service. (§ 12.6)
  - **Adversarial Crisis:** Contests, initiated by an opponent, usually attacking a view, position, or policy held by the organization. (§ 12.9)
  - **Image Crisis:** A questioning of the ethics of an organization's leader or leaders, such as allegations of illegal activity, unethical conduct, or questionable judgment. (§ 12.10)
- Handle a systemic crisis by: communicating freely; focusing on the victims; being available at all times; coordinating all messengers behind the same message; and using all means available to disseminate information. (§ 12.6)
- Handle an adversarial crisis by: putting your best argument forward and not padding it; and by defining your motive and that of your opponents. (§ 12.9)
- Handle an image crisis by: fully disclosing all information, possibly in a marathon news conference; advancing facts to friendly reporters; and engaging in an end-run around adversaries by releasing negative information before they do. (§ 12.10)
- When in an image crisis, admit all errors quickly and forthrightly. Use third-party defenders when in the right. (§§ 12.12, 12.14)
- Maximize the use of online communication and social media in any communication crisis. Create special sections for the public and reporters. (§ 12.8)
- The eight mistakes to avoid in a crisis are (§ 12.15):
  1. Ignoring the problem and not changing priorities.
  2. Not changing the decisionmaking apparatus and team.
  3. Letting lawyers direct the public relations policy.
  4. Allowing systemic crises to become image crises.
  5. Withholding information.
  6. Not correcting errors immediately.
  7. Using the wrong spokesperson.
  8. Not being honest.

- In communication crises, motive is transparent. If a public figure or organization is not motivated by public interest, this will be discovered. If a public figure or organization does not clearly define their motive, they will have just established a negative one that will be promoted and distributed by the media or opponents in the vacuum they have created. (§ 12.16)

Chapter Thirteen:
Honest Spin:
The Ethics of Public Relations

Honest Spin: The Ethics of Public Relations

§ 13.1 Introduction

For years I taught a course at the American University in Washington, DC, titled, "Ethical Persuasion: The Ethics of Public Relations." The title of the course has been a constant source of humor over the years, and one of the best straight lines in Washington: "Must be a short course." Other comments: "That's an oxymoron, isn't it?" and "There is no such thing." These are the common retorts to the assertion that, yes, there is such a thing as the ethics of public relations.

In fact, it is far easier to be an ethical practitioner of public relations than many other professions. Doctors and hospitals have to balance weighty bio-ethical issues, lawyers contend with complicated problems involving justice and civil liberties, even journalists wrestle with a myriad of ethical challenges every time they edit a sound bite from a newscast or choose a word to put on a page. Most reporters must consider more ethical issues in one month than congressional press secretaries must consider in one year. This is due, in part, to the fact that the ethics of public relations is a simpler code to follow.

At the heart of public relations ethics is one overriding principle: don't lie. Beyond the moral value in doing the right thing, being ethical is also the most effective way to do your job. "Credibility is the coin of the realm," said Mike

McCurry, former President Bill Clinton's spokesman. Once a spokesperson is no longer believed by the media, his value to his principal or organization is significantly diminished.

This chapter addresses the larger questions beyond the simple truth-telling lesson you got in the first grade. The who, what, when, where, why, and how of conducting a public relations job carries ethical implications. Sometimes daily conversations with reporters are laden with ethical questions that a public relations professional must resolve in a split second. This chapter will help you focus on those questions in advance, consider how you deal with ethical issues associated with your daily work, and offer guidance on potential solutions to the thorny problems you may face.

§ 13.2 The Current Ethical Environment in Public Affairs

Throughout American history, those seeking to influence public opinion have had to understand and contend with the prevailing ethical environment of their times—what amounts to the population's perceptions of the credibility of public figures and public institutions. This environment can be shaped by outside circumstances (such as wars or natural disasters), the policies and behavior of our leaders, and how those leaders characterize those policies and behavior in the mass media.

For example, while there were no polls to measure public opinion, one could surmise that the population was generally supportive of government leaders immediately following the War of Independence in 1776. This was the environment in which the advocates of a new Constitution launched a public relations campaign (through the *Federalist Papers*) to support its adoption. In contrast, the corruption in government and business in the late-nineteenth and early-twentieth centuries, and criticism of that behavior by popular commentators like Will Rogers, created an environment of public distrust in America's institutions.

Prior to the introduction of mass media, this ethical environment was more a product of leaders' policies and the simple articulation of those policies. But as communication has become omnipresent and more complicated, how leaders characterize their policies and behavior, and the public relations strategies they choose, are increasingly the dominant influences in shaping our ethical environment.

In much of the post-World War II era, Americans held government and other major institutional leaders in high regard. Since the 1950s, the Gallup

Poll has asked a question to gauge Americans' trust in government. The question is:

> *How much of the time do you think you can trust*
> *the government in Washington to do what is right?*
> *Always, most of the time, or only some of the time?*

For thirty years, the numbers held steady. About two-thirds of all Americans answered "yes," they trusted the government to do the right thing most of the time or always. But two historic and tragic series of events changed everything. Watergate and the Vietnam War altered Americans' attitudes about government.

Beginning in the late 1960s and early '70s, answers to the "trust" polling question shifted: instead of two-thirds of all Americans saying they trusted government most of the time, two-thirds said they trusted the government only some of the time or not at all. The polling numbers on this question remain unchanged from the early 1970s, ranging to a low of 23 percent trusting government in 1992 to 42 percent in 2000.

After Watergate, the default setting for most Americans had become one of cynicism and suspicion toward public institutions and leaders. Frank Mankiewicz, former president of National Public Radio and press secretary to Senator Robert Kennedy, noted: "Nixon aides kept saying, 'We may have committed illegal, unconstitutional acts, and then lied and covered them up—but we were only doing what all leaders do.' And the American public somehow believed this." Mankiewicz argued that Americans had a "changed, less indignant attitude toward antisocial behavior in their leaders—from school boards to the president." (*Communications Ethics*, by James Jaksa and Michael Pritchard (Wadsworth, 1994).)

Subsequent revelations in the post-Watergate era confirmed what Nixon had argued were standard operating practices in politics. John F. Kennedy's infidelities became common knowledge; Lyndon Johnson's own Oval Office taping system was made public; and Jimmy Carter's early scandal involving allegations of financial improprieties by his budget director, Burt Lance, seemed to further cement this cynical belief in the minds of Americans.

As new presidents and congresses took office, new scandals added weight to citizens' distrust of their leaders in all positions of public trust. The Iran-Contra Affair, the House Banking-Checks Scandal, the Bill Clinton-Monica Lewinsky Scandal, allegations of child abuse in the Catholic Church, allegations of sexual abuse and coverup by prominent college athletic coaches, insider trading and below-market rate mortgages by members of Congress, and the Enron collapse, Hurricane Katrina, Deepwater Horizon, Fast and Furious, and the Solyndra bankruptcy. After each of these incidents, commentators said that public confidence in America's leadership was at a new low. But, in fact, public trust hasn't changed much since Richard Nixon resigned from office—most Americans don't trust the government.

Moreover, Watergate and Vietnam did more than initiate a change in government and the public's perception of leaders—it changed the practices, attitudes, and standards of the profession largely responsible for that perception: the media. James Jaksa and Michael Pritchard, in their book *Communications Ethics*, said: "Prior to Watergate, government officials had been successful in controlling the press in wartime, citing security concerns. The abuse of power during Watergate, the unwillingness of the White House to provide the press and the nation with information, and the rampant deceit all prompted the press to more aggressively assert its responsibility to the public."

Thousands of young people graduated from college with journalism degrees, dreaming of becoming the next Woodwards and Bernsteins. Television stations hired investigative units to root out local corruption. The entire tenor of the relationship between the governing class and the watchers had changed—the watchers had taken down a president, and no public figure could escape their scrutiny or wrath. A British observer commented on the differences between their parliamentary system and our constitutional system, and the effect it has on the media. "We have a permanent opposition party in Great Britain—you have *The Washington Post*."

While the media may have seen itself as a public crusader charged with cleaning up government in the post-Watergate years, their actions and excesses in this pursuit have led to a drop in their own public esteem. Sixty-four percent of Americans rate the honesty and ethical standards of members of Congress as "low" or "very low," tying the record "low"/"very low" rating Gallup has measured for any profession historically. Gallup has asked Americans to rate the honesty and ethics of numerous professions since 1976, including annually since 1990. In the same Gallup Poll, from November 28–December 1, 2011, journalists were rated "low" or "very low" by 27 percent of Americans, compared to 9 percent for clergy, 15 percent for building contractors, and 1 percent for nurses.

Beginning with Watergate and Vietnam, and extending to the Fast and Furious, Solyndra, and Penn State scandals of the early twenty-first century, the ethical environment in which public relations practitioners work has been dominated by mistrust of the major American institutions in every corner of leadership. This lack of trust defines every interaction that public figures and their spokespeople have with reporters. It helps shape every story that is written about public affairs. And the pervading negative view has the earned status of "conventional wisdom" in the minds and attitude of nearly every citizen.

Our distrust of government and the media was interrupted by one short blip of confidence in the last three decades. In the weeks following the tragic attacks of September 11, 2001, the American people for a short time turned to their government for support. The Gallup Poll in October 2001 showed that 60 percent of Americans trusted the government to do the right thing most of the time, which was the first time since Richard Nixon resigned that a majority of the nation had faith in its leaders to do the right thing. The media enjoyed a similar bump in popularity—some speculated because they went back to their roots and did more straight reporting and less commenting of the news. Whatever the effect, it was short-lived. A CBS/*New York Times* survey a year later in 2002 indicated that only 37 percent trusted the government always or most of the time.

Public relations practitioners seeking to engage in completely ethical practices must be prepared to be met by skepticism from reporter and citizen alike. This sets the bar enormously high for anyone in public affairs, and requires us to work harder to regain the public trust that has been battered for decades.

§13.3 Ethical Duties of a Public Relations Professional

Philip Seib and Kathy Fitzpatrick's book, *Public Relations Ethics*, enumerates five categories of ethical duties: duty to self, duty to client organization, duty to employer, duty to profession, and duty to society. For the public relations practitioner in public affairs, three of these figure most prominently: duty to self, duty to employer, and duty to society.

Duty to Self. It may sound trite, but Washington might be a better place if we all followed Jiminy Cricket's advice to Pinocchio, "Let your conscience be your guide." As experienced public relations professionals know, it isn't always that easy. Yet, we all have an ethical duty to reconcile our behavior with our own personal value systems and beliefs. For those lucky enough to spend a long and fruitful career in public service communication, one of the yardsticks we will use to measure our achievements will be based on our own notions of right and wrong.

Duty to Employer. Matching your convictions with a job (§ 1.2) is one of the most important decisions in your communication career when dealing with your duty to your employer. The bulk of ethical issues are handled upfront when you agree to be an advocate for a person or organization, and hopefully your views are in sync with theirs. Ethical questions can arise when your employer engages in activity that crosses a legal or ethical line, such as violating the law, an institutional rule, or knowingly misleading the public. How a public relations specialist responds to this kind of employer behavior often depends upon the employer's intentions on how to deal with the ethical violation. If an employer has made a mistake, he may choose to admit to the wrongdoing and make amends. In this case, your loyalty may be called upon to assist him through the crisis. However, if the employer is not repentant, and intends to continue with his unethical actions, then, depending upon the seriousness of the mistake, resignation may be the only ethical course of action.

Disagreements between public relations specialist and employer are usually not confined to ethical lapses. You may disagree with your boss on policy decisions or individual actions. If you agree with the overall mission of the organization, and do not find yourself in conflict too often, you can usually live with the occasional divergence of opinion without it requiring a serious ethical analysis. However, when working for an elected official, it is that official's responsibility to promulgate policy.

Duty to Society. The opening sentence of the Public Relations Society of America Member Code of Ethics Pledge states, "I pledge to conduct myself professionally, with truth, accuracy, fairness, and responsibility to the public." Most public relations practitioners in Washington aren't in it for the money—they are passionate believers in a cause or ideology and have chosen the communication profession as the best avenue to advance the issues and institutions that they believe are beneficial to society. Private public relations experts, while often engaged in worthwhile work, often don't carry the same degree of ethical burden. It's a lot easier to get worked up over a public relations campaign related to restricting a woman's right to an abortion than it is to get excited about the unveiling of a new laundry detergent.

How you interpret your duty to society is based on your own moral and ethical code. While there are some standard public relations codes, they must be viewed through your own personal prism of right and wrong. One person's blatant fabrication is another person's white lie.

How one analyzes these situations, and the resulting decisions, have a collective impact on society and how the public relations profession is viewed by the public. In public affairs, misleading or lying to the public has significant implications. Not only can individuals be harmed, caretakers of the public trust diminish citizens' faith in democracy with every deceitful action or statement. While there can be no absolute ethical yardstick to measure one's duty to society, it is important that it be included in any ethical analysis, and your interpretation of your societal responsibilities can often be the best guidance in a situation involving ethical questions.

Ethical challenges arise when these duties come into conflict with one another. Your employer wants you to say or do something that you think is wrong. Or, your organization has taken a public position on an issue that you think is harmful to society. There are no easy answers to these challenges, and often your choices result in some sacrifice. Some options for addressing these challenges are covered in § 13.5, Ethical Choices.

Tips for PAOs and PIOs

Public trust trumps all.

§13.4 Common Ethical Challenges

Use of Language. Sometimes the simple selection of words can have ethical implications. Exaggerating the impact of legislation or minimizing its effect can be viewed as misleading the public. Members of Congress and advocacy groups are in a constant struggle over defining their own and their opponents' agenda, and are sometimes accused of crossing the ethical language line in their zealousness to win media attention and favorable public opinion.

In Chapter Ten, we reviewed how Newt Gingrich and the GOP image-makers in 1995 sought to portray their reduction in planned Medicare spending as "strengthening" seniors' health-care system. Similarly, Republicans accused Democrats of foul play when seniors in a close congressional race received official-looking direct-mail pieces emblazoned on the cover, "Please Open Immediately. Notification Regarding Denial of Your Health Care Coverage." Inside was a letter outlining the Democratic candidate's support for a patients' bill of rights and the Republican candidate's opposition to the bill.

Surprisingly, keeping language honest and undistorted by hyperbole is not only more ethical, it's often more effective. Reporters have become so accustomed to exaggerated claims that doses of clean, straight communication can be a refreshing and convincing tool.

Language issues are the most common ethical challenge faced in media relations. Communication specialists have to weigh internal issues, impact on the public, potential damage to the credibility of the principal, and effect on your own reputation. Often the best ethical measurement in these instances is also tied to effectiveness. Will the language pass the media's "smell test"? Will they question the veracity of the statement we're issuing? Can our data be refuted, and what is the credibility of the sources challenging it? These are the questions reporters will ask, and the ones public relations specialists should ask as well. When assessing whether you are using the correct language in a publicly released document, make sure it will withstand the withering examination that accompanies any public figure's statements.

Misappropriation (Stealing) of Credit. They say failure is an orphan and success has a thousand fathers. Often when an accomplishment is about to be unveiled in Washington, the delivery room suddenly becomes crowded with parents not present at the conception or at any stage of development. This is a particularly delicate matter for members of Congress, whose survival depends on demonstrating achievement to voters.

Consequently, ethical problems arise when public relations professionals are pushed to enhance the role or work of an organization or principal in public affairs beyond what they legitimately did. Congressional press secretaries often struggle with the verb in the lead of the press release after legislation is passed. Did the member "sponsor," "vigorously support," "push through," "champion," or merely "vote for" the bill in question?

However one settles on how to portray a public figure's role in a success, it is important that the public relations specialist back up all claims of credit with proof and documentation. You may be called upon to justify your boss' heroics in the court of public opinion.

Interactions with Political Campaigns. Our governmental system has established an important, but sometimes vague, dividing line between official activity and campaign activity. Government communication specialists are often in the toughest spot, since much of their work can be easily translated into political value. Congressional press secretaries and communication directors are pulled in to craft campaign press releases that refer back to official activity. Federal agency public affairs deputies coordinate campaign visits of cabinet secretaries and other officials during presidential election years.

While the interpretation of the rules and laws governing public relations professionals' actions vary, there can be no debating the consequences for violating them. Crossing these lines not only damages your credibility, it will reflect poorly on your entire organization. If you are interacting with a campaign organization, it's best to be briefed on all provisions that cover your actions from an expert on the interpretation of the requirements. After starting in a new position, or prior to initiating a regular working relationship with a campaign, ask your supervisor or office counsel to provide you with a comprehensive review of all the laws, regulations, and advisory opinions covering your activities.

Leaking, or Use of Anonymity. The efficacy of leaking was discussed in Chapter Nine. But the ethical use of leaking is—forgive the pun—another story. Journalistic ethical standards on the use of unnamed sources have changed over the last quarter-century. Prior to the 1970s, news organizations felt it was unethical to quote unnamed sources except when it was necessary to protect them from reprisal for speaking to the media. Today, using unnamed sources is a common practice in journalism, and it allows individuals with a variety of motives to use the media to further their goals. And Wikileaks provides anonymously sourced documents that have included classified information.

Because the journalistic ethical standard has changed on the propriety of using unnamed sources, it's ridiculous to think that those who deal with reporters will not use leaks to further their aims. However, when leaking information or speaking to the media anonymously, there are some good rules to follow.

First, just as misleading the media on the record is unethical and ineffective, lying in an off-the-record setting carries a similar ethical weight, and a loss of credibility with the reporter if the lie is discovered. In addition, you should not use the cloak of anonymity to unfairly hurt another's reputation or image. It's one thing to secretly attack a policy position because your identification would cause unacceptable reprisals; it's another thing to unjustly attack another person's character behind a veil of secrecy.

Finally, there are serious ethical questions surrounding the use of leaked or anonymous sourcing when critiquing a policy position of your own organization. Large entities, such as the federal government, always have policy debates as to the appropriateness of a particular official action. Internal processes are established to consider a variety of viewpoints and filter reasonable debate through an organized decisionmaking process.

If that process is extremely flawed, or results in an illegal policy, using the media to correct a societal wrong can be considered the most ethical choice. In 2002, *Time* magazine chose the three whistle-blowers at Enron, the FBI, and Worldcom as their Persons of the Year for challenging organizational doctrine and using both internal communication systems and the media to reveal wrongdoing. Regrettably, this type of character is the exception, and more often people in Washington speak anonymously to the media with less noble motives. Usually, public relations professionals should avoid secretly critiquing their own organization and, when appropriate, discourage the practice within their organization.

Lying for a Principal or Organization. I don't believe there is a public relations professional in Washington who hasn't had to tell a lie for their boss. Most are probably the garden variety, such as telling a reporter that he's not in the office—when he really is, and just wants to avoid talking to the reporter. Hopefully, there will be no cataloguing and atonement for white lies come Judgment Day, or we're all probably in a whole lot of trouble. But there are also pressures in the public affairs community to go beyond the simple covering for a colleague or boss.

There are few black-and-white examples of public relations professionals lying to reporters. Usually the circumstances are murkier. Sometimes reporters will have pieces of stories, merging incorrect facts with correct ones—but still possessing the general thrust of the story (which usually is negative). There are some in the public relations profession who argue that if the reporter does not ask the question just right, they can legitimately respond to the reporter, "That's not correct." This seems to me to be a few steps over the ethical line, in addition to being a formula for a bad relationship with the reporter in the long term. There is no hard-and-fast rule such as, "If the reporter's got 50 percent of the story right, you have to come clean." Each interaction is a judgment call.

Communication specialists have to balance their ethical obligation to the truth with their obligation to their client. For example, your nonprofit organization may be planning to release a report outlining the persistent errors in a government agency's ability to collect child support payments from deadbeat parents. A reporter with a very small newspaper has learned a few key findings of the report, but has some important statistics wrong. Your public relations goal is to release the report in a grand press conference in two days, with mothers and kids to testify to the hardship that the lack of payments causes. The reporter asks you to confirm the findings and statistics, and you imply that she's got some relevant facts wrong, but will say no more, hoping to discourage her from running a story before you're ready. You know that if your organization gets good coverage, it will put pressure on the government agency to improve its record, thereby making the lives of some women and children a little better. As long as you don't provide untruthful answers to direct questions, you've probably stayed on the right side of the ethical line.

In contrast, you may also be faced with a situation where the member of Congress you work for was seen having a seemingly romantic dinner in a public Washington restaurant with a woman who wasn't his wife, and was observed passionately nibbling on various body parts in between various courses. A reporter asks you about the circumstances, but gets the name of the restaurant wrong. You are probably not following an ethical route if you reply, "You've got your facts wrong," and leave it at that. As discussed in Chapter Twelve, when faced with a crisis, especially one involving the image or reputation of the principal, it is usually best to come clean as quickly as possible.

§13.5 Ethical Choices

When faced with an ethical dilemma, public relations professionals have four choices: avoidance, compliance, ignorance, and resignation.

Avoidance. While it may sound cowardly to avoid reporters because you don't want to answer their questions, it sometimes may be the most ethical choice. Capitol Hill press secretaries' quality of life improved measurably when Caller-ID was installed in congressional offices, offering spin doctors the capability of forcing that pestering reporter to suffer in voice mail hell forever. I'm sure reporters were equally gleeful at the new technology, allowing them to dispense the same justice to bothersome press secretaries.

When faced with a reporter asking questions that will require a public relations professional to make a difficult ethical decision, one option is to avoid the question altogether. Some questions will persist, making the choice unavoidable. But, circumstances change, bosses change their minds on courses of action, and reporters lose interest. Don't force yourself into an ethical dilemma until you really have to—and avoiding difficult choices is a perfectly acceptable option in some circumstances.

Some difficult decisions are candidates to be foisted onto other colleagues. In the early 1990s, when the debate over flag-burning was raging in America, a congressman asked his press secretary to draft a statement on the topic in favor of a constitutional amendment to ban flag burning. The press secretary—a former reporter—strongly opposed the amendment. He didn't want to draft the statement, but was new to the office and did not want to engage in a major conflict with his boss. Moreover, he knew the amendment was scores of votes away from passing, so the statement and vote had very little impact on the policy outcome.

The young press secretary resolved the issue by asking a colleague in the office to draft the statement. It may not have been a perfect choice, but aides are never going to be 100 percent in sync with the policies of their bosses, and they must merely come to a common understanding on those issues where they agree (and hope that the issues where they substantially agree outweigh those where they disagree).

Compliance. Some public relations professionals, when asked by a principal to engage in unethical activity, comply with the request out of loyalty to their boss. This is a poor choice and usually leads to destroyed reputations or worse. In 1991, Senator Chuck Robb of Virginia and some key aides came into possession of a series of illegally recorded conversations of a political rival, Governor Doug Wilder. Instead of reporting how they came into possession of the tapes, the senator's staff allegedly schemed how to use the tapes to their advantage. Eventually, they were caught, and the aides and the senator were at the center of a criminal investigation. Senator Robb made the extraordinary gambit of testifying before the grand jury in hopes of avoiding indictment—which worked. Three of his aides weren't so lucky and pleaded guilty to violations of wiretap law. The history books are full of loyal aides who, when faced with a conflict between their duty to their boss, to their own conscience, or to the law, made the wrong choice.

Ignorance. For decades, professional public relations practices dictated that communication specialists learn all they can about a principal, especially when faced with an ethical crisis. It was assumed that you are in the best position to assess the potential public damage of the crisis, and you can't do that without all the facts.

In recent years, the convergence of public relations crises and legal crises has rewritten the ethics rulebook. Sometimes the ethically appropriate course is to *not* ask questions in a crisis. Public relations specialists do not enjoy attorney-client privilege; spokespersons can find themselves facing serious legal problems if caught in the web of a legal investigation and forced to divulge secrets that violate their duty of loyalty to their principal. This is why some public relations practitioners have chosen to avoid asking the difficult questions—using ignorance as a shield to protect themselves, and sometimes even their principal.

Clinton Press Secretary Mike McCurry defined this method in a brilliant combination of ethical behavior and effective public relations tactics during the Monica Lewinsky scandal, and through President Clinton's impeachment. Like all Americans and the White House staff, McCurry was caught by surprise by the allegations in January 1997 that President Clinton had some kind of relationship with former White House intern Monica Lewinsky. In the opening days of the scandal, McCurry did all he could just to keep the media sharks at bay with his skill and wit at the press room podium. On the first day the story broke, a reporter asked a question about the White House's next strategic step. "What's your next move?" "To get off of this podium as quickly as possible," McCurry replied.

In the first weeks of the crisis, McCurry made a clear decision to diverge from orthodox public relations strategy suggesting he should learn all he could from the president about the allegations. He determined it was not his responsibility to ask the president of the United States such questions. His role was to focus on the functions of government, and he would not wallow in the pit that the media was pushing him into.

> ### § 13.6 Sources for Ethics and Public Affairs
>
> **National Association of Government Communicators Code of Ethics**
> <*www.nagc.com*> and look for "Code of Ethics" under "About NAGC."
>
> **Public Relations Society of America Code of Ethics**
> <*www.prsa.org*> and look for "Ethics" under "Intelligence." Also see <*TCNMRA.com*> for links and additional resources.

His decision was framed in part by a previous brush McCurry had with scandal as a young man on Capitol Hill. As a twenty-five-year-old congressional press secretary, his boss, Senator Harrison Williams, became a target of the Abscam investigation. FBI agents, posing as Arab sheiks, ran a sting operation on seven members of Congress who were allegedly bribed into trading official favors and votes for cash. Senator Williams was caught on tape, and McCurry was subpoenaed, requiring him to pay lawyers thousands of dollars to help him navigate through depositions with prosecutors.

The incident influenced the future presidential press secretary in handling the Clinton scandal and redefined ethical public relations practices. By not having any knowledge of Clinton's extracurricular activities with the young woman, McCurry became useless to White House reporters obsessed with the story. The only questions that the president's chief spokesman could answer related to the official Clinton agenda, thereby forcing reporters to cover it. By staying above the fray, he not only effectively served the president, he kept his own reputation intact.

Resignation. Many ethics experts argue that when a professional is unable to fulfill his duty to his principal *and* duty to society (as he interprets it), the only ethical choice is to resign. Resignation on principle is so rare in our society these days that the individual who performs the act may not only have found the right ethical solution, he'll probably get a six-figure book contract to boot.

However, in the day-to-day life of public affairs, walking away from a job isn't so easy. You have to consider the repercussions to your immediate family, the consequences to your co-workers, and the effect on your ability to do good in your profession in the future. And the employee who resigns on principle is sending a clear message that his employer is engaging in unethical practices, a public penalty that also dances close to the line of violating your ethical responsibilities to your employer.

The most famous public relations resignation in history was Bernard Kalb's resignation from the State Department in 1986. In August 1986, the Reagan administration let it be known that they believed that Libyan leader Muammar Quddafi was renewing his support for terrorism and that it could lead to a U.S. attack. Later it was conceded that there was no hard evidence for this statement, and that it was part of a disinformation campaign cooked up by Reagan National Security Advisor John Poindexter (who later resigned as a result of the Iran-Contra affair). State Department spokesman and former television network news reporter Bernard Kalb resigned in protest. "You face a choice," he said, "as an American, as a spokesman, as a journalist, whether to allow oneself to be absorbed in the ranks of silence, whether to vanish into the unopposed acquiescence, or to enter a modest dissent." (*Communications Ethics*, by Jaksa and Pritchard.)

§ 13.7 Conclusion

In classes on ethics in public relations, students often get confused between ethical strategies and effective strategies. Often there is an "end justifies the means" mentality. If it works, then it must be okay. This ethical framework has been used to justify many misdeeds in public affairs, and will never hold up in the court of public opinion or in the history books.

Despite the clamoring of pundits and politicians that we live in an unethical world, the public still values honesty and ethics. People reward the public figure who stands up for what is right in the face of negative repercussions. We seek those exemplifying a "profile in courage" not just to witness a noble act, but to remind us of the goodness in all of us.

Public relations professionals have an obligation to reflect that potential for high moral standards in our interactions with others and in the execution of our craft. When our principal is considering a proposed policy or action, we are often called upon to be predictors of the media's and the public's ethical judgment. Our voice carries weight because of our training in speculating on reporters' behavior and attitudes. This gives us the opportunity to go beyond predicting the impact of a particular action and how it will be portrayed. We have a preventive responsibility to our principal, to society, and to ourselves to block proposed malfeasance.

Our resulting view may be extreme, and public relations professionals are often blamed for frequently predicting a worst-case scenario. But our perspective is usually better than the clouded self-interest of a principal who may be the subject of some inquiry or investigation. How would history have been changed if one public relations professional, the day after the Watergate break-in, had said in the senior councils of the White House, "Let's come clean on everything."

Public relations experts counseling for intelligent and honest communication strategies may not be listened to—and often aren't. But lodging the correct position is not an irrelevant act, and often the best way to be true to yourself, your principal, and the public.

§ 13.99 Chapter Summary

* Public relations practitioners operate in an environment shaped by the public mistrust created by the Watergate Scandal and the Vietnam War. Most Americans distrust the government. (§ 13.2)
* Public relations specialists working in public affairs have three duties: duty to self, duty to employer, and duty to society. (§ 13.3)
* Common ethical challenges to public relations specialists include: using language accurately; misappropriating (or stealing) credit for accomplishments of others; ethically interacting with political campaigns; leaking information improperly; and lying for the principal or organization. (§ 13.4)
* The ethical choices available to a public relations specialist when faced with an ethical dilemma are: avoidance, compliance, ignorance, or resignation. (§ 13.5)

Back of the Book

Appendix One:
Thirteen Rules of Media Relations

1. Never lie, falsify, misrepresent, obfuscate, mislead, purposely distort, or commit any other willful act that will hurt your trustworthiness with reporters. Credibility is the coin of the realm.

2. Never underestimate the superficial nature of the media. Simple ideas, well told, get attention. A visual stunt or a celebrity spokesman will usually draw more press—and get your message across better— than a profound policy statement.

3. Sometimes you get blamed for things that aren't your fault; and sometimes you get credit for things you didn't do. Remember, this is a strange business, a lot of which is beyond your control.

4. Don't say anything you don't want to see in print. Never talk to a reporter unless you've carefully thought out your comments or said them previously. Anything you say to a reporter can and will be used against you in the court of public opinion.

5. Always have someone else check your work. Errors destroy credibility.

6. Public policy is too important to leave to policy experts. Don't just communicate the message—influence it.

7. Never say "no comment"—It implies guilt.

8. Return reporters' phone calls. Period.

9. Never overestimate a reporter's knowledge of your issue. Be ready to explain, clearly and patiently, the basics of your story. Have fact sheets available, if appropriate.

10. Before going "off the record" or "on background" with a reporter for the first time, agree on the meaning of the terms. Not all reporters and news organizations use the same definitions.

11. In the eyes of the media, hypocrisy is a public figure's greatest sin. To reporters, being consistent is more important than being right.

12. If caught doing something wrong, admit it—immediately and repeatedly. It is better to reveal a failing and be considered sincere than have it discovered and be considered deceitful.

13. Never get in a war of words with someone who buys ink by the barrel. You can't win a fight with a news organization that ultimately controls the message.

Appendix Two:
Glossary

Actuality—Audio package or sound bite provided to radio stations. (§ 2.19)

Assignment Editor—Air traffic controller of television news, responsible for managing and directing all the assets in the newsroom, assigning reporters, camera crews, and satellite trucks. Often, this person, or the individual show's producer, is the primary target audience for pitches. (Increasingly, this term is used in newspapers for a person with similar responsibilities.) (§ 5.6)

Background, or "on background"—Term used when information may be used, but the source may not be specifically identified. The source may be identified generally, using a description mutually agreed upon.

B-roll—Television footage that is not the interview. Usually includes some kind of action or activity.

Backgrounder—An in-depth memo, more detailed than a press release, providing detailed background information on a particular topic. Backgrounders often provide statistical information, chronologies of events, or contact information and sources. (§ 2.9)

Blog (or Web Log)—Individual commentary, like a running column, posted on a web site.

Booker—Individual responsible on television or radio show for booking guests.

Copy—Written material submitted for publication or broadcast.

Cutaway—Shot in television news segment that is not focused on the principal action, often used to segue between two other important shots.

Daybook—A listing of the major events in a state or city, produced by the Associated Press, Reuters, and United Press International. (§ 5.5)

Deep background, or "on deep background"—Term used when information may be used, but the source may not be identified in any manner. (§ 4.12 and § 4.13)

Earned Media (or free media)—All publicity not paid for.

FAQs (Frequently Asked Questions)—Used on web sites as resources and presented in a question-and-answer format. (Ch. Six)

Feed (Radio or TV)—Material sent to television or radio stations. Usually used for television stations. (§ 2.19 and § 2.20)

FOIA (Freedom of Information Act)—Federal law requiring the disclosure of certain information maintained by the federal government. (§ 11.6)

Flack—Slang term for public relations professional.

Futures File—Chronological file maintained by news organizations to track upcoming events.

Hit (as in "press hit")—Any coverage resulting from a public relations event or activity.

Hit (as in "hits" on web site)—Measurement used to assess traffic on a web site (the measurement is considered somewhat misleading). (Ch. Six)

Inverted Pyramid—Journalistic method for organizing story from most important information to least important.

"Legs" or "The story has legs"—Indication that the story could have various manifestations or run for more than one day.

Message—A succinct articulation of a vision designed to convey a broad theme or to motivate people to a specific action. (Ch. Three)

Off the record—Term used when information is not to be used publicly or shared with any other person, except possibly the reporter's editor. (§ 4.12)

Opt In and Opt Out—Terms used for web site visitors' choice to be added to an email list. (§ 6.41)

Package—A television story that is done by a reporter (as opposed to an anchor) that includes interviews and other material.

Photog—Slang term for television photographer or cameraman. (§ 5.6)

Principal—Public relations term for the leader of an organization. (Ch. Seven)

Rating—Measurement for the number of households in a market, out of the total number of households that have a TV set, watching a particular program. (§ 5.7)

Reader—A television story read solely by the anchor with no interviews included.

Share (as in ratings)—Measurement for the number of households with a television set turned on that are watching a particular program. (§ 5.7)

Stand-up—Portion of a television story where the reporter is talking directly into the camera.

Sweeps Weeks (or Sweeps)—Periods primarily focused in February, May, July, and November when the ACNielsen Company comprehensively tracks the ratings of all the television shows in the nation. (§ 5.6)

Talking Points—Bulleted statements or sentences used for articulating a position or conveying information. (§ 8.4)

Trial Balloon—A process for anonymously floating public policy proposals with the media. (§ 9.9)

Two-shot—The camera shot of a reporter talking to the person he's interviewing, shot from behind the interview subject.

Unearned Media (or paid media)—Advertising.

Viral Marketing—The cascading process of an email message spread by recipients to multiple lists because they like the content and want to share it with others. (§ 6.40)

VNR (Video News Release)—A television package produced by a public relations professional to appear as if it were prepared by an independent reporter. (§ 2.20)

Appendix Three:
Related Resources

Training from TheCapitol.Net

Media Training in Washington, DC
<TCNMR.com>

Capitol Learning Audio Courses™
<http://TheCapitol.Net/CapitolLearning/MediaTraining.htm>

Internet Resources

- Abscam Bribery Scandal (1970s-1980s)—Wikipedia | FBI Documents
- Bhopal/Union Carbide gas disaster (1984)—Wikipedia |
  Bhopal Information Center | Wired | The Big Picture (photos) | DoD
- CAN-SPAM Act: A Compliance Guide for Business—FTC
- Charles B. Rangel Censure (2008-2010)—Wikipedia
- Chicago Tylenol murders (1982)—Wikipedia | Reyna Susi | DoD
- Codes of Ethics—Public Relations Society of America |
  National Association of Government Communicators
- Deepwater Horizon oil spill (2010)—Wikipedia
- Exxon Valdez oil spill (1989)—Wikipedia | EPA | Rich Klein | Ron Smith |
- Factcheck.org
- Fast and Furious, Operation (2009-2010)—Wikipedia
- Federal Records Managers—National Archives
- FOIA.gov—from the Dept. of Justice
- Freedom of Information Act (FOIA)—from the Paul V. Galvin Library
  at the Illinois Institute of Technology
- Fukushima Daiichi nuclear disaster (2011)—Wikipedia
- Gallup—Politics | Congress | Economy | Honesty and Ethics of Professions
- Honest Leadership and Open Government Act—Wikipedia
- "In Recent Scandals, a Rethinking Of Capital's Conventional Wisdom,"
  by John F. Harris, *The Washington Post*, April 12, 2005
- Iran-Contra Affair—Wikipedia | infoplease
- Jack Abramoff (2006)—Wikipedia
- NASA Space Shuttle Challenger STS 51L (1986)—Wikipedia | DoD | NASA

Links for all of these items are online at <TCNMRA.com>

- Office of Government Information Services (OGIS) (reviews agency compliance with FOIA)
- Oklahoma City bombing (1995)—Wikipedia | Chronology (*The Washington Post*)
- OpenSecrets.org
- Political Scandals in Congress—Wikipedia
- Press Area Usability—Jakob Nielsen (The Nielsen Norman Group Report, "Designing Websites to Maximize Press Relations," is available here)
- Public Relations Society of America (PRSA) Member Code of Ethics
- Ruby Ridge (1992)—Wikipedia
- Section508.gov
- Sex Scandals in Congress—Wikipedia | LA Times | *The Washington Post*
- Solyndra loan controversy (2011)—Wikipedia
- The Fact Checker—*The Washington Post*
- useit.com—Jakob Nielsen
- Usability.gov
- Waco siege (1993)—Wikipedia | Chronology (PBS)
- Watergate scandal (1970s)—Wikipedia | *The Washington Post* | PBS
- Web Pages That Suck—Vincent Flanders
- Web analytics—Wikipedia
- Your Right to Federal Records—from GSA (Also available as a 36-page PDF)
- Your Right to Know: Guide to FOIA—ACLU

Books

Ambush at Ruby Ridge: How Government Agents Set Randy Weaver Up and Took His Family Down, by Alan W. Bock, ISBN 1880741482 (1995)

A Place Called Waco: A Survivor's Story, by David Thibodeau, Leon Whiteson, ISBN 1891620428 (1999)

Crisis Communication: Practical PR Strategies for Reputation Management and Company Survival, by Peter Anthonissen, ISBN 0749454008 (2008)

Crisis Communications: A Casebook Approach, by Kathleen Fearn-Banks, ISBN 0415880599 (2010)

Crisis Management: Planning for the Inevitable, by Steven Fink, ISBN 0595090796 (2010)

Links for all of these items are online at <TCNMRA.com>

Dead Last: The Public Memory of Warren G. Harding's Scandalous Legacy, by Phillip G. Payne, ISBN 082141819X (2009)

Designing Brand Identity: An Essential Guide for the Whole Branding Team, by Alina Wheeler, ISBN 0470401427 (2009)

Digital Strategies for Powerful Corporate Communications, by Paul Argenti and Courtney Barnes, ISBN 0071606025 (2009)

Disaster Response and Recovery, by David A. McEntire, ISBN 0471789747 (2006)

Effective Crisis Communication: Moving From Crisis to Opportunity, by Robert R. (Ray) Ulmer, Timothy L. Sellnow, and Matthew Seeger, ISBN 1412980348 (2010)

Emergency Management, by Michael K. Lindell, Carla Prater, and Ronald Perry, ISBN 0471772607 (2006)

Emergency Management: Principles and Practice for Local Goverment, by William Waugh and Kathleen Tierney, ISBN 0873267192 (2007)

Emergency Management: The American Experience 1900–2005, by Claire B. Rubin, ISBN 0979372208 (2007)

Engage, Revised and Updated: The Complete Guide for Brands and Businesses to Build, Cultivate, and Measure Success in the New Web, by Brian Solis, Ashton Kutcher, ISBN 1118003764 (2011)

Ethics in Public Relations: A Guide to Best Practice, by Patricia J Parsons, ISBN 074045332X (2008)

Ethics in Public Relations: Responsible Advocacy, by Kathy R. Fitzpatrick and Carolyn Bronstein, ISBN 1412917980 (2006)

Exxon Valdez: The Great Crisis Management Paradox, by James A. Lukaszewski and Joy Gmeiner, ASIN B000PC6WXC (1993)

Firewall: The Iran-Contra Conspiracy and Cover-up, by Lawrence E. Walsh, ISBN 0393318605 (1998)

Glass Houses: Shocking Profiles of Congressional Sex Scandals and Other Unofficial Misconduct, by Stanley G. Hilton and Anne-Renee Testa, ISBN 0312971028 (1998)

Hardball: How Politics Is Played, Told by One Who Knows the Game, by Chris Matthews, ISBN 0684845598 (1999)

How Come No One Knows About Us? The Ultimate Public Relations Guide: Tactics Anyone Can Use to Win High Visibility, by Robert Deigh, ISBN 0832950173 (2008)

Links for all of these items are online at <TCNMRA.com>

Feeding the Media Beast: An Easy Recipe for Great Publicity,
by Mark E. Mathis, ISBN 1557533970 (2005)

For Immediate Release: Shape Minds, Build Brands, and Deliver Results with Game-Changing Public Relations, by Ronn Torossian, ISBN 1936661160 (2011)

Introduction to Emergency Management, by George Haddow, Jane Bullock, and Damon Coppola, ISBN 1856179591 (2010)

Likeable Social Media: How to Delight Your Customers, Create an Irresistible Brand, and Be Generally Amazing on Facebook (And Other Social Networks), by Dave Kerpen, ISBN 0071762345 (2011)

Making News: A Straight-Shooting Guide to Media Relations, by David Henderson, ISBN 158348468X (2006)

Measure What Matters: Online Tools For Understanding Customers, Social Media, Engagement, and Key Relationships, by Katie Delahaye Paine, ISBN 0470920106 (2011)

Media Ethics: Cases and Moral Reasoning, by Clifford G. Christians, ISBN 0205029043 (2011)

Media Ethics: Key Principles for Responsible Practice, by Patrick Lee Plaisance, ISBN 1412956854 (2008)

Media Law and Ethics, by Roy L. Moore and Michael Murray, ISBN 0805850678 (2007)

Media Training 101: A Guide to Meeting the Press, by Sally Stewart, ISBN 0471271551 (2003)

Media Training A–Z, by BJ Walker, ISBN 1932642366 (2008)

No More Wacos: What's Wrong with Federal Law Enforcement and How to Fix It, by David Kopel and Paul Blackman, ISBN 1573921254 (1997)

Obama's Wars, by Bob Woodward, ISBN 1439172498 (2010)

Political Scandals in the United States, by Robert Williams, ISBN 1579580394 (1998)

Public Relations Ethics, by Phillip Seib, Jerry Hendrix, ISBN 0155019430 (1994)

Ruby Ridge: The Truth and Tragedy of the Randy Weaver Family, by Jess Walter, ISBN 006000794X (2002)

Send In The Waco Killers: Essays on the Freedom Movement, 1993–1998, by Jeanne Suprynowicz, ISBN 0967025907 (1999)

Shadow: Five Presidents and the Legacy of Watergate, by Bob Woodward, ISBN 0684852624 (1999)

Links for all of these items are online at <TCNMRA.com>

Strategic Public Relations: 10 Principles to Harness the Power of PR, by Jennifer Gehrt and Colleen Moffitt, ISBN 1436387256 (2009)

The Corporate Blogging Book, by Debbie Weil, ASIN B003B654MO (2010)

The Economics of a Disaster: The Exxon Valdez Oil Spill, by Bruce M. Owen, David Argue, et al., ISBN 0899309879 (1995)

The Federal Siege at Ruby Ridge: In Our Own Words, by Randy Weaver and Sara Weaver, ISBN 0966433408 (1998)

The Four Stages of Highly Effective Crisis Management: How to Manage the Media in the Digital Age, by Jane Jordan-Meier, ISBN 1439853738 (2011)

The Future of War: Organizations as Weapons, by Mark D. Mandeles, ISBN 1574886304 (2005)

The McGraw-Hill 36-Hour Course: Online Marketing, by Lorrie Thomas, ISBN 0071743863 (2010)

The New Rules of Marketing and PR: How to Use Social Media, Blogs, News Releases, Online Video, and Viral Marketing to Reach Buyers Directly, by David Scott, ISBN 1118026985 (2011)

The Old Rules of Marketing Are Dead: 6 New Rules to Reinvent Your Brand and Reignite Your Business, by Timothy R. Pearson, ISBN 0071762558 (2011)

The Politics of Disgrace: The Role of Political Scandal in American Politics, by Nancy E. Marion, ISBN 1594605084 (2010)

The Siege at Ruby Ridge, Starring Laura Dern and Randy Quaid, ASIN B000AM6OO4 (2005)

The Zen of Social Media Marketing: An Easier Way to Build Credibility, Generate Buzz, and Increase Revenue, by Shama Kabani, Chris Brogan, ISBN 1935251732 (2010)

Torture and Truth: America, Abu Ghraib, and the War on Terror, by Mark Danner, ISBN 1590171527 (2004)

Toxic Sludge Is Good For You: Lies, Damn Lies and the Public Relations Industry, by John Stauber, Sheldon Rampton, ISBN 1567510604 (2002)

Waco—The Rules of Engagement, Starring Clive Doyle, Dan Giffird, ASIN B0000DIJOO (2003)

Why Our Drug Laws Have Failed: A Judicial Indictment of the War On Drugs, by James Gray, ISBN 1566398606 (2001)

Winning PR in the Wired World: Powerful Communications Strategies for the Noisy Digital Space, by Don Middleburg, ISBN 0071363424 (2000)

Links for all of these items are online at <TCNMRA.com>

Remember
Gunter Schabowski

Even with all the examples and tools offered in this book, public relations professionals might still feel they perform a lesser role in our democratic process. Because policy-makers often consider communication an afterthought and not central to the policy creation process, we are sometimes relegated to the back room, to scribble and spin and jawbone with reporters until our skills are deemed required. While this view is increasingly a relic of the last century, it still pervades many of the halls of Washington, DC.

For those communication specialists caught in a debate over the primacy of public relations in our world and the relevance of the guidance offered in this book, I offer three words that will definitively end every argument: Remember Gunter Schabowski.

Gunter Schabowski was a spokesman and local party chief for East Germany in 1989, when the Soviet empire was nearing its end. Soviet leader Mikhail Gorbachev's reform campaign had begun to significantly relax Russia's hold over neighboring countries. Hungary and Czechoslovakia were loosening travel restrictions, and East Germans were looking for cracks in the Iron Curtain, hoping to emigrate to their neighbors and seek a new life in the West. The East German government was trying to keep pace with the rapid developments—hoping to appear in step with the Soviet leader's new policies, while not losing its grip on the control of its borders, which was essential to the government's survival.

On November 9, 1989, East Germany was planning another relaxation in what had become a series of reforms to its policies. The government was about to initiate a new plan that would hopefully quell the demand for travel to the West, but still keep tabs on its citizens. On Thursday night, at 7:00 p.m., East Berlin party leader and spokesman Gunter Schabowski was briefing the press on the new policy the government was instituting to allow "private trips" to other countries. That was when Gunter made his crucial error and changed the course of history.

An Italian reporter asked when the new policy would take effect. Gunter fumbled, not knowing the answer. His superiors had intended the new rules to take effect in the coming days, when an orderly process for setting up passports and visas could be established. But Gunter had not been told this detail.

Violating one of the basic rules of public relations, he guessed. "Immediately, without delay," he replied. When asked what his predictions were about the effect of the new policy, he violated another rule, and speculated. "No one can know what will happen next." It became the understatement of the century.

Within minutes, word spread and masses of people began to appear at the Berlin Wall. Young, confused East German border guards had seen such swift changes in their government in recent months that they did not know exactly what to do. Crowds began to appear on the West side of the Wall as well. The East German guards, thinking that the policies had been changed without their being told, opened the gates.

Crowds began to converge at the magnificent Brandenburg Gate, separating East and West Berlin. People started to climb on the Wall itself, and an atmosphere of celebration ensued. Soon, people started chipping at the Wall with knives and hammers. Sledgehammers and pick axes appeared. Before too long heavy-construction equipment came from nowhere and huge chunks of the wall were being ripped apart. Television cameras captured this astonishing event for the world to see, as the symbol of the Cold War, the tangible instrument of the confinement and suppression of millions of people, was shattered by joyous throngs. And all because a spokesman screwed up a press briefing.

This is not to suggest that such monumental stakes exist every time a public relations specialist talks to a reporter. Yet we cannot escape the impact our words and strategies have on the world. Thomas Paine's words helped create a nation; Gunter Schabowski's words helped bring down an empire.

As you find your role in the world of public affairs, it is helpful to remember the immensely constructive or destructive power that accompanies the responsibilities you accept, and to appreciate the extraordinary opportunity that is before you.

Remember Gunter Schabowski.

Index

References are to chapter and section numbers.

References are to chapter and section numbers.

References are to chapter and section numbers.

References are to chapter and section numbers.

References are to chapter and section numbers.

CPSIA information can be obtained
at www.ICGtesting.com
Printed in the USA
LVHW100202170821
695405LV00011B/1110

9 781587 331671